Explorations in Marx's Theory of Price—Why Marx Is Still Relevant for Understanding the Modern Economy

Howard Nicholas

Explorations in Marx's Theory of Price—Why Marx Is Still Relevant for Understanding the Modern Economy

Volume I: Money and Money Prices

palgrave
macmillan

Howard Nicholas
International Institute of Social
Studies
Erasmus University Rotterdam
Rotterdam, Zuid-Holland
The Netherlands

ISBN 978-1-137-56563-1 ISBN 978-1-137-56564-8 (eBook)
https://doi.org/10.1057/978-1-137-56564-8

This Palgrave Macmillan imprint is published by the registered company Springer Nature Limited
The registered company address is: The Campus, 4 Crinan Street, London, N1 9XW, United Kingdom

Preface

This book is the first volume of a three-volume series borne out of a dissatisfaction I felt after writing *Marx's Theory of Price and its Modern Rivals, 2011.* The dissatisfaction came from an awareness that a number of aspects of Marx's theory of price required greater attention than I was able to accord them in this work. These included his analyses of money, profits, and the cyclical movement of the capitalist economic system. Although I was aware of this neglect while writing the book, I felt it did not do serious damage to my main purpose in writing it; to refute what I considered to be unwarranted charges of unintelligibility, inconsistency, and irrelevance levelled against Marx's explanation of price. I now feel these omissions are consequential, and undermine my defence of Marx's theory of price in the book.

My hope is that this volume and the next will remedy the shortcomings of Nicholas (2011). As the title of the present work suggests its purpose is to expand on Marx's theory of price by expanding on his explanation of money. The second volume builds on this by expanding on his explanation of profits and the movement of prices over cycles. The third volume extends this explanation to the level of the world market, explaining international value and price, world money and exchange rates, and the cyclical movement of world market prices.

My more general purpose in writing these three volumes is to contribute to the construction of a coherent body of economic thought based on Marx's later economic writings (viz., *Grundrisse*, *Contribution to a Critique of Political Economy*, *Capital*, and *Theories of Surplus Value*) and not simply parroting these. In doing so, I follow Joan Robinson's approach to interpreting Marx's work as outlined in her 1953 'Open letter from a Keynesian to a Marxist' as quoted in Begg (2012, pp. 22–23);

> What I mean is that I have Marx in my bones and you have him in your mouth...Again, suppose we want to recall some tricky point in *Capital*, for instance the schema at the end of Volume II. What do you do? You take down the volume and look it up. What do I do? I take the back of an old envelope and work it out...Robinson (1980).

I have used many backs of envelopes in preparing the present volume and laying the ground work for the other two, trying to work out the logical implications of Marx's analysis for the subject under consideration. Hence the relative dearth of quotes from Marx in respect of certain aspects of the investigation at hand.

As with my previous book, I need once again to extend an ocean of gratitude to my family, and in particular to my wife Nicolien and my children Jeske, Bram, and Kasper. A special thanks to Bram who spent long hours listening patiently to me trying to explain this or that problem I was grappling with, and who provided me with a reservoir of empirical support for many of the theoretical propositions contained in the present and forthcoming books. Thanks also to Josephine Valeske for her thorough reading of the initial script and making countless suggestions for its improvement in terms of intelligibility and coherence, and to Eri Ikeda for doing the needful with the references and indices. Needless to say, I absolve Bram, Josephine, and Eri from responsibility for any remaining weaknesses. Last, but not least, I owe a huge debt of gratitude to several generations of my students. Many have generously shared with me their experiences in business and policy-making, and have enthusiastically embraced, and helped me develop, the alternative economics courses I have taught over the past twenty-five to thirty years.

Rotterdam
The Netherlands

Howard Nicholas

Contents

About the Author

Howard Nicholas retired in 2020 as associate professor in economics at the International Institute of Social Studies, Erasmus University of Rotterdam, The Netherlands. He has published in the areas of inflation, development theory, financial markets, the global economy, and the macro dynamics of a number of countries. He is the author of *Marx's Theory of Price and its Modern Rivals* (Palgrave Macmillan).

Acronyms

MC	Monetary Circuit (Marxists)
MIMs	Monetary Interpretation Marxists
MM	Modern Marxists
NI	New Interpretation (Marxists)
OVNs	Objective Value Neoclassicals
PK	Post-Keynesian
SVNs	Subjective Value Neoclassicals
TI	Traditional Interpretation (Marxists)
TIMs	Traditional Interpretation Marxists
TSSI	Temporal Single System Interpretation (Marxists)

CHAPTER 1

Introduction

This book is part of a three-volume work looking in greater depth at Marx's theory of price, a theory that is one of the two foundations on which his explanation of the functioning of the capitalist economic system rests, the other being the theory of profit. Taken together the three volumes seek to expand on and develop the interpretation of Marx's theory of price in Nicholas (2011).

1.1 Nicholas (2011)

My primary purpose in Nicholas (2011) is to defend Marx's explanation of price against charges of unintelligibility, inconsistency, and redundancy that have been levelled against it by foes and friends alike. I argue that while there may be some basis for the unintelligibility charge,[1] there is no basis for those of inconsistency and redundancy. The inconsistency charge is usually made in the context of what is deemed to be his flawed transformation procedure.[2] I argue that the basis for this charge, by friends and

[1] See Wheen (2006).

[2] See Böhm-Bawerk (1975) as one of the earliest among those hostile to Marx's economic analysis making this charge, and Foley (1986), Fine, and Saad-Filho (2004) are among those sympathetic to Marx's economic analysis making the same charge.

H. Nicholas, *Explorations in Marx's Theory of Price—Why Marx Is Still Relevant for Understanding the Modern Economy*, https://doi.org/10.1057/978-1-137-56564-8_1

foes alike, is a misunderstanding of what Marx is trying to do with this procedure. The generally accepted interpretation of Marx's transformation procedure is that he is trying to show how the values of commodities are transformed into prices of production in the context of the formation of the general rate of profit (see Nicholas, 2011, p. 39). For me this is mistaken since it suggests Marx sees the value of the commodity disappearing with the formation of the general rate of profit, mutating into the price of production. I argue that what Marx is trying to do with his transformation procedure is to show how the determination of the exchange value or price of the commodity by its value is modified in the context of the formation of the general rate of profit and the resulting transfer of surplus value between sectors. I further argue that the basis of the redundancy charge is the erroneous contention that Marx's explanation of price is essentially the same as Ricardo's,[3] and the journey from value to price is entirely unnecessary since price can be calculated far more simply and consistently by reference to the technical conditions of production in the manner of Sraffa.[4] I contend that this charge stems from a misunderstanding of Marx's explanation of price as well as those of Ricardo and Sraffa.

In the substantive part of Nicholas (2011) I consider other major approaches to the explanation of price, and other Marxist interpretations of Marx's theory of price. The other approaches I consider are those of Smith, Ricardo, Sraffa, Post-Keynesians (PKs), and the Neoclassicals. My purpose in considering the work of both Smith and Ricardo is to bring out the distinctiveness of Marx's explanation of price with respect to what are generally acknowledged to be the two most important Classical explanations of the price of the commodity, as well as laying the foundations for my criticisms of various Marxist interpretations of Marx's explanation of price and their attempts to 'rescue' it.[5] I argue that without realising it most Marxists interpret Marx explaining the price of the commodity in the manner of Ricardo, and then attempt to 'rescue' him by reinterpreting this explanation as akin to that found in the work of Smith, or at least a

[3] Samuelson (1957), Rodrik (2015).

[4] Steedman (1977, 1991), Roncaglia (1978, 2009), Keen (2001), Sinha (2003, 2010).

[5] Dobb (1973, p. 142) notes "The school of Classical Political Economy was a term coined by Marx himself to describe the theoretical system constructed by Adam Smith and Ricardo and their immediate contemporaries…".

modified version of this explanation. My purpose in considering the explanations of price in the works of Sraffa and PKs is to argue that these do not provide more logically sound explanations of price than that of Marx. My purpose in considering the Neoclassical approach is to highlight the general weakness of the explanation of price in what is considered to be the dominant school of thought with a view to reinforcing the relevance of my interpretation of Marx's alternative explanation of price.

1.2 What Is to Be Done

Reflecting on my interpretation of Marx's explanation of the price of the commodity in Nicholas (2011), I came to realise that at best it allowed me to cast doubt on the alleged fatal flaws in his transformation procedure and Marxist attempts to rescue his theory of price. What I failed to do was to expand on his theory of price as the money price of the commodity. I came to realise my focus on the debate surrounding Marx's transformation procedure caused me to treat rather superficially, and even neglect, certain crucial elements of his explanation of the money price of the commodity that require far more attention than I accorded them in Nicholas (2011). These elements are his theories of money and profits. I expand on the former in the present work and the latter in Nicholas (forthcoming).

In the process of writing this book I also came to realise that paying greater attention to Marx's theory of money in the explanation of the money price of the commodity required me to revisit his theory of the value of the commodity. Specifically, it required me to bring out the link Marx sees between the value of the commodity and money, without interpreting Marx seeing money as a token of the value of the commodity or collapsing the value of the commodity into the value of money. Bringing out the link between the value of the commodity and money in this way has, in turn, required me to pay more attention to Marx's theory of money and the functions it performs, especially money's function as the measure of the exchange value of the commodity. This function is the use of money by producers to denote the general exchangeable values of their commodities prior to putting them into the process of circulation with a view to facilitating their reproduction. It is a function of money that Marx alone sees as the primary and defining function of money, something that has been overlooked by most, if not all, interpreters of his work.

As with Nicholas (2011), I begin the present work with an elaboration of Marx's explanation of the money price of the commodity and then expand on and critically assess what I consider to be the major alternative explanations (viz., the explanations of Smith, Ricardo, Sraffa, the PKs, and Neoclassicals) as well as other Marxist interpretations of Marx's explanation. When expanding on the explanations of money price by Marx and all other approaches, as well as Marxist interpretations of Marx's explanation, I begin with an outline of the general focus and approach they adopt, then move to a consideration of what I perceive to be the foundations of their explanations of the money price of a commodity, ending with a consideration of these explanations. I take the foundations of the explanation of the money price of the commodity in all approaches to be their explanations of the value and exchange value of both the commodity and money, as well as their explanations of the nature of production, exchange, and money. I pay particular attention to the conceptions of the value of the commodity and its link to money, seeing this as the source of the various problems with all other approaches to the explanation of the money price of the commodity from the perspective of Marx's analysis.

When interpreting the explanations of the value and exchange value of the commodity and money in all approaches, including that of Marx and other Marxist interpreters of Marx, I begin by focusing on the underlying conceptions of what is being explained, viz., the conceptions of the value and exchange value of the commodity and money, and then consider their measures, historic emergence and formation, and the determination of their magnitudes. I attach particular importance to the **conception** and **measure** of what is being explained, especially to the conceptions and measures of the values of the commodity and money, whether or not adherents of the different approaches admit to these. I see the source of the deficiencies of the other explanations of the money price of the commodity their erroneous conceptions of the value of the commodity and corresponding conceptions of the value of money. For the sake of conceptual and theoretical clarity I ascribe to all of the approaches, including that of Marx and Marxist interpreters of his work, certain aspects of what I take to be part and parcel of their explanations of the value and exchange value of the commodity and money in the absence of explicit accounts of these. The most common of these ascriptions are the historic emergence and formation of the value and exchange value of the commodity and money. Most approaches are silent on these. I argue, however, the logic of their general explanations of the values and exchange values of the commodity and money allows for the derivation of these.

The mode of presentation I have adopted in the book is, admittedly, quite formal. I see this as necessary since one of my purposes in writing the book is to bring clarity to the relevant literature; to make clear the building blocks of the major explanations of the money price of the commodity and the essential differences between them. In the course of a lifetime of reading on the subject, I can say, without much fear of contradiction, that explanations of money price are among the most opaque in a body of literature (i.e., economics) that is renowned for its opacity. The debates over the veracity of different explanations have become increasingly confused and confusing, with less attention paid to scientific rigour and more to political and other expediency. A recent example of this is the debate over the role of the supply of money in the explanation of inflation. Not only has the theory purporting to explain the link between the two changed over time, so have the policy implications stemming from it. It was not long ago that the causal link between changes in the quantity of money and inflation was seen as one cast in stone, with central banks required to be prudent with respect to the amount of money they injected into the economic system. Now there is no such certainty about this supposedly hallowed relationship, and the behaviour of those responsible for monetary policies in the largest of the advanced countries has been anything but prudent since the Great Financial Crisis (GFC) of 2008–2009.

The basic argument I develop in the book is that Marx's explanation of the money price of the commodity is the most logically consistent and intuitively plausible explanation among all the competing explanations. It is the only explanation that allows changes in the relative money prices of commodities to be conceived of as taking place in the context of changes in the aggregate money price level as well as independently of the latter, and brings the productivity of labour into the explanation of both. All other approaches conceive of changes in the relative money prices of commodities taking place independently of changes in the aggregate money prices of commodities, and downplay, if not entirely ignore, the impact of changes in the productivity of labour on money prices, especially the aggregate money price level. Logically, changes in the money prices of commodities relative to one another must be related to changes in the aggregate money price level, and changes in the money prices of commodities in general related to the productivity of labour. If the productivity of labour is deemed not to have a bearing on the money prices of commodities, what could possibly explain the trend fall in the money prices of commodities in the period after 2009, a period when governments of the advanced countries have adopted some of the most expansive fiscal and monetary policies seen since the end of World War II?

References

Böhm-Bawerk, von E. (1975). Karl Marx and the close of his system. In P.M. Sweezy (Ed.), *Karl Marx and the close of his system by Eugen von Böhm-Bawerk & Böhm-Bawerk's criticism of Marx by Rudolf Hilferding* (pp. 3–118). Merlin Press (originally published in 1896).

Dobb, M. (1973). *Theories of value and distribution since Adam Smith: Ideology and economic theory*. Cambridge University Press.

Fine, B., & Saad-Filho, A. (2004). *Marx's 'Capital'* (4th ed.). Pluto Press.

Foley, D.K. (1986). *Understanding 'Capital': Marx's economic theory*. Harvard University Press.

Keen, S. (2001). *Debunking economics: The naked emperor of the social sciences*. Zed Books.

Nicholas, H. (2011). *Marx's theory of price and its modern rivals*. Palgrave Macmillan.

Nicholas, H. (forthcoming). *Explorations in Marx's theory of price, Volume 2: Profits and business cycles*. Palgrave Macmillan.

Rodrik, D. (2015). *Economics rules: The rights and wrongs of the dismal science*. W. W. Norton.

Roncaglia, A. (1978). *Sraffa and the theory of prices* (Trans. from Italian by J. A. Kregel). Wiley.

Roncaglia, A. (2009). *Piero Sraffa*. Palgrave Macmillan.

Samuelson, P. A. (1957). Wages and interest: A modern dissection of Marxian economic models. *American Economic Review, 47*(6), 884–912.

Sinha, A. (2003). Some critical reflections on Marx's theory of value. In R. Westra & A. Zuege (Eds.), *Value and the world economy today: Production, finance and globalization* (pp. 171–187). Palgrave Macmillan.

Sinha, A. (2010). *Theories of value from Adam Smith to Piero Sraffa*. Routledge.

Steedman, I. (1977). *Marx after Sraffa*. New Left Books.

Steedman, I. (1991). The irrelevance of Marxian values. In G. A. Caravale (Ed.), *Marx and modern economic analysis, Vol I: Values, Prices and Exploitation* (pp. 205–221). Edward Elgar.

Wheen, F. (2006). *Marx's Das Kapital: A biography*. Atlantic Books.

CHAPTER 2

Marx's Explanation of Money Price

2.1 Introduction

Marx did not leave behind a clear explanation of the money price of a commodity, not even in *Capital*, considered to be the most complete of all his writings on political economy. What he did leave is the foundations for the construction of such an explanation, with certain indications of its core elements. These foundations are his explanations of the value and exchange value of the commodity and money in both the simple circulation of commodities and the circuit of capital. The core elements of his explanation of the money price of the commodity are the emphasis he places on the productivity of labour and money's function as the measure of the exchange value of the commodity. My purpose in this chapter is to use these foundations and core elements to outline what I consider to be the explanation of the money price of the commodity found in his work.

The original version of this chapter was revised: Typographical errors in page 23 have been corrected. The correction is available at https://doi.org/10.1057/978-1-137-56564-8_10

H. Nicholas, *Explorations in Marx's Theory of Price—Why Marx Is Still Relevant for Understanding the Modern Economy*, https://doi.org/10.1057/978-1-137-56564-8_2

2.2 Object and Approach

2.2.1 Object

Marx's study of the capitalist system is part of his more ambitious plan to study world history.[1] His initial excursions into this more ambitious study lead him to conclude that it requires him to get a firmer grasp of economy, and in particular the economic dynamics of the current economic system, the capitalist economic system. For this task Marx considered himself fortunate to be in exile in Britain from late 1840 onwards, since for him Britain was clearly the epicentre of the world capitalist system at that time.

According to Marx (1976, p. 92) his purpose in *Capital* is "...to reveal the economic laws of motion of modern society...". The laws of motion he refers to are the long-term tendencies of the system and its cyclical movement, both of which are the result of the drive of capitalists to accumulate wealth on the basis of the production of ever-increasing quantities of commodities. The long-term tendencies Marx sees resulting from the process of capital accumulation include; continuous technological change and accompanying increases in the capital intensity of production, the intensive and extensive expansion of capitalist production alongside the increasing commodification of all economic activity, the increasing concentration and centralisation of capital, and the relative immiserisation of the working classes (albeit in the context of rising living standards). He sees the cyclical movement of the capitalist system resulting from the tendency of the rate of profit to fall. Marx sees his explanation of price as one of the foundations on which his explanation of the laws of motion of the capitalist system is built. He sees the important prices to be explained as trend and cyclical money prices.

2.2.2 Approach

The approach Marx adopts in his analysis of the capitalist system has three pillars; a materialist understanding of history, abstraction, and a critical appraisal of the works of other scholars, especially those he sees as reflecting the views of the dominant classes.

Marx explains his materialist understanding of history as the identification of different historical epochs on the basis of production systems

[1] See Rosdolsky (1977, pp. 12–13).

founded on a division of labour, with class systems being those production systems in which a surplus product is produced and appropriated by one class as a result of the efforts of another.[2] He sees the capitalist system as one such class system, with its defining feature the purchase and sale of labour power as a commodity that is used in the production of commodities for the purposes of their sale and the appropriation of a profit by the owners of these commodities—the capitalist producers.

Marx conceives of his method of abstraction as an attempt to capture the essence of the phenomena being investigated.[3] It is not one of temporarily ignoring certain phenomenal forms while focusing on what are perceived to be the most important of these phenomenal forms. For Marx, this form of abstraction results in a distorted understanding of the phenomena being investigated, as does the failure to abstract at all. Accordingly, his analysis of the capitalist system in *Capital* should be understood as the analysis of an integrated world capitalist system and not a closed capitalist economy. Similarly, Marx's analysis of the simple circuit of commodities at the beginning of Volume 1 of *Capital* should be understood as his attempt to capture the essence of the circuit of capital as the circulation of commodities and money, and not the study of a system that is historically antecedent to capitalism or in some way distinct from it. Moreover, when Marx analyses the simple circulation of commodities he begins by abstracting from money not only to capture the essence of money but also to capture what he considers to be the essence of the entire capitalist production system; the value of the commodity. Abstracting from money in the first instance enables Marx to conceive of the commodities that are produced in the context of a division of labour mediated by exchange as the products of the expenditure of labour time. Money is the objectification of this labour time. On the basis of this understanding of both commodities and money Marx undertakes his analysis of the circuit of capital in *Capital*. Defining capital as a certain magnitude of value that expands in size over the course of its circuit, Marx analyses this circuit in the first instance as the production and circulation of productive capital-in-general (Volumes 1 and 2), and then extends this to competition between individual productive capitals and the different

[2] See Marx (1964).

[3] See Marx (1970, pp. 205–214).

forms capital-in-general assumes in its circuit (Volume 3).[4] Marx uses his analysis of the circuit of capital to explain various economic phenomena in terms of what he considers to be the processes underlying them. He sees these processes as the production of commodities as receptacles of value and surplus value as well as the distribution of the surplus value between owners of non-labour inputs.

It is important to emphasise that the distinction Marx draws between the underlying forces driving the system and the economic phenomena they give rise to should not be seen as akin to the distinction between real and monetary forces and phenomena in orthodox (Neoclassical) economics.[5] For Marx, the capitalist economy is a money-based economy. The real and monetary phenomena of orthodox economics are all phenomenal forms that arise from the functioning of the capitalist economy. They are explained by the above-mentioned underlying forces and the various tendencies they give rise to. They cannot, and should not, be clustered into real and monetary phenomena and explained by real and monetary forces, respectively.

Similarly, it is also important to emphasise that the distinction Marx makes between trend and cyclical economic phenomena is not analogous to that between **equilibrium** and **disequilibrium** economic phenomena also found in orthodox (Neoclassical) economics literature, where the former are seen as corresponding to balance between supply and demand and acting as a sort of centre of gravity of disequilibrium phenomena corresponding to imbalances between supply and demand and fluctuating around equilibrium phenomena. Which is not to say that Marx ignores the forces of supply and demand in his explanation of economic phenomena. There can be no doubting he sees these as important, especially given the frequency of his references to them. However, his concern is to uncover the forces underlying shifts in the supply of, and demand for, commodities which result in alternating tendencies towards, and away from, equilibrium. To quote Marx (1976, p. 476);

[4] See Rosdolsky (1977) for an insightful account of the structure, logic, and contents of Marx's *Capital*.

[5] Real phenomena in orthodox (Neoclassical) economics are seen as phenomena such as output and employment, and explained by real factors (the quantity decisions of individuals), while monetary phenomena are seen as phenomena such as inflation and the balance of payments, and explained by monetary factors (the decisions of individuals in respect of monetary variables).

> It is true that the different spheres of production constantly tend towards equilibrium, for the following reason. On the one hand, every producer of a commodity is obliged to produce a use-value, i.e. he must satisfy a particular social need (though the extent of these needs differs quantitatively, and there exists an inner bond which attaches the different levels of need to a system which has grown up spontaneously); on the other hand, the law of the value of commodities ultimately determines how much of its disposable labour-time society can expend on each kind of commodity. But this constant tendency on the part of the various spheres of production towards equilibrium comes into play only as a reaction against the constant upsetting of this equilibrium.

Lastly, there can be little doubt that in the development of his own economic analysis Marx draws considerably from the works of other economists, including those belonging to the Psysiocratic and Classical schools of economists, and in particular the works of Adam Smith and David Ricardo. However, it warrants emphasising that he does so by way of a critical appraisal of these works, indicating what he considers to be their shortcomings.

2.3 Production and Value of the Commodity

2.3.1 Production

Marx sees all economic systems, except the most primitive, based on cooperation between individuals in the production of the mass of products required to reproduce the material bases of these systems. That is to say, Marx sees all economic systems involving the cooperation between individuals as producers based on a division of labour. He famously argues,

> The solitary and isolated hunter of fisherman who serves Adam Smith and Ricardo as a starting point, is one of the unimaginative fantasies of eighteenth-century romances *à la* Robinson Crusoe... (1970, p. 188)

Marx sees the capitalist economic system too founded on an extensive division of labour, but one mediated by money-based exchange. As noted above, Marx distinguishes between different economic systems or modes of production according to whether or not a surplus product is produced and the manner in which it is appropriated. He refers to all economic systems in which a surplus product is produced as class-based systems. He sees the products produced in all non-class-based systems, e.g., the communal or rural patriarchal systems, as directly social products, and those produced in class-based systems, e.g., feudal and capitalist systems, as indirectly social.[6] Marx sees products becoming social use values in capitalism in the context of their exchange for money.

Marx conceives of the organisers of the processes of production in non-class-based economic systems as the direct producers, e.g., the head of a family or village elders, and in class-based systems as the appropriators of the surplus product, e.g., the owners of land in feudal systems and the owners of the means of production in capitalism.

Marx conceives of the inputs into production in all modes of production as labour and means of production, and not simply labour. He argues in this respect,

> It would be wrong to say that labour which produces use-values is the *only* source of the wealth produced by it, that is of material wealth. Since labour is an activity which adapts material for some purpose or other, it needs material as a prerequisite. Different use-values contain very different proportions of labour and natural products, but use-value always comprises a natural element. As useful activity directed to the appropriation of natural factors in one form or another, labour is a natural condition of human existence, a condition of material interchange between man and nature, quite independent of the form of society. (Marx, 1970, p. 36)

And again,

> Labour is, first of all, a process between man and nature, a process by which man, through his own actions, mediates, regulates and controls the metabolism between himself and nature. (Marx, 1976, p. 283)

Marx conceives of the processes of production in economic systems based on divisions of labour as involving the expenditure of simple labour time in the context of the productive consumption of means of production. He defines simple labour time as the labour time expended by an ordinary person with ordinary abilities in a given society and a given historical epoch, and the expenditure of skilled labour time as certain multiples

[6] Marx (1970, p. 33).

of the expenditure of simple labour time. He conceives of the labour time expended as directly social labour time, i.e., the labour time needed to produce products for which there is social demand, in all modes of production where the division of labour is not mediated by exchange. In capitalism, where the division of labour is mediated by exchange, the labour time expended only counts as social labour time, and the use values produced as social use values, when the commodity is exchanged for money. For Marx, the exchange of commodities for money in capitalism presupposes the labour time expended is qualitatively equivalent or *abstract* labour time.[7] Specifically, Marx sees the expenditure of all labour time as physiologically speaking the same even though it is necessarily useful concrete labour producing a variety of use values. It is this that permits the different products to be exchanged for money in capitalism, although it is not something producers are aware of when they exchange their products for money.[8]

Lastly, Marx conceives of the products comprising both consumption goods and means of production. He stresses that one of the problems with Classical economists is their adherence to Smith's exclusion of the means of production in what is produced. As I will expand on below, Marx sees this exclusion as the result of Smith's income cost explanation of the price of the commodity.

2.3.2 *Value of the Commodity*

Following Smith and Ricardo, Marx sees the basis for the explanation of the magnitude of the price of the commodity as its cost of production, and this in turn its value. Marx differs from both Smith and Ricardo with respect to his **conception** of value and his understanding of the link between the value of the commodity and its price.

For Marx, products have values whenever they require the expenditure of labour time for their existence. As noted above, for Marx the expenditure of labour time constitutes the expenditure of simple labour time that is simultaneously the expenditure of social labour time in all economic systems where goods are produced on the basis of the cooperative efforts of producers, i.e., in the context of a division of labour. Social labour time

[7] Marx (1970, p. 32; 1976, p. 166).

[8] Marx (1976, pp. 166–167).

is the labour time that needs to be expended to meet the social demand for the product.[9] As also noted above, for Marx the expenditure of labour time in capitalism is not directly social, unlike in economic systems such as feudalism. The labour time expended in capitalism counts as social labour time when the product that is produced, the commodity, is exchanged. For Marx, the production of the commodity for the purposes of its exchange causes the labour time expended to acquire the character of general or abstract labour time—qualitatively equivalent labour time. It is the expenditure of labour time as abstract latently social labour time that is the source of the value of the commodity. The expenditure of this labour time allows the commodity to be exchanged for other commodities and, in the final instance, the universal equivalent commodity or money, causing the latently social labour time expended to count as actual social labour time expended. Marx stresses that one of the problems with deciphering the existence of value in capitalism is that it is "invisible". The commodity does not have a sign on it indicating that it has value in the sense of being the product of the expenditure of social labour time. Rather this value only becomes manifest in the form of the exchange value of the commodity, and evidenced by the impact of changes in the former on the latter—the impact of changes in the value of the commodity on its exchange value.[10]

Two additional points need noting in the context of the above. First, for Marx the expenditure of labour time in capitalism that causes a product to have value is the expenditure of labour time that adds use value to the product.[11] Which means he sees some labour time expended in the circulation of commodities, e.g., on their transport, as also contributing to the formation of the values of commodities since this expenditure of labour time, like that in the immediate process of production, adds use value to the commodity. Second, Marx distinguishes between *real* and *relative* value of the commodity. He sees the former as the labour time required to produce the commodity *per se*, and the latter as this labour

[9] "…the real amount of labour (materialized and immediate) it costs to produce a commodity, is its value. It constitutes the real production cost of the commodity itself" (Marx, 1972, p. 513).

[10] See Marx (1976, p. 167).

[11] Marx (1976, p. 131).

time relative to what is required to produce other commodities.[12] Marx argues that one of the weaknesses of Ricardo and Smith is that they lose sight of the former and focus their attention on the latter.[13]

Marx's conception of the value of a commodity leads him to see its **measure** as a certain quantity of social labour time objectified in the commodity. He sees this quantity as the quantity of social labour time directly expended in the production of the commodity in pre-capitalist systems and the quantity of latently social labour time that needs to be expended in capitalism. Marx sees the quantity of labour time that measures the value of the commodity in capitalism as a quantity of abstract simple labour time that is necessary for the production of any commodity. Marx stresses that this labour time is not what is actually expended in the production of the commodity but rather what needs to be expended. He sees the labour time expended by skilled labour being reduced to multiples of simple labour in the context of the determination of wages, when skilled labour is rewarded proportionately more than simple labour.[14] To emphasise that the labour time constituting the measure of the value of the commodity is what is needed to be expended given the technical conditions of production, Marx refers to this measure as 'socially necessary' labour time. For Marx, this measure is the immanent measure of the value of the commodity since, like the latter, it cannot be seen. Marx argues this labour time becomes the immanent measure of the value of the commodity when producers use money to denote the general exchange value of the commodity causing money and commodities to become the embodiments of certain magnitudes of this labour time.[15] Of particular note here is the emphasis Marx places on the labour time used to measure the value of the commodity itself having no value.[16] He argues labour time is an ideal measuring rod of value since its magnitude does not change with the magnitude of value of the commodity whose value it is tacitly being used to measure. This is not the case with a commodity

[12] "If the values of all commodities rose or fell simultaneously, and in the same proportion, their relative values would remain unaltered. The change in their real values would be manifested by an increase or decrease in the quantity of commodities produced within the same labour-time" (Marx, 1976, p. 146).

[13] See Marx (1969b, p. 172).

[14] See Marx (1972, p. 165).

[15] See Marx (1976, p. 188).

[16] Marx (1976, p. 677).

or money as the alleged measures of the value of a commodity. These measures must logically have values that will change with changes in the factors impacting on the magnitude of value of the commodity. Marx makes this point explicitly with respect to Smith's corn measure of value of the commodity (see below).[17]

What should already be evident from the preceding is that Marx sees products **acquiring values** when they are produced in the context of a division of labour. Which means, contrary to other Marxist interpretations of his work that I will discuss below, he does not see products acquiring value in relation to one another with the emergence of capitalism *per se*, or even the exchange of products as commodities for one another in pre-capitalist economic systems. Rather, he sees products acquiring values when they begin to be produced in the context of a division of labour. Marx (1973, pp. 170–171) argues,

> Thus, economy of time, along with the planned distribution of labour time among the various branches of production, remains the first economic law on the basis of communal production.

Marx's conception of value also leads him to see the value of the product in pre-capitalist systems formed in the process of its production while the value of the commodity in capitalism is **formed** after its production and before it is put into the process of circulation, and not either in the processes of its production or its circulation/exchange. For Marx the value of the commodity formed in capitalism is the labour time *required for* the production of the bulk of commodities of a certain type. It is the transformed form of the labour time actually expended in the production of the commodity. This transformation takes place when money is used by the producer to denote the general exchange value of the commodity. Capitalist producers use money to denote the general exchange values of their commodities after their production and just prior to putting the commodities into the market to be sold.

Lastly, Marx argues that the **magnitude of value** of a commodity is determined by the quantity of the 'socially necessary labour time' required to produce it. He sees this socially necessary labour time as the quantity of abstract simple labour time required to produce the bulk of the

[17] Marx (1969a, pp. 70–71).

commodity of a certain type.[18] To repeat, the point Marx makes in this regard is that what matters is not the labour time actually expended in the production of the commodity but what is *necessary* to produce a representative commodity of a certain type. Although Marx does not discuss the matter in the first three chapters of *Capital*, he makes it clear in the course of his analysis of the circuit of capital that the socially necessary labour time required to produce the commodity includes the labour time transferred from the means of production that need to be used in its production. This labour time is what is objectified in the money needed to repurchase the means of production.[19] That is, he sees the current money prices of means of production determining the value transferred from the means of production to the value of the commodity produced with these, and the money prices of the means of production determined by their values in the manner of the money prices of all commodities (see below).

The most important implications Marx draws from his explanation of the magnitude of value of a commodity is the role of changes in the (technologically induced) *productivity of labour* in explaining changes in this magnitude. For Marx, changes in the productivity of labour have a fundamental bearing on both the absolute and relative value of the commodity, and, *via* this, on the value of money and money prices of commodities. Sectoral changes in the productivity of labour cause values of commodities to change relative to one another. Economy-wide increases in the productivity of labour cause the values of all commodities to fall, with differences in increases in productivity between sectors explaining differences in reductions in magnitudes of values of commodities produced in them. For Marx, changes in the values of commodities that result from economy-wide and relative sectoral changes in productivity are not influenced by accompanying changes in the distribution of income.

A second important implication Marx draws from his explanation of the magnitude of value of the commodity concerns the *value transferred* from the non-labour commodity means of production used in its production. This transfer can involve the transformation of the use values of the means of production into the use values of outputs, as well as the productive destruction of the former—the use values of the means of production.

[18] Marx (1981, pp. 283–284).

[19] Marx (1976, pp. 317–318).

Since, for Marx, something cannot have value unless its production requires the expenditure of labour time, there cannot be a transfer of value from the means of production to the value of the commodity produced with them unless the means of production are themselves produced. Marx emphasises that the value transferred is the current replacement value of the means of production and not their historic values. In the case of non-produced means of production such as land and raw materials, no value is transferred. Instead, the owner of the non-produced means of production appropriates as income part of the surplus labour time that needs to be expended in the production of the commodity with the aid of these means of production. This income is rent. The private ownership of non-produced means of production presumes their supply can be limited, allowing for the appropriation of a certain amount of absolute rent. Different qualities of the inputs and/or different productivities of labour expended in the production of commodities with these inputs allow for different amounts of rent to be appropriated by owners of the means of production. Marx (1976, p. 312) argues that if the input used

> ….is not the product of human labour, it transfers no value to the product. It helps create use-value without contributing to the formation of exchange-value. This is true of all those means of production supplied by nature without human assistance, such as land, wind, water, metals in the form of ore, and timber in virgin forests.

Critics of Marx's economics have long argued that, he, like many of the Classical economists whose work he is seen as following, ignores the usefulness of, or demand for, the commodity when explaining value.[20] Even a cursory reading of Marx's explanation of value suggests this criticism stems from a crass misinterpretation of his explanation of the value of a commodity. Marx is clear that a commodity will not have value unless it is useful—socially useful. He argues that if a commodity loses its use value it loses its value, something that is particularly important in the explanation of the value of long-lasting material inputs and depreciation charges pertaining to these.[21] What Marx is at pains to emphasise, however, is that while usefulness is a necessary condition for a commodity to possess value it is not a sufficient condition. The usefulness of a commodity is not

[20] See for example Bowles and Gintis (1981, p. 5), Rodrick (2015, pp. 118–119).

[21] See Marx (1976, p. 310).

what causes the commodity to have objective worth in relation to other commodities as manifest in the standard prices attached to all commodities of a given kind irrespective of their particular usefulness to different individuals. Instead, it is the expenditure of labour time that causes the commodity to have value, albeit in a way that adds social usefulness to the product.

Other critics of Marx's economics have argued that like many Classical economists he mistakenly sees the expenditure of labour time as the only source of value of a commodity. Gehrke and Kurz (2018, p. 435) quote Sraffa arguing that "…it is a purely mystical conception that attributes to labour a special gift of determining value". G. Hodgson (1982, pp. 77–78) argues that "neither Marx, nor anyone else, has demonstrated that labour is the only social and objective common substance embodied in commodities". However, these critics are interpreting Marx confusing the explanations of the value of the commodity with explanations of material wealth. For Marx, the production of material wealth requires material as well as labour inputs, while the production of value only requires the expenditure of labour time in the production of the commodity.

2.4 Exchange and Exchange Value of the Commodity

2.4.1 *Exchange*

Marx's purpose in **conceiving** of the process of exchange in the context of a simple circulation of commodities at the beginning of volume 1 of *Capital* is to capture the essence of the exchange process that facilitates the circuit of capital. This circuit is money (M) outlaid on commodities (C) in the form of the labour power and means of production needed to produce consumer goods and means of production (C'). These are then sold for an amount of money (M') that is in excess of the money outlaid allowing the producer to appropriate a money profit. The complete circuit of capital is then M-C-C'-M'. Marx conceives of the essence of this circuit as C-C', the simple circulation of commodities abstracting from money and capital. This essence, together with his conception of value, provides the basis for his explanation of money and capital; money being the materialisation of value and capital being the expansion of value on the basis of the reproduction of the commodity.

Marx conceives of the process of commodity exchange **emerging** prior to capitalism, and the nature of this exchange changing with the emergence of the capitalist mode of production. He sees the process of exchange prior to capitalism as that between self-sufficient communities exchanging their surplus products with a view to enhancing their consumption satisfaction. Production in these communities is typically for direct consumption. With the transition to capitalism, production is for exchange and, therefore, exchange becomes widespread. For Marx, when production is increasingly for exchange the exchange of commodities becomes increasingly the exchange of particular commodities for one representing general exchange value—the universal equivalent commodity. At the same time the commodities being exchanged for this universal equivalent commodity acquire the form of general exchangeable worth, i.e., the form of the universal equivalent commodity.

It warrants noting here that when Marx analyses the simple circulation of commodities he conceives of the commodities exchanged for one another as the products of socially necessary labour time. Marx refers to the commodity being commanded in the process of exchange as 'the equivalent form', the bodily form of which is the materialisation of this labour time, and the commodity that commands the equivalent form as 'the relative form of value'.[22] He argues that when all producers express the exchange values of their commodities as general exchange values in one and the same commodity, one and the same equivalent form, this commodity becomes the 'universal equivalent' form and, as such, the materialisation of socially necessary labour time *par excellence*.[23] This commodity is the general commodity or money.

Lastly, although Marx conceives of the essence of the process of exchange in capitalism as one commodity for another, he should not be interpreted as conceiving of this process as one of **barter**, in the manner of the Classical economists. This is not because Marx sees the process of exchange of commodities for one another mediated by money in capitalism, but rather because he sees the commodities put into the process of exchange, or rather circulation, possessing the forms of general exchange values indicating their general exchangeability. For Marx, the exchange of commodities in pre-capitalist social systems are barter exchanges, with

[22] See Marx (1976, pp. 140–151) for an extensive discussion of these concepts.

[23] See Marx (1976, p. 161).

the exchange ratios between the commodities determined in the process of exchange by the strength of demand for the commodities relative to the quantity of the commodities supplied. In capitalism the exchange value of the commodity is set before it is put into the process of circulation. I will expand on this point below.

2.4.2 *Exchange Value of the Commodity*

Although Marx most certainly **conceives** of the exchange value of the commodity that needs explaining in the final instance as the money exchange value or money price of the commodity, as noted above he begins his explanation of the exchange value of the commodity by abstracting from capital and money. He conceives of the exchange value of the commodity to be explained in the first instance as the commodity exchange value; the quantity of another commodity a given commodity commands in the process of exchange. He sees the exchange value of the commodity as the form assumed by the value of the commodity when its reproduction is facilitated by exchange. It is the explanation of the commodity exchange value of the commodity that for Marx provides the basis for understanding its money exchange value or money price since the latter is the more general form of the former.

Conceiving of the exchange value of the commodity as its commodity exchange value causes Marx to conceive of the **measure of this exchange value** as the commodity that serves as the 'equivalent' in the exchange of any two commodities. This equivalent is the 'materialisation' of the labour time expended in the production of the commodity constituting the relative form of exchange value.[24] For Marx, the use of a particular commodity to measure the exchange values of all commodities (i.e., to denote their general exchange values) causes this commodity to become the *universal equivalent* or *general commodity* and the labour time expended in its production to become socially necessary labour time. When this commodity is used to measure the general exchange values of all commodities, the labour expended in its production becomes the immanent measure of their exchange values and, therefore, the measure of their values. Although Marx conceives of particular commodities as measures of the exchange values of one another in the first instance, i.e.,

[24] See Marx (1976, pp. 147–152).

when abstracting from money, he is clear that with the development of the exchange-based reproduction of commodities one commodity becomes the 'general equivalent form' and measure of the exchangeable worth of all commodities.[25] This commodity is the money commodity. It becomes the general equivalent form when it is used by all producers to set the prices of their commodities prior to putting them into the process of circulation.[26]

Marx sees the production of the commodity for exchange as the necessary condition for it to **acquire** the form of certain magnitude of exchange value that serves to facilitate its reproduction. He refers to the products of labour that possess exchange values as 'commodities', to distinguish them from the products of labour that are intended for immediate consumption. He argues that a necessary condition for commodities to acquire exchange values is that they possess values. Marx accepts products can acquire exchange values even if they are not produced for exchange. He argues, however, that these exchange values would not be of such magnitudes as to facilitate the reproduction of these commodities. Rather, for Marx, they would reflect the mutual desires of those exchanging the products, with what is exchanged typically being the product surpluses of self-sufficient communities and the exchange ratios between the products being determined in an *ad hoc* fashion.[27]

A further important implication of Marx's analysis of the commodity exchange values of commodities in developed exchange-based systems is that they are **formed** prior to being put into the process of circulation. In fact, they are formed when producers use the commodity that becomes the general equivalent to denote the general exchange values of their commodities with a view to facilitating their reproduction. It has to be admitted, however, that Marx does not make this point explicitly in the context of the exchange of the commodities for one another since for him it is most appropriately made in the context of money-based exchange and the use of money as the measure of the exchange values of commodities (see below).

[25] See Marx (1976, pp. 158–161).

[26] Marx (1976, pp. 162–163, 180–181).

[27] Marx (1976, p. 182).

Lastly, when explaining the magnitude of the exchange value of the commodity Marx begins by abstracting from, money, capital and supply-demand imbalances, and explains the magnitude of the exchange value of the commodity in the first instance as the trend magnitude of the universal equivalent exchange value of the commodity in the context of the simple circulation of commodities. He explains this magnitude by the magnitude of the value of the commodity or the socially necessary labour time required for its production. When Marx brings money into the analysis he continues to explain the magnitude of the exchange value of the commodity in the simple circulation of commodities, but now as the magnitude of its trends money exchange value. He explains this magnitude, like that of the magnitude of the universal equivalent exchange value of the commodity, by the magnitude of its value. When Marx brings capital into the analysis he explains the magnitude of the exchange value of the commodity in the first instance as the trend magnitude of its money exchange value in the context of the circuit of capital-in-general, and then subsequently as the trend money exchange value or money price of production of the commodity in the context of competition between capitals (firms) and the formation of the general rate of profit. Marx then completes his explanation of the magnitude of the exchange value of the commodity by bringing into the analysis supply-demand imbalances and explaining this magnitude as that of the money market price of the commodity. I will elaborate on Marx's explanation of the trend magnitude of money price of production of the commodity below and the magnitude of the money market price of the commodity in Nicholas (forthcoming). What requires consideration here is Marx's explanation of the trend magnitude of the money exchange value of the commodity in the context of the circuit of capital-in-general. Marx depicts this explanation as;

$$EV = MP + Lw + S \tag{1.1}$$

where EV is the quantity of money commanded by a unit of the commodity, MP is the money expended on the means of production used to produce a unit of the commodity, L is the quantity of labour time required to produce a unit of the commodity, w is the economy-wide money wage rate, and S is the money form of surplus value. The money exchange value of the commodity must equal the money paid for means of production (MP) and appropriated as wages and surplus value in the context of the production of a unit of the commodity, with the money form of surplus value being the money value of unpaid labour appropriated by the capitalist producer. For Marx, as I will expand on below, since money comes to embody a certain quantity of (socially necessary) labour time, the money value commanded by the commodity can be seen as translated into a certain quantity of (socially necessary) labour time and determined by the transformed form of the labour time expended directly and indirectly in the production of the commodity, i.e. the quantity of socially necessary labour time required for the production of a unit of the commodity. Marx derives the importance of the labour time expended in the production of the commodity as the major determinant of the magnitude of its exchange value by an extensive and detailed consideration of the process of production and the actions of the capitalist producer in the pursuit of profit. He sees these actions as in one way or another resulting in the reduction of the unit labour time required for the production of the commodity.[28] He stresses that the socially necessary labour time required for the production of the commodity is not visible, hence its impact on the money exchange value of the commodity needs to be deduced by the correspondence between changes in the money exchange value of the commodity relative to another commodity and changes in the relative productivity of labour in their production. Marx uses the analogy with gravity to explain this link, arguing that the value of the commodity acts as a centre of gravity for its money exchange value.[29]

Of note in the context of the above is that for Marx the value transferred to the value of the commodity from the means of production is given by the value of money required to repurchase these, and not the labour time expended in their production or the value of money used to purchase them prior to their use in the process of production, i.e., their historic costs. I will return to this point below when discussing Marx's explanation of the money price of the commodity in the context of the

[28] See Nicholas (forthcoming) for a discussion of Marx's analysis of the capitalist process of production and the drive of the capitalist producer to reduce unit labour costs.

[29] Marx (1976, p. 168).

formation of the economy-wide rate of profit, and in Nicholas (forthcoming) in the context of a discussion of Marx's so-called transformation problem.

A final point that needs to be made here concerns Marx's rationale for abstracting from supply–demand imbalances and focusing on the trend magnitude of the exchange value of the commodity in the first instance. For Marx the trend magnitude of the exchange value of the commodity is the average of movements in the magnitude of the money exchange value of the commodity (or money market prices of commodities) in the context of supply–demand imbalances. Marx sees short term movements in the money exchange values of commodities as resulting in changes in the methods of production and, therefore, the value and corresponding trend money exchange value of the product. Hence, his justification, like that of Smith and Ricardo, for abstracting from supply–demand imbalances in the first instance.[30]

2.5 Money and Its Functions

2.5.1 Money

Marx is often accused of neglecting money in his economic analyses and, as a result, having a fairly poor theory of money compared to other Classical economists.[31] However, even a cursory glance at his major works on political economy belies this contention. Indeed, what Marx's writings indicate is that he pays considerable attention to money, seeing it as pivotal to his explanation of the dynamics of the capitalist system. A case in point is the *Grundrisse*. This is a compilation of seven of Marx's Notebooks that are arguably his first serious attempt to set down in writing the results of his extensive research into political economy over the period 1850–1857.[32] The core of this work comprises two lengthy chapters amounting to well over one hundred pages and is almost exclusively devoted to money. Marx's concern with the role of money in the

[30] See Marx (1981, p. 266).

[31] Schumpeter (2003, p. 27) refers to Marx's "distinctly weak performance in the field of money, in which he did not succeed in coming up to the Ricardian standard", and Blaug (1985, p. 285) argues that "Marx's theory of money, even on its own reading, fares badly next to the best work of his predecessors".

[32] See Nicolaus (1973) for details of Marx's purpose in this work.

workings of the capitalist economy can also be seen in the remainder of this work, as well as the considerable attention he pays to it in *Capital, Theories of Surplus Value* and *Contribution*. In fact, the basis for accusing Marx of neglecting money is perhaps to be found in the neglect of this aspect of his work by many Marxist interpreters of his economic analyses (see below).

What Marx makes clear in his various writings on political economy, beginning with *Grundrisse*, is that the basis for understanding money and the role it plays in the capitalist system is an understanding of the reproduction of the commodity. Marx **conceives** of money in capitalism as whatever is used by producers to denote the exchange values of their commodities as certain magnitudes of *general* exchange values with a view to facilitating the reproduction of these commodities (i.e., enabling the producers to repurchase all the commodity means of production, including labour power). He sees the values of commodities assuming a money form, i.e., the form of money prices, and money becoming the representative of general exchange value and the objectification of a certain quantity of value (socially necessary labour time) when producers use money to denote the exchange values of their commodities as general exchange values.

Marx is particularly concerned to argue that money does not *represent* value *per se*, but is the form value necessarily assumes when commodities are produced for exchange. To conceive of money as representing value is, for Marx, to misunderstand both value and money. It implies value is something that is tangible and directly observable, and money is seen as representing a certain magnitude of it by all those using money in the performance of its various functions. For Marx, since value is not directly observable money cannot be seen as representing a certain magnitude of it by those using it. Rather, value as a certain magnitude of economy-wide socially necessary labour time becomes objectified in money when it is used to denote the exchange values of commodities as certain magnitudes of general exchange value, while at the same time becoming objectified in commodities when their exchange values acquire a money form.

Marx sees money **emerging** prior to capitalism with the development of the exchange of commodities for one another when one of the commodities being exchanged is used as a standard of all the other commodities being exchanged, i.e., is used as a numéraire commodity. He sees the numéraire commodity representing particular exchangeable worth and this worth changing with each and every transaction. Marx sees money in the early phases of capitalism assuming in the first instance the form of the numéraire commodity found in pre-capitalist economic systems, but its nature changing. That is, he sees the numéraire becoming the representative of general exchange value as a result of being used by producers to denote the general exchange values of their commodities with a view to facilitating their reproduction.

Marx sees money as the numéraire commodity in pre-capitalist economic systems assuming in the first instance the **form** of one or another of the most frequently traded commodities including salt, hides, slaves, cattle and metals, with metals, especially precious metals such as gold and silver, becoming increasingly the numéraire commodities of choice because of their greater homogeneity, divisibility, transportability, and durability.[33] He sees money in capitalism assuming the form of whatever is used by capitalist producers to denote the exchange values of their commodities as general exchange values, beginning with what was used as the numéraire commodity in the period immediately preceding the emergence of capitalism. Marx argues in this context that gold becomes money in capitalism because it is used by capitalist producers to measure the exchange values of their commodities, and not because it is a produced commodity with intrinsic value.[34] He even explicitly conceives of money assuming the form of credit money resting on an inconvertible fiat currency base arguing that in this case money "would be drafts on the nations stock of products and on the directly employable labour force" (1973, p.121).[35]

It should already be apparent from the preceding, and will become even clearer from the explanations of the value and exchange value of money, that Marx's conception of money precludes him from conceiving of money as a **veil**, having no link to the reproduction of the commodity. Specifically, since Marx conceives of money as whatever is used by producers to denote the exchange values of their commodities as general exchange values with a view to facilitating their reproduction, it should be readily apparent that for Marx changes in the value and exchange value of money, and corresponding changes in the money prices of commodities, have a profound bearing on their reproduction.

33 See Marx (1973, pp. 165–166).

34 Marx (1970, p. 115).

35 See also Marx (1970, pp. 121–122).

Lastly, given the proclivity of Marxists to interpret Marx conceiving of money as **capital** in the first instance (see Chapter 7), it is also important to note Marx is emphatic that money should not be conflated with *capital*, even though capital assumes the form of money in its circuit. For Marx the conflation of money with capital results in a mistaken understanding of both.[36] It causes money to be seen as yielding a return when it is held by individuals as a reserve of liquidity, i.e., a reserve of means of purchase and settlement of debts. It causes capital to be seen as assuming the form of money alone in its circuit as capital and not money and commodities as the forms value assumes in the process of its (value's) expansion. For Marx, this confusion is the result of a failure to abstract from capital in the first instance when attempting to understand money and the functions it performs.[37]

2.5.2 *Functions of Money*

After explaining the nature and historic emergence of money in the course of his discussion of the form the value of the commodity assumes in the process of its simple circulation in *Capital I* and *Contribution*, Marx proceeds to a consideration of the functions performed by money when facilitating the reproduction of the commodity. These functions are 'the measure of value', 'means of circulation', and 'money', where the function of money as money comprises 'hoard', 'means of payment' and 'world money'. When analysing these functions Marx considers it necessary to assume money to be gold because reference to more advanced forms of money, e.g., credit-money, requires a prior exposition of the circuit of capital and the different forms assumed by capital in this circuit, forms that he has yet to develop in his analysis.[38]

I begin with Marx's measure of value function, a function he considers to be its most important and defining function.[39] This function is the use of money to denote the general exchange value of the commodity, causing the latter to assume a money form. Assuming money to be gold Marx (1973, pp. 205–208) argues:

[36] Marx (1970, p. 66; 1976, p. 188).

[37] Marx (1973, p. 121).

[38] Marx (1976, p. 224).

[39] Marx (1976, p. 188).

> A commodity is exchange value only if it is expressed in another, i.e., as a relation....The same is true of money as measure, as the unit in which the exchange values of other commodities are measured....Exchange values (commodities) are transformed by the mind into certain weights of gold or silver and are ideally posited as being = to this imagined quantity of gold...

and,

> Hence, when money begins to function as a measure of value, when it is used to determine prices.... (Marx, 1976, p. 214)

I have argued elsewhere (see Nicholas, 2011, p. 17) that, as such, it would be more appropriate for this function of money to be referred to as **the measure of the exchange value** of the commodity function. For Marx, the performance of this function by money causes the labour time actually expended in the production of the commodity, i.e., the useful individual labour time, to be converted into a certain quantity of socially necessary labour time and money to become the form of a certain quantity of socially necessary labour time as the measure of the value of the commodity and the representative of general exchange value. Marx argues that the price form allows for a divergence between the labour time required for the production of the commodity and that objectified in the money commanded by the commodity.[40] It causes the link between the price form, as the labour time commanded by the commodity, and the value of the commodity, as the labour time actually expended in its production, to disappear. In fact, it even allows products to have money prices without being produced. Marx (1976, p. 197) comments,

> The price-form, however, is not only compatible with the possibility of a quantitative incongruity between magnitude of value and price, i.e., between the magnitude of value and its own expression in money, but it may also harbour a qualitative contradiction, with the result that price ceases altogether to express value, despite the fact that money is nothing but the value-form of commodities. Things which in and for themselves are not commodities, things such as conscience, honour, etc., can be offered for sale by their holders, and thus acquire the form of commodities through

[40] Marx (1976, p. 196).

> their price. Hence a thing can, formally speaking, have a price without having a value.

Although Marx sees the price form allowing for the possibility of a commodity acquiring general exchange value without being produced, he should not be interpreted as arguing that commodities in general can be seen as acquiring exchange value without being produced, without having labour time expended in their production. Far from it. The norm is that if labour time is not expended in the production of the commodity in the first place, this labour time cannot be translated into a certain magnitude of necessary labour time in the context of the commodity acquiring general exchange value in the form of money. Only in certain exceptional circumstances do products acquire money forms that bear little or no relation to the quantity of labour time expended in their production. For Marx, these exceptions do not prove the rule. He argues that it is the money form of exchange value that creates the illusion money is the source of value and, as such, confers value on commodities when it is exchanged for them.[41]

An important implication Marx draws from his analysis of money's function as measure is, as noted above, that it does not need to have a physical presence to perform this function. Rather, what functions as measure only needs to have a presence in the minds of those using it to set prices, it only needs to exist as money of account. Marx (1976, pp. 189–190) argues, "Since the expression of the value of commodities in gold is purely an ideal act, we may use purely imaginary or ideal gold to perform this operation".

Marx's measure function should not be confused with its numéraire function. Money is used as a numéraire in pre-capitalist economic systems to convert the exchange values of commodities in terms of one another into their exchange values in terms of one commodity, the numéraire commodity, to facilitate the exchange of these commodities for one another. Money is used as a measure of the exchange values of commodities in capitalism by producers of these commodities to facilitate their reproduction. Producers do this by denoting the exchange values of their commodities as magnitudes of money exchange values that reflect the money costs of producing them allowing them to appropriate the necessary money revenues to repurchase all the inputs, including labour

[41] Marx (1976, p. 187).

power, used up in the production of the commodities. As noted above, even though what serves as the numéraire commodity in pre-capitalist systems becomes the form assumed by the measure of the exchange values of commodities in the first instance in capitalism, money's function as measure is not the same as its function as a numéraire. The distinction between the two is manifest in the fact that the numéraire function is necessarily performed by a commodity while the measure function is not.

Marx's measure function of money is also not to be confused with its functions as a *standard of price* and *money of account*. As the measure of the exchange value of the commodity money serves to convert the exchange values of commodities into certain magnitudes of the substance of money, while as the standard of price money is used to denominate this price in terms of certain units of itself. Assuming gold to be money, gold as measure is used to convert the exchange value of the commodity into a certain magnitude of gold, while as a standard of price this magnitude is denominated in terms of units of gold, the units being certain weights of gold. These unit weights are then given names and the names serve as money of account.[42] Marx observes that the less the money of account is subject to variations, the better it serves the purpose of being a standard of price, while as measure the exchange value of the commodity the value of money is necessarily variable.[43]

The second function of money Marx pays considerable attention to is what he refers to as its **means of circulation** function. He sees this function as essentially one of validating the money prices set by producers. That is, he sees this function as the use of money to purchase goods in accordance with the money prices set by producers. Hence, it can also be referred to as a **means of purchase** function. The validation of price takes place when the commodity is put into circulation with a determinate money price and exchanged for money. Marx refers to this function as the means of circulation (means of purchase) and not medium of exchange function to draw attention to money's role as one of circulating commodities with determinate money prices and not one of facilitating their exchange for one another.

Marx sees the measure function of money as a prerequisite of its means of circulation function. As measure of the exchange values of commodities

[42] Marx (1976, pp. 194–195).

[43] Marx (1976, p. 192).

money converts the exchange values of commodities into money prices. As means of circulation it then facilitates the exchange of these commodities for money in accordance with the magnitudes of their money prices. This means that for Marx the quantity of money in the process of circulation depends on the quantity and money prices of commodities put into this process.

Marx argues that the performance of the means of circulation function of money does not require its material presence. Indeed, as a means of circulation, gold can be, and is, usually replaced by less valuable or even valueless tokens of itself.[44] What matters is that these tokens are accepted as being either convertible into money as gold, when they are issued as tokens of gold, or accepted as convertible into commodities when they are issued as tokens of commodities by the state. Marx argues that the form money assumes in its functioning as means of circulation leads to all manner of mistaken explanations of the determination of the magnitude of its value and corresponding money prices of commodities. This is because money as the means of circulation appears to be a token of either itself as a numéraire commodity or the commodities it circulates, giving the appearance of it acquires value as money in the process of the circulation of commodities.[45] Marx argues it is an appearance that is strengthened when money is a commodity by the ability of the state to push into circulation any quantity of valueless paper issued by it with a certain legal rate of exchange with the commodity that constitutes money, viz., gold. For Marx, this appearance is an illusion since the increase in the issue of tokens of gold in relation to the quantity of gold backing the tokens causes the value of the tokens to fall and prices in terms of these tokens to rise.[46]

Marx conceives of the third function of money as one where it is required to exist in its bodily form as opposed to when it has an ideal existence as measure or when it is capable of being replaced by tokens of itself when it functions as a means of circulation.[47] Marx conceives of this **function of money as money**, and sees it performing this function when it is called upon to function as hoard, means of payment, and world

[44] Marx (1970, p. 114).

[45] Marx (1976, pp. 212–213).

[46] Marx (1976, p. 225).

[47] Marx (1976, p. 227).

money. I will consider Marx's conceptions of money's functions of hoard and means of payment below, and take up his conception of money's function as world money in the third volume of the present work.

For Marx, money functions as **hoard** when it is accumulated as general exchange value. This function of money arises quite naturally from the fact that money commands any and all use values (and settles debts). He sees the economic significance of hoarding as one of providing a reserve of means of purchase (and settlement of debts) that allows the ebb and flow of money and tokens of money into and out of the process of circulation according to the needs of this process. This, as a number of Marxists have noted, is an important element of Marx's criticism of the Classical Quantity Theory of Money (CQTM) explanation of inflation which suggests that money put into circulation remains in circulation irrespective of the quantity and money prices of commodities. However, as I will argue below, it is certainly not the most important basis for his criticism of this theory.

Marx is also quite explicit that the hoard function of money mutates into a function of money capital with the development of the capitalist mode, in much the same way that its function as means of purchase mutates into the function of money capital at the outset of the production process. He argues,

> With the development of the credit system, which necessarily runs parallel with the development of modern industry and capitalist production, this money no longer serves as a hoard but as capital, though not in the hands of its proprietor, but rather of other capitalists at whose disposal it is put. (Marx, 1978, p. 261)

These mutations of the functions of money into the functions of capital have caused many Marxists to ignore Marx's repeated admonitions regarding the confusion of the functions of money with the functions of capital.[48] I will return to the point in Chapter 7 in the discussion of Marxist interpretations of Marx's explanation of the functions performed by money.

Marx sees money's function as **means of payment** as that of settling debts resulting from the extension of credit, a function that is logically coupled with that of denominator of debts. Although Marx focuses in

[48] Marx (1970, pp. 186–187).

the first instance on gold and tokens of gold as media of circulation, he is quite explicit that with the development of the capitalist mode commodities are increasingly circulated by credit and tokens of credit. Crucially for him this means that there is necessarily a disjuncture between the money value of all commodities and the quantity of money and tokens of money in the process of circulation at any point in time, with the extent of this disjuncture varying over time. Of importance in this regard is the quantity and time duration of debt contracts, both of which are likely to vary quite considerably over the course of the business cycle.

As noted above, an important implication Marx derives from his analysis of the functions money is required to perform as money is that its physical presence is required in the performance of this function, unlike that of measure of exchange value and means of circulation. A concomitant of this is that the performance of its function as hoard and means of payment requires its value to be relatively stable, unlike the performance of its measure function.

2.6 Value of Money

Although, as noted above, Marx sees money emerging prior to capitalism, when explaining the value and exchange value of money as well as the money prices of commodities he focuses on capitalism, drawing a distinction between the various forms money assumes in capitalism. He sees these forms as commodity money or gold and credit money resting on an inconvertible fiat currency base. Marx **conceives** of the value of money in capitalism when it is a commodity, much like the value of any commodity, as the quantity of labour time required for the production of the bulk of it,[49] and the value of convertible tokens of commodity money as the value of the money commodity they nominally represent. He conceives of the value of credit money resting on an inconvertible fiat currency base, or simply inconvertible fiat currency, as the weighted average values of the commodities whose exchange values it is used to measure.

It follows from this that Marx sees the **measure** of the value of money when it is a commodity as a certain quantity of socially necessary labour time required for its production. He sees the measure of the value of

[49] Marx (1976, p. 161).

money as money, especially when it assumes the form of intrinsically value-less fiat currency, as a certain quantity of economy-wide socially necessary labour time it comes to objectify when used as measure of the exchange values of all commodities.

Marx sees money **acquiring** value historically prior to the emergence of capitalism as the value of whatever is used as the standard of the commodities being exchanged for one another, and this standard becoming increasingly gold or silver with the development and widening of the process of exchange. Marx sees gold and silver coming to possess value as money in addition to possessing values as a particular commodities with the emergence of capitalism when they come to be used by all producers to denote the general exchange values of their commodities with a view to facilitating the reproduction of these commodities. Marx argues that when producers denote the general exchange values of their commodities in terms of gold, both gold and the commodities possessing gold prices come to objectify certain quantities of socially necessary labour time, this labour time being the transformed form of the labour time actually expended in the production of the commodities.

Marx sees the value of money in capitalism **formed** when money is used to measure the exchange values of all commodities. Which means, he sees it formed at the same time and in the same context as the formation of the values and exchange values of all commodities, prior to it being put into the process of circulation to facilitate the circulation of commodities. This in turn means that when money assumes the form of a commodity its value as both a commodity and money is formed after its production and the production of all commodities.

Marx's explanation of the **magnitude** of value of money follows from the preceding. He sees the magnitude of its value as a commodity determined in the manner of any commodity, by the socially necessary labour time directly and indirectly required for its production relative to the socially necessary labour time required for the production of all other commodities.[50] He sees changes in this magnitude determined by changes in the relative productivity of labour used directly and indirectly in the commodity's production as well as changes in the prices of raw materials used in the production of gold relative to those used in the

[50] Marx (1976, p. 161).

production of all other commodities.[51] Marx implicitly sees the magnitude of value of money as money when it is a commodity determined by the average magnitudes of values of commodities whose exchange values it measures, with changes in the magnitude of value of money resulting from changes in the economy-wide productivity of labour and changes in the prices of all raw materials. An increase in the economy-wide productivity of labour or decrease in the money prices of raw materials can be expected to exert upward pressure on the magnitude of value of the commodity as money in much the same way that a decrease in the relative productivity of labour used in the production of the money commodity or increase in the money prices of raw materials used in its production will exert upward pressure on the magnitude of its value as a commodity. This means that when money is a commodity its value as money can deviate from its value as a commodity, but with the latter exerting a gravitational force on the former. Marx sees the magnitude of value of convertible tokens of the commodity money determined by the value of the commodity money they notionally represent. Lastly, Marx sees the magnitude of value of inconvertible fiat currency determined in the same way as the magnitude of value of the commodity as money; by the average values of commodities a unit of the commodity money objectifies when it is used to measure the exchange values of all commodities. Which means, as in the case of gold money, an economy-wide increase in the productivity of labour or decrease in the money prices of raw materials exerts upward pressure on the magnitude of value of inconvertible fiat currency.

The logic of Marx's analysis suggests that an additional factor having a bearing on the magnitude of the value of money is aggregate excess demand, i.e., aggregate demand that does not arise from incomes appropriated in the context of the production of all commodities. When money is a commodity Marx's analysis suggests that structural shifts in the demand for all commodities relative to the money commodity will impact on the magnitude of its value relative to the values of all other commodities *via* its impact on the methods of production used in the production of the money commodity relative to all other commodities. This means,

[51] Marx sees changes in raw material prices having a bearing on trend movements in the magnitude of the value of money in a given country, but only brings this into his analysis when extending it to the circuit of capital and competition between individual capitals.

however, that as long as money is a commodity, it is unlikely this impact will be significant since it is unlikely such shifts in the structure of demand for all commodities relative to the money commodity will have much of an impact on relative methods of production. When money assumes the form of credit money resting on an inconvertible fiat currency base the logic of Marx's analysis suggests the impact of changes in aggregate excess demand on the value of money will be greater, and depend on the extent to which the positive impact it has on the economy-wide productivity of labour and, therefore, upward pressure it exerts on the value of money, offsets the upward pressure it can be assumed to exert on the aggregate money price level and, therefore, downward pressure on the value of money. It suggests the greater the impact increases in excess aggregate demand have on the economy-wide productivity of labour, causing this productivity to increase, the greater will be the upward pressure it exerts on the value of money and the lower the downward pressure exerted on it by the aggregate money price level. I will expand on these points below and more extensively in Nicholas (forthcoming).

2.7 Exchange Value of Money

Marx **conceives** of the exchange value of money in capitalism as the quantity of any commodity with a determinate money price a unit of it commands.[52] He sees any commodity with a determinate money price commanded by money objectifying economy-wide socially necessary labour time and, therefore, being the external **measure** of the exchange value of money, with a certain quantity of socially necessary labour time its immanent measure.[53] It warrants stressing in this context that for Marx the commodity as measure of the exchange value of money, like money as the measure of the exchange value of the commodity, does not *represent* a certain quantity of labour time. If this were the case, as Marx points out, there would be no need for commodities to function as the external measures of the exchange value of money in much the same way there would be no need for money to function as the external measure of the exchange value of the commodity.[54]

[52] Marx (1976, p. 186).

[53] Marx (1970, p. 66).

[54] Marx (1970, pp. 84–85).

Marx sees money **acquiring** exchange value historically prior to the emergence of capitalism as the exchange value of the numéraire commodity. He sees money acquiring exchange value as both a particular commodity and money in the early phases of capitalism when money continues to assume the form of the commodity used as a numéraire in pre-capitalist economic systems. The exchange value the numéraire commodity acquires as money in capitalism results from its use as the measure of the exchange values of commodities by capitalist producers, and is distinct from its exchange value as a particular commodity. For Marx, the exchange value of money as a numéraire commodity possesses no intrinsic link with the values of commodities whose exchange it facilitates in pre-capitalist economic systems, while the exchange value of money in capitalism, whatever form it assumes, possesses an intrinsic link with the commodities whose reproduction it is used to facilitate.

The primacy Marx attaches to money's measure of exchange value function also causes him to see its exchange value **formed** in the context of the performance of this function. That is to say, he sees the exchange value of money formed when it is used by most producers of commodities to denote the general exchange values of their commodities. Which means Marx sees the exchange value of money formed at the same time as its value, before money and all commodities are put into the process of circulation.

Lastly, Marx sees the trend **magnitude** of the exchange value of money, whether or not it is a commodity, determined by the magnitude of its value. This means that when he assumes money to be a commodity he sees its exchange value determined by the relative productivity of labour in the gold sector and relative prices of raw materials used in the production of gold. An increase in the productivity of labour in this sector relative to the productivity of labour in all other sectors, or fall in the prices of raw materials used in the production of gold relative to those used in the production of all other commodities, causes the magnitude of the exchange value of gold to fall and, therefore, the gold prices of all commodities to rise. Marx sees the magnitude of the exchange value of convertible paper reflecting the magnitude of the exchange value of gold in accordance with its nominal exchange ratio with gold. Lastly, Marx sees the magnitude of the exchange value of inconvertible fiat currency also determined by the magnitude of its value. On the basis of what was argued above, this means Marx sees trends in the magnitude of the exchange value of this form of money determined by trends in the economy-wide productivity of labour, raw material prices and aggregate excess money demand for all commodities. An increase in the economy-wide productivity of labour or a fall in the money prices of raw material inputs, implying a fall in the values of all commodities and a corresponding increase in the magnitude of value of money, exerts upward pressure on the exchange value of money and, therefore, corresponding downward pressure on the money prices of commodities (or their rate of increase). That is to say, the implied increase in the value of money resulting from a fall in the magnitudes of values of all commodities is manifest in the lower absolute money prices of commodities, or at least lower rate of increase in them. The transmission of impulses from the value of money to its exchange value, like that from the value of the commodity to its exchange value, takes place in the context of producers setting money prices of their commodities. An increase in aggregate excess demand for commodities, as noted above, exerts downward pressure on the value of money as manifest in upward pressure on the money prices of commodities set by producers. The impact of the increase in aggregate excess money demand for commodities on the magnitude of the exchange value of money will depend on the condition of aggregate production and, ultimately, the stage of the business cycle. This means an understanding of the forces impacting on the magnitude of the exchange value of money requires an elaboration and expansion of Marx's explanation of the circuit of capital in the context of competition between individual capitals (firms), something I will take up in Nicholas (forthcoming).

2.8 Money Price of the Commodity

As I noted above, Marx is concerned to explain the money exchange value of the commodity in the first instance and not its money price of prodution because he sees the explanation of the latter requiring a prior explanation of the circuit of capital in general and the formation of the general rate of profit. The absence of such an explanation does not, however, preclude a bare-bones interpretation of his explanation of the money price of production of the commodity.

To begin with, Marx **conceives** of the money price of production of the commodity as the quantity of money that needs to be commanded by the commodity for the producer to be able to reproduce it while appropriating a rate of profit that is commensurable with the turnover time and risk associated with its production. It is not the commodity exchange value of the commodity where money is a token of the values of commodities being exchanged for one another. For Marx, the relative price of the commodity as well as the general money price level can only be explained on the basis of a prior explanation of the money price of the commodity. He conceives of the relative price of the commodity as its money price relative to the money price of another commodity and not, as for Smith and Ricardo, the quantity of one commodity directly commanded by another. Marx conceives of the aggregate money price level as the weighted average of the money prices of all commodities, and not the quantity of money used to facilitate the exchange or circulation of all commodities comprising the net product relative to the quantity of these commodities. From his explanation of the exchange value of the commodity, it should also be apparent Marx sees the money price of the commodity as the form assumed by the value of the commodity.

The implication of Marx's conception of the money price of production of the commodity is that its **measure** is money, and not another commodity with money a token of the commodities being exchanged for one another. For Marx, when producers use money to denote the general exchange values of their commodities it causes, on the one hand, the labour time expended in their production to be transformed into magnitudes of socially necessary labour time, viz., the labour time required to produce the bulk of commodities of a certain type, and, on the other hand, money to become the objectification of a certain magnitude of socially necessary labour time. This in turn causes a certain magnitude of socially necessary labour time to become the immanent measure of the money prices of production of commodities at the same time it becomes the measure of their values.

Marx sees commodities **acquiring** money prices as gold prices prior to the emergence of capitalism when gold is used as a numéraire commodity to facilitate the exchange of commodities for one another by becoming the standard of all traded commodities as measures of the exchange values of one another. He sees the money prices of commodities continuing to assume a gold form with the emergence of capitalism, but these prices now facilitating the reproduction of the commodities as money prices of production when gold begins to be used by all producers to denote the general exchange values of their commodities for the purpose of facilitating their reproduction. Marx stresses that a necessary condition for commodities to acquire money prices is that they are produced by means of the expenditure of labour time as individual labour time that counts as social labour time when the commodity is exchanged. In pre-capitalist systems where exchange mediates the division of labour the individual labour time expended in the production of the commodity is converted into social labour time when the commodity is exchanged for another commodity. In capitalism the individual labour time expended is converted into *latently* social labour time when the producer uses money to denote the general exchange value of the commodity, and into *actual* social labour time when the commodity is sold for money.

It follows from his conception of the money price of production of the commodity and its measure that Marx sees it being **formed** prior to the commodity being put into the process of circulation. Specifically, he sees the money prices of production of commodities formed at the same time as their values and the value of money, when money is used by producers to set the prices of their commodities. Marx denies that money prices are formed by haggling between the producers and the buyers of commodities in a market setting. For him, commodities are put into the market by producers (or retailers) with given money prices and buyers simply decide on how much, if any, of the commodities they wish to purchase.

Lastly, Marx begins his explanation of the **magnitude** of the price of production of the commodity as the money price of production by explaining its *trend* magnitude. His explanation of this magnitude can be depicted as;

$$P_i = (MP_i + L_i w)(1 + R) \tag{1.2}$$

where P_i is the money price of production a standard commodity of a certain type (i), MP_i is the money expended on the means of production used to produce the standard commodity, L_i is the quantity of labour time required to produce the standard commodity, w is the economy-wide money wage rate, R is the economy-wide general money rate of profit. Marx argues that even though the formation of a general rate of profit causes the quantity of transformed labour time embodied in the standard commodity to deviate from the labour time required for its production, the latter still fundamentally determines the former as manifest in the correspondence between trends in the relative money prices of commodities and the relative productivity of labour in their production. The higher the productivity of labour in one sector relative to another, the lower its relative money price of production. Although Marx develops this argument on the basis of commodity money, the logic of his analysis suggests he sees it also holding in the case of any money form.

When Marx brings capital and the formation of the general rate of profit into the analysis he argues that changes in the latter will have a bearing on the relative money prices of commodities depending on the relative capital intensities of their production, but that this impact on prices will be relatively minor compared to the impact of changes in relative productivities of labour.[55] Marx's justification for seeing this impact as relatively minor is his observation that the trend general rate of profit is relatively stable, certainly as compared to changes in the relative productivity of labour. A related point made by Marx is that trend movements in the money wage rate will only have a bearing on the trend magnitude of the money price of the commodity *via* their impact on the trend general rate of profit.[56] He notes approvingly Ricardo's criticism of Smith's contention that trend movements in the money wage rate have a direct bearing on the aggregate money prices of all commodities (see below). For Marx, the money wage rate is the money price of the commodity labour power that, like the money price of any commodity, is fundamentally determined by the labour time required for its production or rather the production of the commodities needed to sustain labour.[57]

From the interpretation of Marx's explanation of the money exchange value of the commodity outlined above it can be concluded that he sees the money prices of production of the means of production having a bearing on the money prices of the commodities they are used to produce. For Marx what matters in this regard is the *current* money prices of production of these means of production or the money that needs to be paid for their repurchase, and not their historic prices or the quantity of money that was paid for them. An important implication to be drawn from this is that for Marx the current prices of raw materials should be seen as also having an important bearing on the money price of the commodity, and manifest in the correspondence between changes in the

[55] See Marx (1981, p. 266).

[56] See Marx (1981, pp. 303–305).

[57] See Marx (1981, p. 306).

current prices of raw materials used in the production of the commodity and changes in the aggregate money prices of commodities.[58]

Marx's explanation of the trend in the aggregate money price level follows from his explanation of the magnitude of the money price of the commodity since, as argued above, he sees the aggregate money price level as the aggregate of the money prices of all commodities. This means he sees trends in the economy-wide productivity of labour having a fundamental bearing on the aggregate money price level, albeit modified by trends in aggregate excess demand when money assumes the form of credit money. When money is a commodity, gold, Marx explains increases in the aggregate gold price level as resulting from increases in the productivity of labour in the production of gold relative to the productivity of labour in the production of all other commodities. This in turn requires him to see increases in aggregate excess demand for commodities causing increases in the aggregate gold prices of commodities insofar as these increases result in the productivity of gold in the gold sector rising relative to the productivity of labour in the production of all other commodities. Since there is no reason to suppose this, there is no reason to suppose increases in aggregate excess demand exert upward pressure on the aggregate money price level when money is gold. Indeed, if anything, increases in aggregate excess demand are more likely to reinforce deflationary pressures in a gold money setting since such increases are more likely to result in productivity increases in the production of all other commodities than in the gold sector. When money assumes the form of credit money the logic of Marx's analysis suggests that aggregate excess demand is more likely to exert upward pressure on the aggregate money price level, with this pressure being greater at some junctures than others. This is because, when money is credit money increases in aggregate demand arising from increases in budget deficits and expansion in credit are more likely to be protracted, at times exerting continuous upward pressure on the aggregate money price level that are considerably offset when these expansions simultaneously encourage increases in the productivity of labour in all

[58] A second important implication to be drawn from Marx's explanation of the value transferred to the value of the means of production pertains to value transferred from fixed capital and corresponding depreciation charges. I will deal with this in Nicholas (forthcoming).

sectors, and at other times are barely offset when they fail to encourage any significant increases in the productivity of labour.

Whatever form money assumes, the logic of Marx's analysis suggests he sees changes in the money prices of raw materials having a bearing on the aggregate money price level. He sees increases in these prices exerting upward pressure on the aggregate money price level and decreases in these prices exerting downward pressures. The net impact will depend on the state of economy-wide productivity growth and not the magnitude of the increase/decrease in raw material prices *per se*. I will expand on this point in Nicholas (forthcoming) when discussing movements in the aggregate money price level over the course of the business cycle.

As should be apparent from the above interpretation of Marx's explanation of the magnitude of the exchange value of money, not only is it very different from the Classical Quantity Theory of Money (CQTM) it can be seen as fundamentally undermining it. Certainly, this is the way Marx sees his own explanation of the determination of the magnitude of the exchange value of money. For him the problem with the CQTM is that it is founded on a mistaken understanding of money and the functions it performs, which is in turn the result of a mistaken understanding of the value of the commodity. For Marx, adherents of the CQTM approach conceive of the value of the commodity in a way that requires them to see the primary function of money as its medium of exchange function. This in turn causes them to explain the aggregate money price level by the quantity of money used to facilitate the exchange of commodities relative to the quantity of these commodities. What is missed in this regard is that the primary and defining function of money is its measure of exchange value function. This causes commodities to be put into circulation with determinate money prices and circulated by money with a determinate exchange value. That is to say, it causes the quantity of money in the process of circulation to be endogenously determined. Marx notes that to the extent commodity purchases are made on credit and money is held as hoard to meet various contractual obligations, and leaving aside the fact that money is used to purchase financial assets, there can be no reason to suppose that the quantity of money in circulation corresponds with the quantity commodities and their money prices at any point in time. I will expand on this below when considering the explanations of the aggregate money price level by Smith and Ricardo from the perspective of Marx's analysis.

Lastly, from the preceding it should be apparent that Marx sees changes in the relative money prices of commodities accompanying changes in the aggregate money price level as well as taking place independently of the latter. This follows from Marx's conceptions and explanations of the relative money price of the commodity and the aggregate money price level. Specifically, it follows from his conception of the relative price of the commodity as the money price of one commodity relative to the money price of another and the aggregate money price level as the aggregate money prices of all commodities, and his explanation of trends in both as impacted on by trends in the productivity of labour.

References

Blaug, M. (1985). *Economic theory in retrospect* (4th ed.). Cambridge University Press.

Bowles, S., & Gintis, H. (1981). Structure and practice in the labor theory of value. *Review of Radical Political Economics, 12*(4), 1–26.

Gehrke, C., & Kurz, H. D. (2018). Sraffa's constructive and interpretive work, and Marx. *Review of Political Economy, 30*(3), 428–442.

Hodgson, G. (1982). *Capitalism, value and exploitation: A radical theory.* Martin Robertson.

Marx, K. (1964). *Pre-capitalist economic formations* (J. Cohen, Trans.). Lawrence & Wishart.

Marx, K. (1969a). *Theories of surplus value: Part I* (E. Burns, Trans.). Lawrence & Wishart.

Marx, K. (1969b). *Theories of surplus value: Part II* (E. Burns, Trans.). Lawrence & Wishart.

Marx, K. (1970). *A contribution to the critique of political economy* (translated from German by S. W. Ryazanskaya). Progress.

Marx, K. (1972). *Theories of surplus value: Part III* (translated from German by J. Cohen & S. W. Ryazanskaya). Lawrence & Wishart.

Marx, K. (1973). *Grundrisse* (M. Nicolaus, Trans.). Penguin Books.

Marx, K. (1976). *Capital: Volume I* (B. Fowkes, Trans.). Penguin Books.

Marx, K. (1978). *Capital: Volume II* (D. Fernbach, Trans.). Penguin Books.

Marx, K. (1981). *Capital: Volume III* (D. Fernbach, Trans.). Penguin Books.

Nicholas, H. (2011). *Marx's theory of price and its modern rivals.* Palgrave Macmillan.

Nicholas, H. (forthcoming). *Explorations in Marx's theory of price, Volume 2: Profits and business cycles.* Palgrave Macmillan.

Nicolaus, M. (1973). Foreword. In K. Marx (Ed.), *Grundrisse* (pp. 7–63). Penguin Books.

Rodrik, D. (2015). *Economics rules: The rights and wrongs of the dismal science*. W.W. Norton.

Rosdolsky, R. (1977). *The making of Marx's 'capital'* (P. Burgess, Trans.). Pluto Press.

Schumpeter, J. A. (2003). *Ten great economists: From Marx to Keynes*. Taylor and Francis.

CHAPTER 3

Smith's Explanation of Money Price

3.1 Introduction

There can be little doubt, as I have argued elsewhere (see Nicholas, 2011, p. 61), that Marx owed a considerable intellectual debt to the works of the Classical economists, particularly Adam Smith and David Ricardo. It is Smith and Ricardo that Marx pays most attention to in his critical appraisal of the theories advanced by the Classical economists in the course of his attempt to develop his own explanation of the workings of the capitalist system.[1] It is also evident that Marx's consideration of Ricardo's theory of price is usually in the context of Ricardo's critical comments on Smith. Hence, apart from the fact that Smith's work precedes that of Ricardo's in chronological terms, it seems logical to begin the appraisal of other explanations of the money price of the commodity from the perspective of Marx's explanation with that of Smith, particularly since many of the other explanations (e.g., PKs and Marshallian Neoclassicals) take his work as their point of departure.

[1] Marx's criticisms of the Classical economists are mostly to be found in *Theories of Surplus* Value, *Contribution*, *Grundrisse* and Capital.

H. Nicholas, *Explorations in Marx's Theory of Price—Why Marx Is Still Relevant for Understanding the Modern Economy*,
https://doi.org/10.1057/978-1-137-56564-8_3

3.2 Object and Approach

As the title of Smith's most important work on political economy suggests, his major concern is the wealth of nations. For Smith, as for Classical economists in general, wealth constitutes the accumulation of produced commodities requiring labour for their production. When explaining this wealth, he places particular emphasis on the division of labour in the production of the commodities comprising it, arguing that the increasing division of labour enhances the productive power of labour. In fact, at the very beginning of the *Wealth of Nations (WN)* Smith (1976, p. 13) claims,

> The greatest improvement in the productive power of labour, and the greater part of the skill, dexterity and judgement with which it is anywhere directed, or applied, seems to have been the effect of the division of labour.

After elaborating what he sees constituting the division of labour, and noting it tends to advance more rapidly in manufacturing than in agriculture, Smith argues it (the division of labour) arises with the exchange of commodities for one another.[2]

Smith's approach to explaining the nature of the capitalist system is to analyse the mode of producing commodities in this system and compare it with the mode of producing commodities in pre-capitalist systems. He concludes the crucial difference between modes of production is that, except for 'the early and rude' mode of production, pre-capitalist systems are mostly to be characterised by relations of direct economic dependence between classes while in capitalism such relations have largely disappeared. The important point to note here is that Smith does not regard the study of pre-capitalist economic systems modes as providing the analytical basis for the study of the capitalist economic system. Rather, for him, the importance of their study is to understand the different political and institutional organisations of society which these economic systems foster.[3] It is also important to note Smith is not arguing that the distinction between capitalist and pre-capitalist economic systems is analogous to one between

[2] See Smith (1976, p. 25).

[3] Skinner (1976, p. 16) argues that for Smith the significance of changes in the mode of producing means of subsistence is that it implies changes in "...the balance and distribution of political power, with consequent effects on the nature of government".

surplus and non-surplus systems in, for example, the manner of Sraffa (see below).

Smith begins the explanation of the creation of wealth by explaining the prices of the commodities he sees as constituting the material base of the system. When explaining these prices, Smith, like his Classical predecessors and contemporaries, employs the method of abstraction. He abstracts from supply and demand imbalances and money in the first instance, explaining prices as equilibrium relative prices. After explaining these prices, Smith brings supply and demand imbalances and money into his analysis and explains market prices, as the money form of prices that deviate from their equilibrium levels in accordance with supply and demand imbalances.

From the perspective of his materialist understanding of human history Marx certainly approves of Smith's focus on the production of commodities and the expenditure of labour time in their production when explaining the historical evolution of the wealth of nations. For Marx, Smith is correct to argue that the productive powers of labour have been advanced historically by increases in divisions of labour in economic systems founded on divisions of labour, especially capitalism. However, Marx also sees a number of weaknesses with Smith's focus on the driving force underlying the accumulation of wealth. Firstly, for Marx, Smith mistakenly sees the increasing division of labour driven by the process of exchange. For Marx, this allows Smith to deny the expenditure of labour time as the source of the value of the product. Secondly, for Marx, Smith does not see the importance of the way in which a surplus product is produced and appropriated as the basis for an understanding different modes of production.[4] Thirdly, for Marx, Smith does not pay adequate attention to the distribution of wealth, allowing for considerable divergences in interpretations of his explanations of this distribution, particularly in capitalism. However, for Marx the redeeming feature of what attention Smith does pay to the distribution of wealth is his adherence to the labour theory of value when explaining profit, notwithstanding the fact that he abandons it when explaining prices.[5] Lastly, for Marx, Smith does not explain the accumulation of wealth in capitalism in the context of the cyclical movement of the economic system

[4] See Marx (1969b, p. 77).

[5] See Marx (1969b, pp. 74–75).

in this mode of production. Noting this omission in Smith's work, Marx considers it to be excusable given the phenomenon of overproduction, and crises resulting from overproduction, was not evident at the time of his writing.[6]

Marx certainly approves of Smith's use of the method of abstraction when explaining wealth creation in general and capitalism in particular, but he is also critical of the manner of Smith's method of abstraction. Marx praises Smith for beginning his explanation of wealth creation with the commodity as the possessor of both use value and exchange value, and focusing on the source of the latter as the value or 'cost' of producing the commodity.[7] However, he is critical of Smith's failure to abstract from capital as well as the manner of his abstraction from money. For Marx, Smith's failure to abstract from capital in the first instance causes him to have a mistaken conception of capital and explain the exchange value of the commodity in capitalism as determined by its income components, including profits (see below). Marx argues that the manner of Smith's abstraction from money when explaining the exchange value of the commodity in the first instance causes him to explain this exchange value in the context of what is effectively a barter process of exchange, resulting in a distorted explanation of the exchange values of the commodity and money (see below). Marx sees the source of Smith's myopia in both these respects as resulting from his adoption of the viewpoint of the unscientific observer who is unable to penetrate the economic categories thrown up by competition.[8]

3.3 Production and Value of the Commodity

3.3.1 Production

Smith conceives of the production of commodities as undertaken by a producer with the aid of 'factors of production'. He defines the factors of production as inputs used in the production of commodities whose owners appropriate a commodity income for permitting their use by the producer in the process of production. Smith sees production taking place in the context of a division of labour. He sees labour as the sole factor of

[6] See Marx (1969b, p. 525).

[7] See Marx (1969a, pp. 72–73).

[8] See Marx (1969b, p. 165).

production in the early and rude mode of production, and one of several factors of production in the capitalist mode, the other factors being capital (or 'stock') and land.[9] He sees labour appropriating the entire net product in the early and rude mode of production, and sharing the net product with owners of capital and land in the capitalist mode.

When analysing the process of production in capitalism Smith places considerable emphasis on the payment of incomes to factor owners to induce them to supply the factor inputs required to produce the commodity, and in particular the payment of corn for the supply of the labour input. In fact, Smith sees the labour input as the most important input for the production of the commodity even when capital is brought into the analysis since capital for him is a collection of commodities that are also produced with labour.

Smith sees the commodities produced with the aid of factor inputs in capitalism constituting the commodity incomes appropriated by owners of these inputs. To avoid conceiving of the commodities appropriated as income being essentially the same as the commodities used to produce them, Smith tacitly assumes the former to be exclusively those meeting the consumption needs of owners of the factor inputs. Marx (1978, p. 441) argues Smith justifies this by conceiving of the process of reproduction as one of simple reproduction, where

> The whole expense of maintaining the fixed capital must evidently be excluded from the net revenue of the society. Neither the materials necessary for supporting their useful machines and instruments of trade, their profitable buildings, etc., nor the produce of the labour necessary for fashioning those materials into the proper form, can ever make any part of it.

Lastly, Smith sees the precondition for the emergence of capitalism, which he characterises as a production system based on a division of labour, as the process of the exchange of commodities for one another, with the development of this process leading to an increasing division of labour and a corresponding greater efficiency in the production of commodities. In a much-quoted passage from his *WN*, Smith (1976, p. 22) argues;

[9] See Smith (1976, pp. 65–67).

> As it is the power of exchanging that gives occasion to the division of labour, so the extent of this division must always be limited by the extent of that power, or, in other words, by the extent of the market.

From the perspective of Marx's analysis the problems with Smith's explanation of production begin with its **conception**. Smith does not fully, or consistently, recognise the social nature of the system and the pre-eminent importance of the labour input in all social systems of production. The most obvious manifestation of this is that he puts capital and land on the same footing as labour when analysing the capitalist system of production, seeing these as factor inputs in the manner of labour. This is not to say Smith does not at times accord labour particular importance in the process of production in capitalism, especially when explaining profits. In fact, when explaining profits, he reverts to the labour theory of value when doing so.[10]

Smith is also not clear about the **producer** as the entity responsible for the organisation of production in either the early and rude mode or capitalism. He appears to see the owner of the labour factor input as the producer in the early and rude mode, with the tacit assumption being that the labour input is a factor input and labour pays itself an income for its own use in production. Smith conceives of the producer in capitalism as someone other than the owner of capital, who is also not a manager. The reason for the confusion is the explanation of the income appropriated by the producer as profit. To see the producer owning capital requires seeing the profit appropriated by the producer in relation to the capital advanced as resulting from the expenditure of labour time in excess of the labour time commanded by the worker as the wage. It is a conclusion Smith attempts to avoid due to what he sees as flaws in the labour theory of value, but ends up embracing this conclusion in the final instance.

A corollary of Smith's conception of the producer is his conception of the **capital** input, as a stock of long-lasting material inputs whose owners appropriate commodity incomes in relation to the quantity of their holdings of this stock. One problem with this conception is the quantification of the capital stock, and the commodity income appropriated by owners of the capital stock in relation to it. The problem in this regard is the aggregation of the commodities comprising the stock of capital and the commodities appropriated as incomes by owners of

[10] See Marx (1969a, pp. 74–75).

capital. Smith's solution to the problem is to tacitly see the capital stock reducible to quantities of corn, and corn incomes appropriated in relation to this corn stock. Smith does not explain why he does not use money to reduce the capital stock to a homogeneous quantity. A second problem with Smith's conception of the capital input is he sees it as borrowed, with the income paid to the owner of this input being interest. That is, he denies capital is owned by the producer. He also denies that the income appropriated in relation to this capital, i.e., profit, is the revenue appropriated by the producer of commodities using this capital less the capital outlaid, where the capital outlaid is what is needed to replace the inputs used up in production includes the value of labour power.

Even though Marx praises Smith for the importance he accords to the **labour** input in all modes of production including the capitalist mode, he sees Smith incorrectly conceiving of this input as something that is bought and sold in all modes of production, including the early and rude mode. For Marx what Smith overlooks is that the labour input, or labour power (the capacity of labour to expend labour time in the production of a good), is only a commodity input that can be bought and sold in capitalism. The purchase and sale of labour power is in fact a defining characteristic of the capitalist system. It is only in capitalism that all reproducible inputs, including the labour input, are commodities that can be bought and sold.

Although Smith recognises the importance of the labour input in the process of production, he tacitly sees this process as the productive consumption of commodities *per se*. This is because he sees the inputs into production, including labour, as marketable factors of production that are purchased with the commodities produced by them. Indeed, given the importance he attaches to the labour input, seeing all commodity inputs reducible in the final instance to this input, and given that he sees corn as the commodity required to purchase this input, he ends up tacitly conceiving of the production system as essentially a corn-based one; the use of corn to produce either corn or other commodities that are readily convertible into corn. Smith does not see that the essence of all social production systems is not the expenditure of commodities *per se* but the expenditure of labour time. In fact, to the extent that the production process can be conceived of as involving the productive consumption of commodities, it is the productive consumption of means of production in the context of the expenditure of labour time.

A related problem is Smith's conception of the nature of the commodities produced. Marx repeatedly criticises Smith for seeing aggregate output excluding the means of production.[11] He argues Smith's exclusion of the means of production from the net product in capitalism is mistakenly premised on the assumption of simple reproduction, i.e., abstracting from an expansion in the scale of reproduction. For Marx, in all systems of production where produced material inputs are used in the process of production, there is need for the replacement in kind of used-up means of production.[12] He argues that Smith's exclusion of the means of production from the net product leads him to the 'absurd conclusion' that the whole of capital can be resolved into variable capital, i.e., capital outlaid on wages, and not both constant and variable capital. For Marx it causes Smith to see the whole of the net product consumed by the worker in the form of means of subsistence.[13]

An additional problem with Smith's conception of the nature of the commodities produced from the perspective of Marx's analysis is that he sees these produced for exchange whether in the early and rude mode or capitalism. For Marx, it is only in capitalism that commodities are systematically produced for exchange and have the form of exchange values or prices. Although products produced in pre-capitalist economic systems can possess prices, these typically only constitute the surpluses over and above what is produced to meet subsistence requirements. Moreover, the prices of these surplus products do not facilitate their reproduction. Rather, they reflect the strength of the desires of the exchanging parties. The important implication of this is that it cannot be argued, as Smith does, that it is the emergence of exchange that brings about a division of labour in production. There have been divisions of labour in virtually all production systems involving human beings.[14] What is different

[11] See for example Marx (1969a, p. 99).

[12] See Marx (1981, p. 988).

[13] See Marx (1976, pp. 736–737).

[14] Roll (1973, pp. 154–155) points out "There can be little doubt that Smith confused cause and effect. However true it may be that exchange cannot exist without division of labour, it is not true, at least in theory, that division of labour requires the existence of private exchange. It is logically demonstrable that a certain social organization...can have a technology using division of labour without exchange. And communities of this type can be shown to have existed".

about capitalism is that the division of labour is extensively mediated by exchange.

3.3.2 *Value of the Commodity*

It is in the context of the preceding interpretation of Smith's explanation of production that his explanation of the value of the commodity is best understood. Like most other Classical economists, Smith formally sees commodities only having use values and exchange values, and not also values. He argues,

> The word value, it is to be observed, has two different meanings, and sometimes expresses the utility of some particular objective, and sometimes the power of purchasing other goods which the possession of that object conveys. The one may be called 'value in use'; the other, 'value in exchange'. (1976, pp. 44–45)

However, when explaining the exchange value of the commodity it is evident he sees commodities having values as distinct from exchange values, with these values being the basis for explaining the exchange values. Specifically, Smith conceives of the value of the commodity as the *cost of producing it*, and this cost as the *corn incomes* appropriated by the owners of the factor inputs used in the production of the commodity. Smith conceives of the value of the commodity as the corn commanded as wages in the early and rude mode. He conceives of it in capitalism as the corn commanded by wages and the corn equivalent of the commodity incomes commanded by owners of other factor inputs. Smith's justification for choosing corn instead of any other commodity as the most important of all wage goods consumed by labour is the relative stability he allegedly observes in its exchange ratio with labour.[15] Since the corn commanded as incomes can be interpreted as commanding a certain quantity of the labour input, Smith's conception of the value of the commodity can be interpreted as the quantity of labour commanded as incomes in the context of its production.

Although Smith gives the impression of changing his concept of the value of the commodity when he shifts from a consideration of the early

[15] See Smith (1976, p. 54).

and rude state to capitalism,[16] in fact this conception remains fundamentally the same, i.e., the quantity of labour commanded by owners of inputs required to produce the commodity. Smith (1976, p. 47) argues,

> Every man is rich or poor according to the degree in which he can afford to enjoy the necessaries, conveniences, and amusements of human life. But after the division of labour has once thoroughly taken place, it is but a very small part of these with which a man's own labour can supply him. The far greater part of them he must derive from the labour of other people, and he must be rich or poor according to the quantity of that labour which he can command, or which he can afford to purchase.

For Smith, the only difference between the early and rude mode of production and capitalism is that in the former the quantity of labour commanded by owners of the labour input (in the form of the net product) is equal to the quantity of labour expended in its production—the production of the net product—while this is no longer the case in capitalism.

The ambiguities surrounding Smith's conception of the value of the commodity manifest themselves in similar ambiguities with respect to his understanding of its measure. He argues a distinction is warranted between the 'real' and 'nominal' measures of the value of a commodity, with the former being labour and the latter another commodity or even money.[17] The implication to be drawn from this distinction is that he sees the labour measure pertaining to the value or cost of production of the commodity and corn or money as the measure pertaining to its exchange value.

Although Smith does not explicitly discuss either the emergence or formation of the value of the commodity, his implicit understanding of these can be derived from his general analysis in *WN*, especially his analysis of the production of the commodity. This suggests he sees commodities acquiring values historically when they are produced with factor inputs, with labour historically the first such input to be used. Analogously, since Smith sees the value of the commodity as the commodity income cost of producing it, it follows he sees its value formed and

[16] Ricardo (1973, pp. 9–11), among others, can be argued as interpreting Smith in this manner.

[17] See Smith (1976, p. 51).

reformed prior to the production of the commodity, whether the mode of production is the early and rude mode or capitalism.

Smith's explanation of the magnitude of the value of the product follows from the above. He sees this magnitude as the relative quantity of corn commanded as incomes by owners of factors used in production.[18] This means he sees the magnitude of value in the early and rude mode of production, when labour is the sole factor input used in production, determined by the relative quantity of corn directly commanded as incomes in the context of the production of the product. When production requires additionally the advance of capital and use of privately owned land, Smith sees the magnitude of value determined by the relative quantity of corn or corn equivalent of the incomes appropriated by owners of all factor inputs, where corn is seen as purchasing a certain quantity of the labour input. Which means Smith sees the magnitude of value of the commodity in capitalism determined by the methods of producing the commodity, the rates of remuneration of the factor inputs (especially the corn wage rate), and the exchange ratios between corn and the other commodities commanded by the owners of the non-labour factor inputs. A fundamental implication of Smith's explanation of the magnitudes of the values of commodities is that it requires him to see changes in these resulting from changes in the corn income costs of producing them, especially changes in the corn wage and the corn exchange values of all commodities. Thus, Smith sees an increase in the corn wage rate for a given (or falling) rate of profit resulting in an increase in the magnitudes of values of commodities produced in relatively more labour-intensive industries and a decrease in the values of commodities produced in less labour-intensive industries.

From the perspective of Marx's analysis the problems with Smith's analysis of the value of a commodity begin with its **conception** as the corn or corn equivalent of commodities commanded as incomes by owners of factors of production used to produce the commodity, where corn is seen as commanding a certain quantity of the labour input. Marx argues Smith adopts this conception of the value of the commodity because he recognises the labour time expended in the production of the commodity is not equal to the labour time commanded by it in the context of the formation of a general rate of profit in capitalism. This is because the

[18] Roll (1973, p. 158) argues that the origin of Smith's explanation of the magnitude of value of the product can be traced to the work of Petty, Steuart, and Cantillion.

labour time commanded as profits by owners of capital in the different sectors in the context of the formation of a general rate of profit is not equal to the labour time expended in the production of the commodity in excess of what is needed to reproduce the wage goods paid to labour. The labour time expended can be more or less than what is appropriated. Marx even praises Smith for recognising the problem in this regard, criticising Ricardo for failing to acknowledge Smith's recognition of the problem.[19] At the same time Marx criticises Smith for abandoning the labour time explanation of the magnitude of value of the commodity, and praises Ricardo for continuing to adhere to this explanation, albeit in a misguided way.

For Marx the consequence of Smith's conception of the value of the commodity, as the corn income costs of producing it, is that he collapses the value of the commodity into its exchange value, and, more specifically, into its corn exchange value.[20] The quantity of corn commanded by the commodity in the process of exchange must equal the quantity of corn (directly and indirectly) commanded as incomes in the context of the production of the commodity. Marx argues this conflation of the value of the commodity with its exchange value in turn causes Smith to lose sight of the *source of value* of the commodity as the labour time expended in its production, and instead see this source as the corn incomes appropriated by factor owners, especially that appropriated by labour. Marx (1969a, p. 94) argues Smith does not see,

> … it is labour and not the wages of the labourer that creates value. Wages are already existing value, or if we consider the whole of production, the part of value created by the labourer which he himself appropriates; but this appropriation does not create value.

Losing sight of the labour input as the source of value results in Smith paying little attention to this input. The labour input in Smith's analysis has no quantitative dimension and cannot be aggregated. Smith does not see that the labour input that is the source of value in general is an average labour input possessing average skills and expending an average amount of effort over a certain period of time, viz., the working day, considered normal for a given society. He does not see that the source of the value

[19] See Marx (1969b, p. 403).

[20] See Marx (1969b, p. 200).

of a particular commodity is the labour time that needs to be expended by this average labour input in the production of the bulk of this type of commodity. Lastly, Smith's collapse of the value of the commodity into its exchange value causes him to focus on the *relative* value of the commodity, ignoring its *absolute* value. This in turn precludes him from conceiving and explaining changes in the aggregate values of commodities (see below).

Smith's conflation of the value and exchange value of the commodity causes him to have a similarly confused understanding of the **measure** of the value of the commodity; as whatever is deemed to be the measure of its exchange value. It causes him to conceive of the measure of the value of a commodity as any commodity commanded in the process of exchange, and corn as the standard of these measures or numéraire commodity. As the numéraire commodity, corn possesses a value of one. Smith's formal justification for choosing corn and not gold as the standard or *numéraire* commodity is that corn allegedly purchases a more stable quantity of labour than gold or silver over the long term.[21] However, it is more likely his real reason for seeing corn and not gold as the numéraire commodity is his recognition that assuming gold to be the numéraire commodity would require him to assume its value, and therefore its exchange value, is one, preventing him from explaining the deviation of its exchange value as money from its exchange value as a commodity. It is a problem that is arguably recognised by Keynes, hence his denial that money is a commodity (see Chapter 6). It is a problem that is also arguably recognised by Walras, hence his insistence that the numéraire commodity is not money (see Chapter 8).

Smith's conflation of the value of the commodity with its exchange value also causes him to see commodities **acquiring** values historically after they acquire exchange values and not before as for Marx. Like Marx, Smith sees commodities acquiring values when they are produced in the context of a division of labour, but unlike Marx he sees the latter presupposing exchange. For Smith, as noted above, it is exchange that permits a division of labour and drives its further development, and it is exchange that allows income recipients to obtain the commodities they desire.[22] For Marx, Smith does not see that goods are produced in the context of

[21] See Smith (1976, p. 41).

[22] See Smith (1976, p. 25).

a division of labour prior to exchange mediating it, and therefore acquire values historically prior to acquiring exchange values.[23]

Smith's conception of the value of the commodity requires him to see it **formed** both prior to the process of production and in the process of exchange. It requires him to see the value of the commodity formed prior to its production because the incomes paid to factor owners are paid, or at least agreed upon, at the outset of production. At the same time, it requires him to see these values formed in the process of exchange because the relative magnitudes of incomes paid are by definition equal to the magnitude of the exchange value of the commodity and this magnitude is necessarily determined in the process of exchange. To resolve this problem Smith sees changes in the value of the commodity resulting in changes in the quantity of it put into the process of circulation, causing changes in the magnitude of the exchange value of the commodity to adjust to its value (see below). From the perspective of Marx's approach, Smith does not see the magnitude of the value of the commodity, like the magnitude of its exchange value, formed after the production of the commodity and prior to it being put into the process of exchange, when money is used to denote the general exchange value of the commodity. Crucially, like all other approaches, Smith does not see the formation of the value of the commodity linked to money.

The problems with Smith's explanation of the **magnitude** of value of the commodity follow from the preceding. To begin with, for Marx, Smith constantly confuses the determination of the magnitude of value of the commodity with the determination of its exchange value.[24] He confuses the explanation of the magnitude of the value of the commodity, as the corn incomes appropriated by owners of factor inputs used in its production, with the explanation of the magnitude of its exchange value, as the corn commanded by the commodity in the process of exchange. This confusion is to be expected since, as noted above, the direct and indirect corn incomes appropriated in the context of the production of the commodity must logically be equal to the quantity of corn appropriated by the owner of the commodity in the process of its exchange. The source of the confusion is, as also noted above, Smith's attempt to avoid explaining the magnitude of value of the commodity by the labour

[23] See Marx (1969b, p. 218).

[24] See Marx (1969a, p. 70).

(time) expended in its production because of what he perceives to be the flaw with such an explanation (see below). To repeat, for Marx Smith's scientific merit is demonstrated by the fact that when he explains profit he reverts to the labour (time) expended explanation of the value and surplus value of the product.[25]

Second, Smith explains the magnitude of the value of the commodity as in the first instance the magnitude of its *relative*, not *its absolute*, value. That is, it causes him to explain the magnitude of the value of the commodity by the *relative* quantity of corn commanded by owners of factors of production in the context of the production of the commodity.

Third, Smith's explanation of the magnitude of value causes him to see changes in the magnitude of value of the individual commodity taking place in the context of changes in the relative magnitudes of values of all commodities at the same time, preventing him from seeing the change in the magnitude of the value of the commodity as due to factors that are specific to the individual commodity.

Fourth, Smith's explanation of the magnitude of value of the commodity requires him to tacitly ignore the impact on it of changes in both the productivity of labour and corn exchange values of all commodities. Smith tacitly ignores the impact of changes in the productivity of labour on the magnitude of values of commodities to bypass what he sees as a flawed labour theory of value. He tacitly ignores the impact of changes in the corn exchange values of commodities on the magnitudes of their values to avoid a circuitous explanation of the magnitudes of both the value and exchange value of the commodity. Specifically, it allows him to avoid explaining the corn income costs of producing the commodity by the corn exchange value of the commodities commanded as incomes, and these in turn by their corn income costs. It warrants noting in this regard, that Smith does not *formally* abstract from the impact on the magnitudes of the values of commodities of either changes in the productivity of labour or the corn exchange values of commodities, let alone provide a justification for these.

Lastly, Smith explains the magnitude of the value of the commodity as its embodied, and not necessary, cost; the corn that is actually appropriated in the production of the commodity and not what needs to be appropriated in the production of the standard commodity. This requires

[25] See Marx (1969a, p. 71).

him to see the value transferred from the means of production as that embodied in the means of production as well the means of production required to produce these means of production, and so on. In other words, it requires him to have a layered corn income cost explanation of the value of the commodity. Aside from there being no reason to suppose this allows for a determinate magnitude of value to be seen as transferred from the means of production to the value of the commodity, Smith's explanation of the value transferred prevents him from seeing this value as the value of what is needed to repurchase the means of production used up in the process of production.

3.4 Exchange and Exchange Value of the Commodity

3.4.1 Exchange

Like most other Classical economists, Smith conceives of the exchange process as essentially the exchange of commodities for one another (i.e., C-C'), even when it is mediated by money (i.e., C-M-C'). He implicitly sees exchange facilitating the production of the commodity by permitting producers (entrepreneurs) to obtain the commodities required to pay incomes to owners of the factor inputs needed to produce the commodities. As noted above, Smith sees the exchange of commodities as a necessary precondition for a division of labour and the production of commodities using factor inputs. Lastly, Smith sees commodity exchange as effectively barter, even when this exchange is facilitated by the use of money.

The problems with Smith's explanation of the process of exchange from the perspective of Marx's analysis begin with its **conception**. First, Smith does not see that the process of exchange that facilitates the reproduction of the commodity in capitalism is the exchange of the commodity for something representing general exchangeable worth. He does not see that it is this process of exchange that facilitates the reproduction of the commodity by allowing the producer of the commodities being exchanged to repurchase the commodity inputs used up in the process of their production. Second, Smith does not see that this process of exchange is characteristic of capitalism and not also pre-capitalist economic systems. The process of exchange found in pre-capitalist economic systems is the exchange of particular commodities for one another with the purpose of enhancing the consumption satisfaction of those exchanging the commodities. It is because he sees the process of exchange as enhancing the consumption satisfaction of those appropriating incomes in the context of the production of the commodities being exchanged that he sees this process as facilitating the reproduction of the commodities being exchanged in all modes of production including capitalism. Lastly, Smith appears to conceive of the commodities being exchanged for one another *excluding* the means of production that need to be replaced. As noted above, Smith's purpose in doing so is to equate the aggregate output produced with the aggregate commodities commanded as incomes by owners of factor inputs used in their production. The problem in this regard is that it leaves unexplained the exchange values of the means of production used in the production of all commodities.

Smith does not see that the process of exchange which **emerges** prior to capitalism is limited in scope and does not facilitate the reproduction of the commodities being exchanged for one another, while the process of exchange in capitalism is widespread and facilitates the reproduction of the commodities being exchanged. As noted above, Smith sees the process of exchange that emerges in pre-capitalist economic systems as essentially the same as that found in capitalism, viz., the exchange of commodities for one another for the purposes of enhancing the consumption satisfaction of those appropriating commodity incomes in the context of the production of the commodities being exchanged.

Lastly, although Smith conceives of the process of exchange as mediated by money, he sees it as essentially one of **barter**. This is because he sees the commodities being exchanged for one another being put into the process of exchange without determinate exchange values, let alone determinate money prices. Which means that even though the commodities being exchanged in the process of exchange can be assumed to be exchanged according to their values, they will only come to reflect their relative values in the context of a process of bartering by those engaged in the process of exchange. I will expand on this point below.

3.4.2 *Exchange Value of the Commodity*

Smith's conception of the process of exchange causes him to see the exchange value of the commodity as the quantity of another commodity a given unit of it commands, where the commodity commanded is used directly or indirectly to purchase a certain quantity of labour. Obviously, the commodity commanded is corn. Smith refers to the quantity of labour a commodity purchases as its 'real' exchange value, and the quantity of another commodity it purchases, say corn (gold), as its 'nominal' exchange value. He argues that in the early and rude mode of production the exchange value of the commodity accords with the former conception, while in capitalism it accords with the latter conception.[26]

These conceptions of the exchange value of the commodity lead Smith to adopt two different conceptions of the measure of the exchange value of the commodity. One of these is labour, as the measure of the real exchange value of the commodity. The other is the commodity commanded in the process of exchange, which Smith refers to as the nominal measure of the exchange value of the commodity, with the standard of all commodities as measures of the exchange values of one another, or numéraire commodity, being corn. Although there are instances in *WN* where Smith suggests that the standard of the nominal measure of exchange value of the commodity is gold,[27] the logic of his analysis suggest it is corn.

Smith's conceptions of exchange and the exchange value of the commodity suggest he implicitly sees the commodity acquiring exchange value historically with the development of the process of exchange, prior to its production in the context of a division of labour. These conceptions also suggest Smith sees the exchange value of the commodity formed in the process of exchange, at the same time or prior to the formation of its value.

Smith's explanation of the magnitude of the exchange value of the commodity follows from the above. He sees this magnitude determined by the magnitude of value of the commodity, where the value of the commodity is the *corn income cost* of producing it. Of note in this regard is the impression Smith gives of seeing the exchange value of the commodity in the early and rude mode of production determined by its value as the *labour required* for its production.[28] He subsequently corrects this impression, no doubt with an eye to his explanation of the magnitude of exchange value in capitalism, arguing that the labour

[26] See Smith (1976, pp. 47–48).

[27] See Smith (1976, pp. 47–49).

[28] See Smith (1976, p. 65).

required for the production of the commodity even in the early and rude mode is the quantity of ***labour commanded*** by the owners of inputs used in the production of the commodity. It is, in any case, this explanation of the magnitude of the value of the commodity that Smith adheres to in his explanation of the magnitude of the exchange value of the commodity in capitalism.[29]

From the perspective of Marx's analysis the problems with Smith's explanation of the exchange value of the commodity begin with its **conception**. The first problem of note with Smith's conception of the exchange value of the commodity in this regard is that he does not see it assuming a money form, i.e., the form of the money exchange value of the commodity. This is because, as noted above, Smith sees the process of exchange as the exchange of commodities for one another and serving the purpose of satisfying the consumption needs of the exchanging parties. For Smith to conceive of the exchange value of the commodity as its money exchange value requires him to conceive of the process of exchange in an entirely different manner; as enabling the producer to repurchase all the inputs used up in the production of the commodity. Second, and related to this, when Smith conceives of the exchange value of the commodity as its gold (or silver) exchange value he is not conceiving of its exchange value as the money exchange value of the commodity, but rather its corn exchange value where gold is an intrinsically valueless token of corn. Lastly, Smith does not see the exchange value of the commodity as the form assumed by its value since for him the value of the commodity is visible and has the same form as its exchange value, i.e., that of corn. The value of the commodity being the corn incomes commanded by those supplying factor inputs for its production and its exchange value being the corn exchange value of the commodity.

The problems with Smith's conception of the **measure** of the exchange value of the commodity follow from the problems with its conception. Most obviously, Smith does not see this measure as representing general exchange value, i.e., money. Instead, he sees it as the particular commodity commanded in the process of exchange, with corn chosen as a standard or numéraire commodity. Even though Smith argues that corn is preferable to gold as this standard because of the relatively greater stability in its exchange with labour over long periods of time, it is likely

[29] See Smith (1976, pp. 65–66).

that his choice of corn and not gold as the numéraire commodity is motivated, as noted above, by his desire to avoid having to conceive of the exchange value of gold as unity. Second, Smith's conflation of the value and exchange value of the commodity prevents him from seeing the measure of the exchange value of the commodity as the form of the measure of its value, In fact, as argued above, this conflation in Smith's analysis requires him to see both measures as the same, i.e., corn.

Smith's conceptions of the process of exchange and exchange value of the commodity requires him to tacitly see commodities **acquiring** corn exchange values historically prior to capitalism and before they acquire values, the value of the commodity being the corn income costs of producing the commodity. As argued above, Smith does not see commodities acquiring values historically when they come to be produced in the context of a division of labour, and acquiring exchange values historically after they acquire values, when the division of labour is mediated by exchange.

Smith's conception of the process of exchange and the exchange values of commodities in capitalism prevents him from seeing the latter **formed** *prior to* commodities being put into the process of exchange (circulation). This is because it prevents him from conceiving of the exchange value of the commodity as representing its general exchangeable worth, and being conferred on the commodity by the producer to facilitate its reproduction prior to putting the commodity into the process of circulation.

Smith's conflation of the value of the commodity with its exchange value suggests the problems with his explanation of the **magnitude** of the exchange value of the commodity follow from those noted above with respect to his explanation of the magnitude of the value of the commodity. To begin with, it follows from what was argued above that the magnitude of the exchange value of the commodity Smith sees as having to explain in the first instance is the magnitude of its commodity or corn exchange value and not, as for Marx, its general or money exchange value. As I argued above, Smith's reason for beginning with the relative magnitude of value of the commodity when explaining the magnitude of the value of the commodity is his attempt to bypass the labour theory of value. When explaining the magnitude of the exchange value of the commodity, this requires him to explain it by the relative quantity of corn the commodity commands in the process of exchange, where the magnitude of the exchange value of corn is tacitly assumed to be unity. As I also argued above, Smith opts for conceiving of the magnitude of the exchange value of the commodity as the quantity of corn a commodity commands to avoid having to assume the magnitude of the exchange value of gold is one or, as in the case of Keynes, having to deny money is a commodity. However, this means his justification for seeing the magnitude of the exchange value of the commodity as its corn exchange value determined by the corn wage rests on the assumption that in capitalism labour is purchased by the producer with a corn wage.

A second problem with Smith's explanation of the magnitude of the exchange value of the commodity is it requires him to ignore the impact on it of changes in the productivity of labour and assume the corn exchange values of all commodities are given. As I noted above, Smith needs to ignore the impact of the productivity of labour on the exchange value of the commodity in order to bypass what he sees as the flawed labour theory of value, and assume the corn exchange values of commodities are given to avoid a circuitous explanation of the corn income costs and corn exchange values of commodities. Of note with regard to the latter is that Smith's implicit assumption of given corn exchange values of commodities requires him to explain changes in the magnitudes of corn exchange values of commodities while at the same time assuming these magnitudes to be given.

A third problem with Smith's explanation of the magnitude of the exchange value of the commodity is that it requires him to see changes in this magnitude resulting from value-induced changes in the quantity of the commodity put into the process of exchange relative to corn. It requires him, as argued above, to see changes in the magnitude of the value of the commodity causing producers to put more or less of the commodity into the process of exchange relative to corn, causing the corn exchange value of the commodity to fall or rise. Ricardo criticises this contention of Smith arguing it is entirely possible for the magnitude of the corn exchange value of the commodity to change without any change in the quantity of it put into the process of exchange.[30] For Marx, as noted above, Smith sees changes in the magnitude of the corn exchange value of the commodity taking place as a result of changes in the quantity of it put into the process of exchange because he does not see commodities entering the process of exchange with determinate exchange values.

[30] See Ricardo (1973, p. 262).

Lastly, Smith's explanation of the magnitude of the exchange value of the commodity by its embodied costs and not those that need to be incurred for its reproduction requires him to deny the magnitudes of the current exchange values of the means of production used in the production of the commodity have a bearing on the magnitude of its exchange value. Instead, it requires him to see the historic layered magnitudes of the exchange values of the means of production that have been directly and indirectly used in the production of the commodity as having this bearing, with the magnitudes of these determined by their respective values and, in the final instance, the corn wage rate. It warrants noting in this context that Sraffa (1960, pp. 14–15) points out there is no reason to suppose changes in the commodity wage rate have a determinate impact on the magnitude of the commodity exchange value of the commodity unless the various layers of means of production are produced with methods of production where the capital to labour ratios can be assumed to correspond to the economy average.

3.5 Money and Its Functions

3.5.1 Money

Smith begins his investigation into money and the role it plays in the economic system in *WN* by explaining its origins.[31] He sees money emerging to overcome the inconveniences of barter. Specifically, for Smith, something becomes money when it is used to facilitate the exchange of commodities for one another. He illustrates his argument with the case of someone wanting to buy salt but having only oxen or sheep to exchange for the salt, requiring the person to buy a quantity of salt equivalent to a whole ox or sheep. He argues,

> If, on the contrary, instead of sheep or oxen, he had metals to give in exchange for it, he could easily proportion the quantity of the metal to the precise quantity of the commodity which he had immediate occasion for. (Smith, 1976, p. 39)

Although Smith sees money in the first instance assuming the form of metals, and in particular gold and silver, he argues there is good reason

[31] See Smith (1976, Book 1, Chapter 4: Of the origin and use of money).

to believe these can be, and are, replaced by a less costly medium, viz., paper, with the development of exchange. He argues,

> The substitution of paper in the room of gold and silver money, replaces a very expensive instrument of commerce with one much less costly, an[d] sometimes equally convenient. (Smith, 1976, p. 292)

Lastly, Smith conceives of the nature of money as a 'veil' in the sense that changes in the quantity of it do not have a bearing on real economic phenomena such as output and employment.

From the perspective of Marx's analysis, the problems with Smith's understanding of money begin with its **conception**. First, Smith sees money in capitalism as what is used to facilitate the exchange of commodities for one another, tacitly assuming the process of exchange in capitalism is the exchange of commodities for one another. Second, conceiving of money as whatever is used to facilitate the exchange of commodities for one another requires conceiving of it as a valueless token of the commodities being exchanged for one another, and in the final instance a valueless token of corn. Third, his conception of money requires Smith to deny that money can be a commodity even though he repeatedly conceives of it as gold and silver. Lastly, Smith's conception of money causes him to see it representing the particular exchange value of the commodity, i.e., the quantity of another commodity it can be exchanged for, and not general exchange value, i.e., the quantity of any and all other commodities it can be exchanged for.

Conceiving of money as an intrinsically valueless token of commodities whose exchange it facilitates also prevents Smith from seeing it **emerging** historically prior to capitalism as a particular commodity, gold, that facilitates the exchange of commodities for one another. He is also unable to see gold emerging historically as the numéraire commodity that is used to reduce the exchange values of commodities to a common denominator since, as noted above, he sees this commodity as corn. In fact, conceiving of corn as the numéraire commodity requires him to conceive of gold emerging historically as an intrinsically valueless token of corn that is used to facilitate the exchange of commodities even though, like corn, it too is a produced commodity.

The preceding requires Smith to be interpreted as seeing money assuming the **form** of an intrinsically valueless token of the commodities whose exchange for one another it facilitates, and in the final instance a token of corn. This means that when Smith conceives of gold facilitating the exchange of commodities for one another, or for corn as the numéraire commodity, he must be conceiving of gold as a valueless token of the commodities being exchanged, and in the final instance a valueless token of corn, even though it is a produced commodity possessing value. What Smith does not explain in this regard is how gold can be conceived of as both a produced commodity possessing value and a valueless token of commodities or corn when it is used to facilitate the exchange of commodities for one another. To avoid this problem Smith would have to conceive of gold and not corn as the numéraire commodity and money a token of gold. However, as I noted above, this would require him to conceive of the exchange value of gold as one, and commodities put into the process of circulation with determinate gold prices.

Lastly, for Marx, Smith's abstraction from money, in the sense of ignoring it, when explaining the exchange value of the commodity in the first instance causes him to see money as essentially a **veil**, having no bearing on the reproduction of the commodity. This is because it causes Smith to bring money into his explanation of the exchange value of the commodity as an intrinsically valueless token of the commodities whose exchange for one another in accordance with their corn exchange values it is used to facilitate. Logically, this means that for Smith changes in the value and exchange value of money, as well as corresponding changes in the money prices of commodities, cannot have a bearing on their reproduction. Their reproduction can only be impacted on by changes in their corn exchange values. From the perspective of Marx's analysis Smith's abstraction from money in the first instance precludes him from seeing the exchange value of the commodity as its money exchange value where money is the representative of general exchange value, i.e., having command over any and all commodities, which in turn precludes him from seeing changes in the value and exchange value of money as well as changes in the money prices of commodities having a bearing on the reproduction of commodities.

3.5.2 Functions of Money

Like most other Classical economists, Smith sees the primary and defining function of money as that of medium of exchange. He argues,

> The butcher seldom carries his beef or mutton to the baker, or the brewer, in order to exchange them for bread or for beer, but he carries them to the market, where he exchanges them for money, and afterwards exchanges that money for bread and beer. (Smith, 1976, p. 49)

Moreover, although he recognises money performs other functions apart from that of medium of exchange, e.g., denominator and settler of debts as well as store of value,[32] there is nothing in his work to suggest that he sees any of them as more important than the medium of exchange function.

The problems with Smith's explanation of the functions of money from the perspective of Marx's analysis begin with his neglect of money's **measure of exchange value** function. Smith certainly conceives of money functioning as the measure of exchange values of commodities as, for example, when he argues,

> ...the exchangeable value of every commodity is more frequently estimated by the quantity of money, than by the quantity of labour or any other commodity which can be exchanged for it. (Smith, 1976, p. 49)

However, his understanding of the measure of the exchange value function of money here is as the standard of all commodities as measures of the exchange values of one another, i.e., as the numéraire commodity, and not the measure of the general exchange values of all commodities. Hence, Smith's reference to money as a commodity performing this function in the manner of any other commodity. Hence, also, his confusion of corn with gold. It will be recalled that for Smith corn is the numéraire commodity and not gold, even though he is aware that gold is used more frequently than other commodities as the standard of all commodities as measures of the exchange values of one another.

Given Smith's concept of the exchange value of the commodity, there is in fact no reason for him to conceive of money as a measure of the exchange value of the commodity. That is to say, since Smith conceives of the exchange value of the commodity as its commodity exchange value, with one commodity, corn, chosen as the standard of all commodities as measures of the exchange values of one another, the measure of the exchange value of the commodity must be the commodity it commands in

[32] See Smith (1976, pp. 57–58, 73).

the process of exchange and not money. Money can only be conceived of as a token of the commodities commanded by one another in the process of exchange, or a token of corn as the standard of commodities as the measures of the exchange values of one another.

Ignoring money's measure of exchange value function causes Smith to assign primacy to its **medium of exchange** function, and deny its **means of circulation** function, even though he formally assigns primacy to the latter function of money. Smith does not see that money as the means of circulation facilitates the circulation of commodities that are put into circulation with determinate money prices, while money as a medium of exchange facilitates the exchange of commodities for one another in proportion to their exchange values. Conceiving of money as a commodity, viz., gold or silver, and seeing commodities being exchanged according to their gold prices, does not mean Smith is conceiving of money performing a means of circulation function. This is because he sees gold as a token of corn that facilitate the exchange of commodities with one another in accordance with their corn exchange values.

Although, as noted above, Smith does not elaborate on money's function of a **store of value**, it should be apparent that his conception of money requires him to see this function performed by something other than money. This is because what is required to perform this function should logically be something possessing intrinsic value and representing a certain magnitude of exchange value. For Smith, as argued above, money is intrinsically valueless and the quantity of exchange value it represents is the particular exchange value of the commodities being exchanged, which changes with each and every transaction.

3.6 Value of Money

In the same way that Smith does not have an explicit explanation of the value of the commodity as distinct from its exchange value, he also does not have an explicit explanation of the value of money as distinct from its exchange value. However, as with the value of the commodity, his work contains an implicit conception and explanation of the value of money that is distinct from its exchange value. In what follows, I will elicit and criticise this implicit conception and corresponding explanation of the value of money.

Since Smith sees money in the first instance assuming the form of a commodity, viz., gold (or silver), he conceives of its value, like the value of any other produced commodity, as a certain quantity of corn incomes appropriated by owners of factor inputs used in its production.[33] He sees this form of money giving way to valueless tokens of gold, whose value depends on their quantitative relation to gold.[34] Although Smith does not explicitly conceive of money assuming the form of an intrinsically valueless token of the commodities whose exchange for one another it facilitates, the logic of his analysis suggests, as I argued above, this is the form money must actually assume. It also suggests the value of this form of money is given by the average quantity of corn commanded as incomes in the context of the production of all commodities whose exchange for one another this form of money facilitates.

The implication of Smith's implicit conception of the value of money, whatever form it assumes, is that its measure is a certain quantity of corn, and, in the final instance, a certain quantity of labour commanded with the corn. That is, he sees corn as the measure of the value of gold as commodity money as well as the measure of value of money as a valueless token of the commodities whose exchange for one another it facilitates. Corn is logically the measure of the value of money as an intrinsically valueless token of the commodities whose exchange it facilitates because it is a measure of the values of the commodities money becomes a token of when facilitating their exchange for one another.

Smith's conception of the value of money also has certain implications for how he sees money as a commodity acquiring value historically and how this value is formed. It implies he sees money acquiring value historically, like any other commodity, when it is produced with factors of production whose owners appropriate corn incomes, and this value formed, like the value of any commodity, at the outset of its production when the owners of factor inputs used in its production are paid corn incomes. It also implies he sees money as inconvertible fiat currency acquiring value when it comes to replace gold as a medium of exchange and its value formed in the context of its performance of this function.

Lastly, Smith sees the magnitude of value of money as a commodity determined in the same way as the magnitude of value of any commodity, by the corn income costs of its production, and the magnitude of value of convertible tokens of commodity money given by the quantity of

[33] See Smith (1976, pp. 55–56).

[34] See Smith (1976, pp. 293–294).

these tokens in relation to the quantity of the commodity money, gold, it replaces in exchange. He implicitly sees the magnitude of value of money as inconvertible fiat currency determined by the values of commodities it commands in the process of facilitating their exchange, i.e., by the corn income costs of producing the commodities comprising the net product in relation to the quantity of money required to facilitate the exchange of these commodities for one another.

From the perspective of Marx's analysis the problems with Smith's explanation of the value of money begin with its implicit **conception**. To begin with, Smith's conception of money as an intrinsically valueless token of corn prevents him from conceiving of its value as that of gold, or even the value of an intrinsically valueless token of gold. It needs recalling that Smith sees corn and not gold as the numéraire commodity. Hence, if he sees money as the numéraire commodity it must be as corn, and if he sees money as an intrinsically valueless token of any particular commodity it can only be that of corn as the numéraire commodity. Moreover, when Smith conceives of money as gold, it must be as a commodity that can also serve as an intrinsically valueless token of the commodities whose exchange for one another it facilitates. The problem is conceiving of gold as both a commodity and an intrinsically valueless token of commodities whose exchange for one another it facilitates when used as the medium of exchange, a function that requires its physical presence. Second, Smith's implicit conception of money, as an intrinsically valueless token of the commodities whose exchange for one another it facilitates, requires him to conceive of its value as the value of the *aggregate* quantity of all money used to facilitate the exchange of commodities for one another, where this value is the values of all the commodities whose exchange for one another it facilitates. At the same time, his conception of money precludes Smith from conceiving of its value as the value of a particular commodity that is used to measure the exchange values of commodities as their general exchange values. This is because Smith's implicit conception of the value of money is premised on his neglect of money's function as measure of the exchange value of the commodity, a function that for Marx causes money and commodities to acquire qualitatively equivalent values.

The problem with Smith's conception of the **measure** of the value of money follows from the problems with his conception of the value of money. Specifically, Smith's conception of the value of money causes him to implicitly, if not explicitly, conflate the measure of the value of money with the measure of its exchange value, seeing both as a certain quantity of corn. This naturally enough follows from Smith's conception of the value of money, as the aggregate values of commodities commanded by the aggregate quantity of money used to facilitate their exchange for one another, as well as his conflation of the value of the commodity with its exchange value and corresponding conflation of their measures. It should be apparent in this regard that Smith's conception of the value of commodity and corresponding conception of the value of money precludes him from seeing both as a certain quantity of labour time—the labour time required to produce a commodity. In fact, to the extent Smith sees the measure of the value of money as what is commanded with the corn appropriated as incomes, it is a certain quantity of labour and not labour time.

Smith's conception of money and its historical emergence prevents him from seeing money **acquiring** value historically when gold is used as a numéraire to facilitate the exchange of commodities by reducing their exchange values to a common denominator. Instead, it requires him to see something acquiring value as money historically when it is used as a medium of exchange to facilitate the exchange of commodities for one another, with the implication being that what is used for this purpose is a valueless token of the commodities being exchanged and, in the final instance, a valueless token of corn. Insofar as Smith sees money assuming the form of gold (or silver), he must see it acquiring value as a medium of exchange and, therefore, a valueless token of the commodities being exchanged, even though it is a produced commodity.

Smith's conception of the value of money prevents him from seeing it **formed** prior to money being put into the process of the circulation of commodities. It prevents him from seeing the formation of the value of money taking place when money is used to denote the general exchange values of the commodities prior to putting them into the process of circulation. Instead, his conception of the value of money requires him to see it formed in the context of money being used as a medium of exchange to facilitate the exchange of commodities for one another, whether in capitalism or prior to it.

The problems with Smith's explanation of the **magnitude** of the value of money follow from the above. To begin with, Smith's explanation of the magnitude of value of money as gold (or silver) is an explanation of the magnitude of gold as an intrinsically valueless token of the commodities whose exchange for one another it facilitates when performing the function of medium of exchange. It is not an explanation of the value of gold as a numéraire commodity, since for Smith this commodity is corn. Second, the logic of Smith's analysis suggests he sees the magnitude of the value of money determined by the magnitude of its exchange value and not *vice versa*. This implication of his analysis stems from his implicit conception of the value of money as the aggregate value of all commodities commanded by all money whose exchange for one another it facilitates. Given his explanation of the magnitude of the exchange value of money, the preceding suggests that Smith must deny aggregate excess demand for all commodities has a bearing on the magnitude of the value of money unless it corresponds to an excess quantity of money used to facilitate the exchange of commodities (see below for an elaboration of this point). Third, the logic of Smith's analysis prevents him from explaining changes in the magnitude of value of money by changes in the magnitudes of values of all commodities whose exchange for one another it facilitates. This follows from Smith's conception of the value of a commodity as its *relative*, and not also its *absolute*, value, precluding the values of commodities being aggregated. Lastly, leaving aside the preceding, Smith's conception of the value of the commodity prevents him from seeing changes in the economy-wide productivity of labour and raw material prices having a bearing on the magnitude of the magnitude of the value of money. It should be recalled that Smith ignores the productivity of labour when explaining the magnitude of the value of the commodity and implicitly sees the value of means of production transferred to the value of the output produced with them as given by the layered income costs of producing them.

3.7 Exchange Value of Money

Commensurate with what was argued above, it is implicit in Smith's analysis of the exchange value of money that he also draws a distinction between forms of money when explaining it. Specifically, he implicitly draws a distinction between the exchange value of money as, on the one hand, a commodity (and convertible tokens of this commodity), and, on the other hand, inconvertible fiat currency. Smith explicitly conceives of the exchange value of the money commodity as the quantity of another commodity it commands in the process of exchange,[35] and the exchange

[35] See Smith (1976, pp. 55–56).

value of paper tokens of the money commodity as the quantity of these tokens in relation to the quantity of gold it replaces in the process of exchange.[36] He *implicitly* conceives of the exchange value of inconvertible fiat currency as the quantity of commodities comprising the net product that it commands.

Smith's explicit and implicit conception of the measure of the exchange value of money follows from this. He explicitly conceives of the measure of the exchange value of the money commodity (viz., gold or silver) as other commodities, with corn being their common standard. He implicitly conceives of the measure of the exchange value of money as money, e.g., money as inconvertible fiat currency, as the cluster of commodities whose exchange for one another money facilitates and that are in principle convertible into certain quantities of corn as the numéraire commodity.

The preceding has in turn certain implications for how Smith implicitly sees money acquiring exchange value historically and how this exchange value is formed. It implies he sees money acquiring exchange value historically as a particular commodity, like any other commodity, when it begins to be exchanged for other commodities. He implicitly sees money as inconvertible fiat currency acquiring exchange value historically when it is used to facilitate the exchange of commodities for one another. Smith's conception of the exchange value of money, and his explanation of the role money plays in the exchange of commodities for one another, suggest he sees the exchange value of money formed in the process of exchange. When money is a commodity he appears to see its exchange value formed when it is exchanged for other commodities as a numéraire commodity. When money is inconvertible fiat currency Smith implicitly sees its exchange value formed in the context of it facilitating the exchange of commodities for one another as a medium of exchange.

Lastly, Smith's explanation of the magnitude of the exchange value of money naturally enough depends on the form money assumes. He explicitly sees the magnitude of the exchange value of money as a commodity determined by the magnitude of its value in the manner of all commodities, i.e., by the relative corn income costs of producing the money commodity.[37] Smith sees changes in the magnitude of the exchange value of money as a commodity, or in the aggregate gold price level,

[36] See Smith (1976, pp. 293–294).

[37] See Smith (1976, p. 255).

resulting from changes in the corn wage rate. He sees the magnitude of the exchange value of valueless tokens of gold determined by the quantity of these tokens in relation to the quantity of gold they are seen as replacing in the process of exchange, with this quantity typically given by the face values of these tokens.[38] Smith implicitly sees the magnitude of the exchange value of money as money, whatever form money assumes, determined the quantity of money relative to the quantity of commodities whose exchange for one another it is used to facilitate.[39]

From the perspective of Marx's analysis, the problems with Smith's explanation of the exchange value of money begins with his **conception** of the exchange value of money. To begin with, in the same way Smith's conception of money precludes him from conceiving of the value of gold as both a particular commodity and money, with the former exerting a gravitational pull on the latter, it also precludes him from conceiving of the exchange value of gold as both a particular commodity and money, with the former exerting a gravitational pull on the latter. Money cannot logically be a produced commodity with intrinsic value when used as a medium of exchange. Second, Smith's conception of money and the priority he accords to its medium of exchange function precludes him from conceiving of the exchange value of money in the manner of Marx, as the quantity of any particular commodity with a determinate price that a unit of money commands. Instead, it requires him to conceive of the exchange value of money as the exchange value of the *aggregate* quantity of money used to facilitate the exchange of all commodities for one another relative to the quantity of these commodities. Smith's neglect of money's measure of exchange value function prevents him from seeing money acquiring a certain magnitude of exchangeable worth when it is used by producers to denote the exchange values of their commodities as general exchange values, and allowing it to be used to circulate commodities with determinate money prices.

Smith's mistaken conception of the exchange value of money results in a corresponding mistaken implicit conception of its **measure**. It requires him to conceive of the measure of the exchange value of money as the measure of the exchange value of the aggregate quantity of money used to facilitate the exchange of commodities for one another, and this measure

[38] See Smith (1976, pp. 293–294).

[39] See Laidler (1981, p. 188).

as the cluster of commodities without money prices whose exchange for one another money facilitates. Leaving aside the conceptual problems with conceiving of a cluster of commodities and/or their reduction to corresponding quantities of corn, what Smith is unable to conceive of is the measure of the exchange value of money as any commodity put into the process of circulation with a determinate money price. This is because he does not see money's primary and defining function as that of measure of the exchange values of commodities. He does not see that when producers use money to measure the general exchange values of their commodities prior to putting them into the process of circulation they simultaneously cause any and every commodity put into the process of circulation with determinate money prices to becomes measures of the exchange value of money.

Smith's conception of money and implicit explanation of its emergence historically prevents him from seeing a particular commodity **acquiring** exchange value as money when it is used as a numéraire commodity to facilitate the exchange of commodities by reducing their exchange values to a common commodity denominator. Instead, it requires Smith to see money acquiring exchange value historically as a valueless token of corn that is used as a medium of exchange to facilitate the exchange of commodities for one another. Insofar as Smith sees money emerging as gold, the logic of his analysis requires him to see gold acquiring exchange value as money when it is used as a valueless token of corn to facilitate the exchange of commodities for one another.

Smith's neglect of money's measure of exchange value function, and the primacy he attaches to its medium of exchange function, prevents him from seeing money's exchange value **formed** when it is used by producers to denote the general exchange values of their commodities *prior* to putting them into the process of circulation, and instead requires him to see the exchange value of money formed in the process of money being used to facilitate the exchange of commodities for one another. Although Smith refers to money's medium function as its medium of circulation function, he does not see that this function is the use of money to facilitate the purchase and sale of commodities that are put into circulation with determinate money prices.

The problems with Smith's explanation of the **magnitude** of the exchange value of money follow from those noted above with regard to his conception of money and explanation of the magnitude of its value. First, since Smith's conception of money precludes him from conceiving of the exchange value of money as the exchange value of commodity money, it must also logically preclude him from explaining the magnitude of the exchange value of money as the magnitude of the exchange value of a commodity as money. This means that when Smith explains the magnitude of the exchange value of gold he is explaining the magnitude of the exchange value of gold as an ordinary commodity and not also as money.

A second problem with Smith's explanation of the magnitude of the exchange value of money as the magnitude of the exchange value of an intrinsically valueless token of commodities whose exchange for one another it is used to facilitate, is that it requires him to deny this magnitude is determined by the magnitude of its value. In fact, as argued above, he explains the latter by the former. This precludes Smith from explaining the magnitude of the exchange value of money by the average corn income costs of production of all commodities.

A third problem with Smith's implicit explanation of the magnitude of exchange value of money is that it precludes him from explaining this magnitude by aggregate excess demand for all commodities, unless the latter corresponds to an excess quantity of money used to facilitate the exchange of all commodities for one another. Crucially, this prevents Smith from seeing credit expansion as a source of aggregate excess demand unless what facilitates the exchange of commodities for one another is seen as including credit.

A last and related problem with Smith's explanation of the magnitude of the exchange value of the commodity is that it is premised on the assumption that commodities are put into the process of exchange for one another without determinate money prices and the quantity of money used to facilitate their exchange for one another in accordance with their exchange values is put into exchange without reference to the quantity of commodities and the magnitudes of their money prices. That is, it requires Smith to see the quantity of money used to facilitate the exchange of commodities for one another as *exogenously* given, something that follows from his neglect of money's measure of exchange value function and the corresponding primacy he attaches to its medium of exchange function. There are most certainly a number of instances in Smith's *WN* where he sees the quantity of money put into circulation as *endogenously* determined. For example, when he discusses the likely consequences of the imposition of a "bounty" (tax) on corn, he argues it would most likely result in an increase in the money price of corn and, consequently, a rise in the money prices of all other commodities.[40] Similarly, when he discusses the likely consequences of the liberalisation of corn imports, Smith argues it would most likely lead to a fall in the money price of corn and, consequently, a fall in the money prices of all other commodities.[41] However, a closer inspection of Smith's discussion of both of these suggests he in fact sees the quantity of money as exogenously determined in spite of appearances to the contrary. In the case of the bounty on corn, Smith sees the increase in the price of corn inducing a fall in the value of the money commodity, i.e., the quantity of corn required to produce it falling below the quantity of corn it commands in the process of circulation. This in turn brings about an increase in the production of the money commodity and its use to purchase all other commodities. The net result is an increase in the money prices of all other commodities and a fall in the magnitude of the exchange value of money as money to its level as a commodity. Similarly, in the case of the liberalisation of corn imports leading to a fall in the money price of corn, the implied rise in the value of the money commodity above its value as money, i.e., an increase in the corn cost of producing money above the quantity of corn money commands in the process of circulation, leads to a fall in the output of the money commodity and, therefore, the quantity of it put into the process of circulation. This causes the money prices of all commodities to fall and the exchange value of money as money to adjust to its exchange value as a commodity.

3.8 Money Price of the Commodity

Smith refers to the money price of a commodity as its 'nominal price' and conceives of it as the quantity of gold commanded by the commodity in the process of exchange. He distinguishes this price from the 'real' price of the commodity, which he conceives of as the quantity of corn, and therefore a certain quantity of labour, a unit of it commands.[42] In fact, he tacitly sees gold as a token of the numéraire commodity, corn, although he is not clear about this. Confusingly, he at times sees gold as

[40] See Smith (1976, p. 509).

[41] See Smith (1976, p. 535).

[42] See Smith (1976, p. 55).

the measure of the exchange value of the commodity and refers to gold prices as the money prices of commodities.[43]

Although Smith does not pay much explicit attention to how commodities acquire money prices historically or how they are formed, these can be deduced from his explanation of the values of the commodity and money as well as various oblique references to them in *WN*. These suggest he sees commodities acquiring money prices historically when money is used to facilitate the exchange of commodities for one another or for gold as the numéraire commodity. It also suggests he sees the money prices of commodities formed in the process of the exchange of commodities for one another or for gold, where this exchange is facilitated by money.

Lastly, Smith explains the magnitude of the money price of the individual commodity by the magnitude of the commodity exchange value of the commodity for a given value of money. As I noted above, Smith explains the magnitude of exchange value of the commodity as its corn exchange value, and the value of money as the average quantity of corn commanded by money in the process of facilitating the exchange of commodities for one another.

From the perspective of Marx's analysis the problems with Smith's explanation of the money price of the commodity begin with its **conception**. To begin with, Smith's conceptions of the value of the commodity precludes him from conceiving of the exchange value of the commodity as its money exchange value and instead requires him to see it as its commodity or corn exchange value. This in turn causes him to conceive of the money price of the commodity as its corn exchange value where money is a token of corn. Second, Smith is unable to conceive of the money price of the commodity assuming a commodity form, as the commodity money price of the commodity, notwithstanding his conception of commodities having gold prices. This is because his conception of money precludes him from conceiving of gold prices of commodities as their money prices. For Smith, the gold prices of commodities can only be numéraire prices, and only insofar as gold and not corn can be assumed as used to pay wages. Since, Smith is clear that he sees corn, not gold, as what is used to pay wages, he must see corn as the numéraire commodity and money a token of it. This means he can only see gold as an ordinary

[43] See Smith (1976, p. 56).

commodity having a certain determinate exchange ratio with corn, like any other commodity. Third, Smith does not see the money price of the commodity as the *form* assumed by its value in the same way he does not conceive of the exchange value of the commodity as the *form* assumed by the value of the commodity. This is partly for the same reasons as he does not conceive of the corn exchange value of the commodity as the form assumed by its value, and partly because there is no reason to suppose any link between the value of the commodity and money. Lastly, Smith's conception of the money price of a commodity, as its corn exchange value where money is a token of corn, precludes him from, on the one hand, conceiving of the relative money price of the commodity as its money price relative to the money price of another commodity, and, on the other hand, conceiving of the aggregate money price level as the aggregate of the money prices of individual commodities. Instead, it requires him to conceive of the relative price of the commodity as its relative corn exchange value (i.e., the corn exchange value of one commodity relative to the corn exchange value of another) where money is a token of corn, and the aggregate money price level as the aggregate quantity of money used to facilitate the exchange of commodities for one another relative to the aggregate quantity of commodities whose exchange for one another money is used to facilitate.

The problems with Smith's conception of the **measure** of the money price of the commodity from the perspective of Marx's analysis follows from the problems noted above with its conception. First, Smith is not able to conceive of money as the measure of the money price of the commodity and this measure the *form* of the measure of the value of the commodity. This is because his conception of the money price of the commodity requires him to conceive of money as a token of corn as the measure of the exchange value of the commodity. Second, Smith is not able to conceive of money *as a commodity* serving as the measure of the money price of the commodity. That is to say, he is not able to conceive of gold as the measure of the money price of the commodity, in the same way he is not able to conceive of the money price of the commodity assuming the form of a gold price. This is because he does not see gold becoming the representatives of the general exchange values of commodities when they are used by producers to denote the general exchange values of their commodities. Instead, he sees whatever functions as the medium of exchange becoming the representative of the exchange value of the commodities whose exchange it facilitates and a token of the numéraire commodity that reduces the exchange values of commodities to equivalence.

Smith's conception of money precludes him from seeing commodities **acquiring** money prices historically as gold prices when gold comes to be used as a numéraire commodity to denote the exchange values of commodities in one and the same commodity. Instead, his conception of money requires him to see commodities acquiring money prices historically as gold prices when gold comes to be used as a valueless token of corn to facilitate the exchange of commodities for one another. As argued above, the source of the problem with Smith's analysis in this regard is his conception of money as an intrinsically valueless token of the commodities whose exchange for one another it facilitates.

Smith's neglect of money's measure function prevents him from seeing money prices of commodities **formed** *prior* to commodities and money being put into the process of circulation. As argued above, this neglect of money measure function stems from Smith's conception of the value of the commodity and the absence of an intrinsic link between it and money, causing him to ascribe primacy to money's medium of exchange function. It is this that requires him to see the money prices of commodities formed in the process of the exchange of commodities for one another, a process facilitated by money as a medium of exchange.

The problems with Smith's explanation of the **magnitude** of the money price of the commodity also follow from the problems with his conception of the money price of the commodity noted above. First, Smith is unable to explain the magnitude of the money price of the commodity as the quantity of money it commands, since it would require him to conceive of money possessing value in itself and not as a token of something that possesses value. Second, the logic of Smith's analysis prevents him from explaining the magnitude of the money price of the commodity as its commodity money price since, as noted above, he denies money can be conceived of as a commodity. Which means that his explanation of the magnitude of gold prices of commodities is not an explanation of the magnitudes of their money prices, but rather an explanation of the magnitudes of their gold exchange values where gold is a particular commodity that is used as the measure of the exchange values of other particular commodities in the same way all commodities are measures of the exchange values of one another. Third, Smith's conception of the value of the commodity prevents him from seeing the direct impact changes in its magnitude have on the magnitude of its money price. Fourth, Smith's conception of the magnitude of the money price of the commodity requires him to see changes in the relative money prices of commodities taking place independently of changes in the aggregate money price level. This is because Smith's conception of the money price of the commodity requires him to explain the relative money price of the commodity as its relative corn exchange value by different factors to those he advances to explain the aggregate money price level. Specifically, Smith explains the relative corn exchange value of the commodity by the relative quantity of corn appropriated as incomes in the context of its production and the aggregate money price level by the exogenously determined quantity of money used to facilitate the exchange of commodities comprising the net product relative to this quantity of commodities. Lastly, and most importantly from the perspective of Marx's analysis, Smith's explanation of the magnitude of the money price of the commodity requires him to deny that changes in the productivity of labour have a bearing on either the relative money price of the commodity or the aggregate money price level, i.e., it requires him to deny that changes in the relative productivity of labour have a bearing on changes in the relative money prices of commodities *via* their impact on the relative value and corn exchange value of the commodity, and changes in the economy-wide productivity of labour have a bearing on changes in the aggregate money price level.

From the perspective of Marx's analysis, the source of the problems with Smith's explanation of the money price of the commodity is his conception of the value of the commodity and its link to money. Smith's conception of the value of the commodity, as the corn income cost of producing it, requires him to conceive of money as a token of corn and its primary function as that of a medium of exchange, as well as to see the value of the commodity formed independently of money. It is this that causes Smith to have a mistaken conception and explanation of the money price of the commodity, as its relative corn price for a given value of money. The most obvious manifestation of this is that it requires Smith to explain changes in the relative money prices of commodities taking place independently of changes in the aggregate money price level, and to deny that changes in the productivity of labour have a bearing on either.

References

Laidler, D. (1981). Adam Smith as a monetary economist. *Canadian Journal of Economics, 14*(2), 185–200.

Marx, K. (1969a). *Theories of surplus value: Part I* (E. Burns, Trans.). Lawrence & Wishart.

Marx, K. (1969b). *Theories of surplus value: Part II* (R. Simpson, Trans.). Lawrence & Wishart.

Marx, K. (1976). *Capital, volume I* (B. Fowkes, Trans.). Penguin Books.

Marx, K. (1978). *Capital, volume II* (D. Fernbach, Trans.). Penguin Books.

Marx, K. (1981). *Capital, volume III* (D. Fernbach, Trans.). Penguin Books.

Nicholas, H. (2011). *Marx's theory of price and its modern rivals*. Palgrave Macmillan.

Ricardo, D. (1973). *The principles of political economy and taxation*. London (Originally published in 1817).

Roll, E. (1973). *A history of economic thought* (4th ed.). Faber and Faber.

Skinner, A. S. (1976). General introduction. In A. Smith (Ed.), *The wealth of nations* (pp. 1–60). Oxford University Press.

Smith, A. (1976). *The wealth of nations*. Oxford University Press (Originally published in 1776).

Sraffa, P. (1960). *Production of Commodities by Means of Commodities*. Cambridge University Press.

CHAPTER 4

Ricardo's Explanation of Money Price

4.1 Introduction

It is evident from even a cursory glance at Marx's critical assessment of the Classical school of economists that he has the highest regard for the work of David Ricardo, suggesting on a number of occasions that he stands head and shoulders above all others in this school. For this reason alone, a consideration of Ricardo's explanation of price is warranted. However, perhaps a more compelling reason is that it has been contended by many scholars that Marx added little, if anything, to Ricardo's labour theory value explanation of price.[1]

4.2 Object and Approach

Ricardo takes for granted that wealth is created by the expenditure of labour time in the context of an increasing division of labour, and focuses his attention on the distribution of this wealth in capitalism. More precisely, his focus is on the distribution of the net product between landlords, capitalists, and labour. Ricardo states in the preface to his *Principles* "To determine the laws which regulate this distribution is the principal problem in Political Economy..." (1973, p. 3). He argues that while

[1] See for example Schumpeter (2006).

H. Nicholas, *Explorations in Marx's Theory of Price—Why Marx Is Still Relevant for Understanding the Modern Economy*,
https://doi.org/10.1057/978-1-137-56564-8_4

much progress had been made by his predecessors in respect of the determination of the wealth of nations, they offered little by way of an explanation of its distribution between rent, profit, and wages.[2] Hence, the justification for his *Principles* is an attempt to fill this lacuna. A particular concern of Ricardo in explaining the distribution of the net product is to explain the link between this distribution and the price (exchange value) of the commodity. For Marx one of the merits of Ricardo's work is the way in which he explains the distribution of the net product between classes as one founded on the expenditure of labour, even resulting in him being referred to by a fellow Classical economist as "the father of communism".[3]

The preceding should not, however, be interpreted as suggesting Marx is uncritical of Ricardo's focus and approach in his study of the economy. In fact, it is readily apparent Marx considers Ricardo's focus to be too narrow, i.e., the distribution of the net product, and founded on a perfunctory acceptance of Smith's view of the causes of increases in wealth. Moreover, although Marx praises Ricardo for his method of abstraction, he is also critical of the latter's failure to fully investigate the inner essence of the phenomena being investigated. Marx argues that Ricardo, more than any other Classical economist, is able to use the method of abstraction to penetrate the level of appearances when explaining the distribution of income, and it is in fact his particular method of scientific inquiry "that represents Ricardo's great historical significance for science" (1969a, p. 166). The problem Marx sees with Ricardo's method, however, is his failure to investigate more thoroughly the links between the inner essence and surface appearance of economic phenomena. Most importantly for Marx is Ricardo's concern to explain the magnitude of the exchange value of the commodity by its value, causing him to overlook the precise nature of the relationship between the two and consequently blinding him to the link between the commodity and money. For Marx, Ricardo does not see that when production is mediated by money-based exchange money develops a link with the value of the commodity, one that manifests itself in the link between the value of the commodity and its money price.

[2] See Ricardo (1973, p. 3).

[3] See Marx (1969a, p. 166).

4.3 Production and Value of the Commodity

4.3.1 Production

For Marx, Ricardo recognises more than other Classical economist the social nature of production and the importance of conceiving of production requiring the expenditure of labour time in all modes of production. He shares Smith's conception of the production of commodities based on the use of factor inputs and his distinction between modes of production in terms of differences in the factors of production used. Like Smith, Ricardo sees labour as the sole factor of production used in the early and rude mode of production with the wages accruing to labour accounting for the whole of the net product. Also like Smith, Ricardo sees labour used alongside capital and land in capitalism with owners of these factors of production sharing in the net product produced in this mode. Where Ricardo deviates from Smith is in seeing rent as part of profit as well as the emphasis he places on the expenditure of labour time in the process of production. It is this emphasis Marx sees as setting Ricardo apart from Smith and most other Classical economists.[4] Marx argues, however, that it does not prevent Ricardo from seeing the commodities produced excluding the means of production in the manner of Smith.[5]

For Marx the problems with Ricardo's explanation of production stem in most part from his uncritical acceptance of Smith's explanation of production. These problems are his lack of clarity regarding the producer, the inputs used in production, and the outputs produced. Like Smith, Ricardo is not clear who the **producers** are and how they are distinguished from the owners of capital. The implication to be drawn from his analysis is, as for Smith, that producers are *managers* who do not own capital. The money they outlay to undertake production is borrowed by them from capitalists. For Ricardo, as for Smith, the outputs produced possess exchange values in all modes of production and exclude the means of production.[6] Although Ricardo, unlike Smith, sees the process of production in capitalism as involving the expenditure of labour time, he does not see that this labour time must assume the form of the money exchange value of the commodity before the commodity is put into the

[4] See Marx (1972, p. 181).

[5] See Marx (1978, p. 466).

[6] See Marx (1976, pp. 736–737).

process of circulation. This *lacuna* in Ricardo's work causes him, like Smith and most other Classical economists, to misunderstand money and the money prices of commodities in capitalism.

4.3.2 Value of the Commodity

Ricardo's explanation of production leads him to conceive of the 'absolute value', or simply the 'value', of the commodity as the quantity of labour time which is used for its production, and distinct from the exchange value of the commodity as the quantity of another commodity it commands in the process of exchange.[7] When elaborating his conception of the value of the commodity, Ricardo emphasises the difference between his concept of value and that of Smith, criticising the latter's concept in the process.[8] Sraffa (1951) notes that several interpreters of Ricardo's work have cast doubt on his adherence to the labour theory of value in the later years of his life, but argues the evidence suggests otherwise. He quotes Ricardo in one of his last known correspondences on the subject stating "I am fully persuaded that in fixing on the quantity of labour realized in commodities as the rule which governs their relative value we are on the right course" (Sraffa, 1951, p. xl).

Ricardo sees the measure of value as the quantity of labour time used to produce the commodity and not, as for Smith, the quantity of labour commanded by corn. He argues this measure of the value of the commodity, unlike the measure of value adopted by Smith, is an invariable measure. For Ricardo the labour commanded by corn must vary in the same way, and as a result of the same forces, as the labour commanded by other commodities.[9] Somewhat confusingly, there are instances when Ricardo too appears to conceive of the measure of value of the commodity as the labour commanded by it. Upon closer inspection, however, these instances are when the measure he is referring to pertains to the exchange value of the commodity rather than its value.

The implication of Ricardo's conception of the value of the commodity is that he sees commodities acquiring values historically when their production requires the expenditure of labour time. He even quotes

[7] See Ricardo (1973, p. 6).

[8] See Ricardo (1973, p. 7).

[9] See Ricardo (1973, pp. 7–10).

Smith to this effect arguing that from the earliest mode of production onwards the source of the exchange value of the commodity is "the exertion of human industry" (1973, p. 6). It also follows from this that Ricardo sees the value of the commodity formed in the context of the process of production and not, as for Smith, prior to the process of production.

Ricardo sees the magnitude of value of a produced commodity determined by the quantity of labour time used in its production, whether the mode of production is conceived of as akin to the early and rude state or capitalism. That is to say, Ricardo sees the magnitude of value of the commodity determined by its labour time cost of production and not, as for Smith, its commodity income cost of production. An important conclusion Ricardo draws from his explanation of the magnitude of value of the commodity is that changes in it are fundamentally explained by changes in the productivity of labour.[10] He recognises there can be differences between the labour expended by different producers in terms of the skill and intensity of work, but argues that over time these are reduced to equivalence by the market such that, for example, the work of a skilled worker counts as imparting value of a greater magnitude than that of a less skilled worker.[11]

Although Marx is positive in his appraisal of Ricardo's explanation of the value of the commodity, arguing that this explanation is far in advance of his Classical peers, including Smith,[12] Marx argues it too has major shortcomings, beginning with Ricardo's **conception** of the value of the commodity. For Marx, one problem with this conception is Ricardo's tendency to at times adopt Smith's conception of the value of a commodity, i.e., the commodity income cost of producing it,[13] and therefore, like Smith, collapse the value of the commodity into its commodity exchange value.[14] This problem, as I will elaborate on below, stems from Ricardo's recognition that the magnitude of value of the commodity does not equal the magnitude of its exchange value in the context of the formation of an economy-wide general rate of profit. A second problem with

[10] See Ricardo (1973, p. 15).

[11] See Ricardo (1973, p. 13).

[12] See Marx (1969a, p. 166; 1972, p. 181).

[13] See Marx (1972, p. 138).

[14] See Marx (1969a, p. 208).

Ricardo's conception of the value of a commodity for Marx is that Ricardo sees it as the labour time ***embodied*** rather than the labour time ***required*** for the production of the commodity.[15] For Marx the source of this problem in Ricardo's analysis is his failure to understand the link between the value of the commodity and money.[16] Ricardo does not see that when producers denote the general exchange values of their commodities in terms of money, i.e., when they set the money prices of their commodities, they transform the labour time actually expended in its production into the labour time necessary for its production—into certain quantities of the simple labour time required for the production of the bulk of the commodities of a certain type using normal techniques and methods of production. A third problem with Ricardo's conception of the value of the commodity for Marx is his tendency to conceive of it as the relative value of the commodity, and not also its absolute value, seeing this value as the relative labour time expended in the production of the commodity and not also the absolute quantity of labour time required to be expended in its production.

Ricardo's occasional adoption of Smith's conception of the value of a commodity and corresponding conflation of the value of the commodity with its exchange value causes him to also occasionally conflate their **measures**. Most of the time Ricardo sees the measure of the value of a commodity as a certain quantity of labour time, but on occasion he sees it as another commodity, even the money commodity—gold. For Marx the problem with Ricardo's conception of the measure of the value of the commodity is that he sees it as the labour time actually expended in the production of the commodity and not what needs to be expended, not the labour time required to produce the bulk of commodities of a certain type using standard techniques and methods of production—not the socially necessary labour time. Ricardo also does not see that this labour time is what is objectified in money and serves as the measure of the value of the commodity when producers use money to denote the general exchange values of their commodities.[17]

[15] Marx interprets Ricardo as referring to 'labour-time' when he refers to the 'labour' expended.

[16] Marx (1969a, p. 164).

[17] Marx (1969a, p. 164; 1972, p. 138).

It should hardly be surprising in the context of the above, Ricardo has at times a similarly confused understanding of the historical **acquisition** of values by commodities as well as their formation. Ricardo appears at times, like Smith, to see commodities acquiring values historically when they are produced with factors of production, beginning with the use of the labour factor in the early and rude mode of production, when labour is the sole factor of production. That is, like Smith, Ricardo erroneously sees commodities acquiring values in pre-capitalist systems because they are produced with inputs whose owners appropriate incomes in much the same way as in capitalism. Which means, as for Smith, he sees commodities acquiring values in pre-capitalist economic systems when labour pays itself a wage. Ricardo does not see that products acquire values in all modes of production because they are produced in the context of a division of labour and their production involves the expenditure of labour time, even though this logically follows from his conception of the value of the commodity.

Although for the most part Ricardo sees the value of the commodity **formed** in the process of production, there are times when he sees it formed prior to this process. These instances are when he adopts Smith's conception of the value of the commodity. In either case, what Ricardo does not see is that the formation of the value of the commodity takes place in the context of producers using money to denote the general exchange values of their commodities prior to putting them into the process of production. He does not see that when producers use money to denote the general exchange values of their commodities, it causes the actual labour time expended in their production to be transformed into the labour time expended in the production of the bulk of the commodities of the type the individual producers are producing. It causes the labour time expended to be converted into socially necessary labour time.

The problems with Ricardo's explanation of the **magnitude** of value follow from the preceding. To begin with, he sees the quantity of the labour time that determines the magnitude of the value of the commodity as the quantity of it *embodied* in, and not *required* for, the production of the commodity. For Marx it is Ricardo's failure to see the importance of the labour time *required to* produce a commodity determining the magnitude of its value that results in his failure to see the link between the value of the commodity and money. Marx (1969a, p. 164) argues,

> Ricardo starts out from the determination of the relative values (or exchange values) of commodities by "the quantity of labour".... [But] .... does not grasp the connection of this labour with money or that it must assume the form of money. Hence he completely fails to grasp the connection between the determination of the exchange value of the commodity by labour time and the fact that the development of commodities necessarily leads to the formation of money. Hence his erroneous theory of money. Right from the start he is only concerned with the magnitude of value....

That is, for Marx, Ricardo does not see that the labour time embodied in the production of the individual commodity is transformed into the labour time required for its production when producers use money to denote the general exchange values of their commodities prior to putting them into circulation. It also follows that for Marx Ricardo does not see what matters in the explanation of changes in the magnitude of value of the commodity is changes in the productivity of labour in the production of the bulk of commodities and not changes in the productivity of labour in the production of the particular commodity.

A second problem with Ricardo's explanation of the magnitude of value of the commodity, and one that also follows from his conception of it, is that he explains this magnitude as the relative magnitude of value of the commodity and not, in the first instance, its absolute value. That is to say, he explains the value of the commodity by the relative quantity of labour time required for its production and not, in the first instance, the quantity of labour time required for its production *per se*. This, as I will elaborate on below, has important implications for Ricardo's explanation of the magnitude of the value of money. It prevents him from explaining changes in this magnitude as resulting from changes in the economy-wide productivity of labour.

A last problem with Ricardo's explanation of the magnitude of the value of the commodity is his implicit understanding of the magnitude of value transferred to the value of the commodity from the means of production used in its production. The logic of his analysis suggests this is determined by the labour time expended in the production of the means of production as well as the labour time expended in the production of the means of production used in the production of these means of production, and so on. In other words, as for Smith, the value transferred from the means of production for Ricardo is the layered values of the means of production used in the production of the commodity. As for Smith,

Ricardo's analysis does not permit him to see the value transferred from the means of production to the commodity as the value of what is needed to purchase the means of production used up in the production of the commodities. This is because his embodied cost explanation of the value of the commodity prevents him from seeing the value of the commodity formed when producers use money to denote the exchange values of their commodities, with these exchange values including the value of what is required to repurchase the means of production used in the production of the commodities.

4.4 Exchange and Exchange Value of the Commodity

4.4.1 Exchange

Ricardo sees the process of exchange through similar lenses to those of Smith. Like Smith, he sees the process of exchange as the exchange of commodities for one another (C-C'), even when money is brought into the analysis. He sees the purpose of exchange as the satisfaction of the consumption needs of those exchanging the commodities, these being the owners of the factor inputs. Like Smith he sees the exchange of commodities as a characteristic of all modes of production, whether it is the early and rude mode or capitalism. And, like Smith, Ricardo sees the formation of the exchange values of commodities taking place in the context of the exchange of commodities. Where Ricardo differs from Smith, as I will expand on below, is when it comes to explaining the magnitudes of the exchange values of commodities, although, as noted above, even here he occasionally adopts Smith's explanation of these magnitudes.

Since Ricardo's explanation of the process of exchange is broadly similar to that of Smith, the problems with his explanation of this process from the perspective of Marx's analysis are similar to those noted above with Smith's explanation. To begin with, like Smith, Ricardo does not see that the process of exchange in capitalism as fundamentally the commodity for money (C-M) and not commodities for one another (C-C'). He also does not see that the purpose of the process of exchange in capitalism is the reproduction of commodities, and not one of meeting the consumption needs of the exchanging parties. In fact, like Smith, it is this view of the purpose of the process of exchange that causes Ricardo to misconceive of the process of exchange that characterises capitalism as one commodity for another and not the commodity for money. Ricardo does not see that for commodities to be reproduced producers must exchange them for something that represents general exchange value. It is Ricardo's conception of the process of exchange as one commodity for another, and its purpose as meeting the consumption desires of the exchanging parties, that causes him, like Smith, to erroneously see the process of exchange as characteristic of all economic systems, including the early and rude mode of production. What Ricardo, like Smith, does not see is that widespread exchange is only a characteristic of capitalism, since it is only in capitalism that it becomes the basis for the reproduction of the commodity. Lastly, Ricardo's conception of the process of exchange as one commodity for another causes him, like Smith, to see this process as essentially one of barter, because it requires him to deny commodities are put into the process of exchange with determinate (money) prices.

4.4.2 *Exchange Value of the Commodity*

Commensurate with his conception of the process of exchange, Ricardo conceives of the exchange value of the commodity as the quantity of another commodity commanded by it in the process of exchange where the commodity commanded is produced with an equivalent quantity of labour time to that of the commodity commanding it. He sees the measure of the exchange value of the commodity as a commodity with an invariable exchange value; "the standard commodity". The invariable exchange value of the standard commodity is with respect to the factors deemed as influencing the exchange value of any commodity. If the exchange value of the commodity that is used as the standard varies in the same way as the exchange values of the commodities whose exchange values are being assessed, it would be difficult to establish the cause of the change in the exchange value of the commodity under investigation. It would be difficult to establish whether this change is due to factors influencing the commodity in question or those influencing what is used as the standard of its exchange value.[18] Ricardo (1973, p. 27) admits the search

18 "When commodities varied in relative value it would be desirable to have the means of ascertaining which of them fell and which rose in real value, and this could only be affected by comparing them one after another with some invariable standard measure of value, which should itself be subject to none of the fluctuations to which other commodities are exposed". (Ricardo, 1973, p. 27).

for such an invariable standard is futile since "there is no commodity which is not itself exposed to the same variations as the things the value of which is to be ascertained…". However, he contents himself with the presumption that gold is the nearest approximation one can get to such an invariable standard.[19]

Ricardo's conceptions of exchange and the exchange value of the commodity require him to implicitly see commodities acquiring exchange values historically when they are produced in the context of a division of labour mediated by exchange, and these exchange values formed in the process of the exchange of commodities for one another. This means he sees commodities acquiring exchange values historically after they acquire values, and these exchange values formed in the process of exchange. It needs acknowledging, however, that on occasion he gives the impression he sees the exchange values of commodities formed prior to them being put into the process of exchange.[20]

Lastly, when explaining the magnitude of the exchange value of the commodity, Ricardo focuses on its trend magnitude and explains this by the trend magnitude of its value; by the trend quantity of labour time expended in the production of the commodity. In opposition to Smith, Ricardo argues that the impact of a change in the value of the commodity on the magnitude of its exchange value may or may not take place *via* a change in the quantity of the commodity put into the process of exchange. Much will depend on the extent to which demand permits this expansion. Ricardo (1973, p. 281) gives the example of bread, arguing;

> If the natural price of bread should fall 50 per cent from some great discovery in the science of agriculture, the demand would not greatly increase, for no man would desire more than would satisfy his wants, and as the demand would not increase, neither would the supply; for a commodity is not supplied merely because it can be produced, but because there is a demand for it.

Ricardo sees a second factor having a bearing on the trend magnitude of the exchange value of the commodity as the money wage rate. He argues that an increase in the money wage rate will cause some money prices to

[19] See Ricardo (1973, pp. 28–29).

[20] See Ricardo (1973, p. 282).

rise and others to fall, unless the increase in the money wage rate results from a fall in the value of money.[21] The money prices it causes to rise will be the money prices of those commodities whose labour intensity of production is greater than that of the money commodity, and the money prices of commodities it causes to fall will be those whose labour intensity of production is less than that of the money commodity. Ricardo is at pains to stress that the impact of such changes in the money wage rate on the exchange value of the commodity will in any case be of a much lesser magnitude than that of changes in the productivity of labour.[22] It is important to note in this context that one of Ricardo's concerns in emphasising the impact of changes in the money wage rate on the exchange values or relative prices of commodities is to oppose Smith's contention that an increase in the money wage rate results in an increase in the money prices of all commodities.

Marx makes it abundantly clear that he considers Ricardo's explanation of the exchange value of the commodity superior to that of Smith, and most of the rest of the Classical school for that matter.[23] However, he also sees serious flaws in this explanation, some of which he is explicit about, and others that are only implicit in his comments on Ricardo's explanation. He sees these flaws beginning with Ricardo's **conception** of the exchange value of the commodity. For Marx, the major problem with this conception is that Ricardo, like Smith, does not see what is commanded in the process of exchange representing general exchange value.[24] Specifically, Ricardo does not see that what is commanded in the process of exchange is money and, therefore, the exchange value of the commodity is its money price. Instead, he sees what is commanded as another particular commodity representing particular exchange value, even when the commodity commanded is gold. That is, like Smith, Ricardo conceives of the exchange value of the commodity as its commodity exchange value, even when the exchange value of the commodity is its gold exchange value. For Marx, a second problem with Ricardo's conception of the exchange value of the commodity is that, also like Smith, Ricardo does not see it as the *form* assumed by the value of the commodity. Although,

[21] See Ricardo (1973, pp. 22–27).

[22] See Ricardo (1973, p. 22).

[23] See Marx (1972, p. 181).

[24] See Marx (1969a, p. 164).

unlike Smith, Ricardo conceives of the value of the commodity as the quantity of labour time expended in its production, he does not see this labour time linked to money and, therefore, the money exchange value of the commodity as the form assumed by the labour time expended in the production of the commodity. As I will expand on below, for Marx, Ricardo does not see the exchange value of the commodity as the form of its value because he does not see that when producers use money to denote the general exchange values of their commodities it causes money to become the embodiment of a certain magnitude of socially necessary labour time and, therefore, money prices to become the form of the socially necessary labour time required to produce the commodity.

It follows from the preceding that Marx sees Ricardo having a correspondingly mistaken conception of the **measure** of exchange value of the commodity. For Marx, Ricardo does not see this measure as the general equivalent form or money. In fact, for Marx, Ricardo does not see that his search for 'an invariable standard commodity' as measure of the exchange values of all commodities is in fact a search for money as this measure. Which is not to say that for Marx the magnitude of the exchange value of money is, or should be, invariable. On the contrary, for Marx this magnitude is not only variable but necessarily so in order to perform its function as money (see below). A second problem with Ricardo's conception of the measure of the exchange value of the commodity from the perspective of Marx's analysis is that Ricardo does not see this measure as the form of the measure of the value of the commodity. This particular myopia in Ricardo's analysis follows, naturally enough, from his failure to conceive of the exchange value of the commodity as the form assumed by its value.

Although Ricardo formally sees commodities **acquiring** exchange values historically after they acquire values, at times he sees commodities acquiring exchange values historically prior to them acquiring values. This is because, as noted above, at times he follows Smith in seeing commodities acquiring values when they begin to be produced with wage labour. Wage labour presupposes that the commodities paid to workers are exchangeable. Ricardo does not see that the widespread acquisition of exchange values by commodities occurs with the emergence of capitalism and the use of money by producers to denote the general exchange values of their commodities in something that represents general exchange value prior to putting the commodities into the process of circulation.

The logic of Ricardo's analysis prevents him, like Smith, from seeing the exchange values of commodities necessarily **formed** prior to them being put into the process of circulation with determinate money prices. That is, for Ricardo as for Smith, commodities are put into the process of exchange for one another without determinate exchange values, only acquiring these in the process of exchange. The source of the problem in this regard is Ricardo's tacit acceptance of Smith's conception of the process of exchange as the exchange of commodities for one another, with the purpose of exchange being the satisfaction of the consumption desires of those exchanging the commodities. This conception of the process of exchange and its purpose prevents Ricardo, like Smith, from seeing the exchange values of commodities formed prior to the commodities being put into the process of circulation, at a point when producers use money to denote the general exchange values of their commodities with a view to facilitating their reproduction.

Finally, although Marx considers Ricardo's explanation of the **magnitude** of the exchange value of the commodity to be superior to others in the Classical school, he (Marx) is clear that Ricardo's explanation too has a number of shortcomings. To begin with, and following from the problems noted above with Ricardo's conception of the exchange value of the commodity, he does not see the exchange value of the commodity that needs explaining in the first instance as its general or money exchange value. When Ricardo conceives of the exchange value of the commodity to be explained in the first instance as its gold exchange he gives the impression that he is explaining the money exchange value of the commodity. However, the logic of his analysis suggests that when he explains the gold exchange value of the commodity he is explaining its numéraire exchange value and not its money exchange value.

A second problem with Ricardo's explanation of the magnitude of the exchange value of the commodity is that he does not explain how the magnitude of the value of the commodity can be conceived of as determining the magnitude of its exchange value when the two magnitudes diverge from one another in the context of the formation of the general rate of profit. Marx notes Ricardo's solution is to tacitly assume the two are roughly equal to one another.[25] For Marx, Ricardo does not see that even though the two magnitudes diverge from one another,

[25] See Marx (1969a, p. 403).

the magnitude of value of the commodity continues to determine the magnitude of its exchange value as manifest in the relationship between changes in the productivity of labour and changes in the magnitude of the exchange value of the commodity. For Marx, Ricardo does not see the link between the two because he does not see the producer setting the prices of commodities before putting them into the process of circulation. He does not see that when producers set prices, they base these prices on unit production costs, with the most fundamental of these costs being unit wage costs, and the most fundamental determinant of the latter being the quantity of the labour input required to produce the bulk of commodities of a certain type. He does not see that when producers attempt to expand profits they try in one way or another to increase the productivity of labour—to decrease unit labour times required to produce the commodity. That is to say, they try in one way or another to reduce the quantity of labour time used to produce the commodity. While there are limits to individual producers reducing wage rates of workers in an attempt to reduce unit wage costs, there are considerably less constraints on the ways in which they are able to increase the productivity of labour.

A related point Marx makes is that Ricardo does not see clearly enough the labour time that determines the magnitude of the exchange value of a commodity is what *needs* to be expended in the production of the bulk of commodities of a certain type, and not what is *actually* expended in the production of the particular commodity. As argued above, Ricardo does not see that when producers use money to denote the general exchange values of their commodities they transform the costs they actually incur in the production of the commodity into industry standard costs and, correspondingly, the labour time that is actually expended in the production of the commodity into industry standard quantities of socially necessary labour time.

For Marx, the consequence of Ricardo's failure to explain the link between the magnitude of the exchange value and the value of the commodity in the context of the formation of a general rate of profit is, as noted above, his tendency to at times adopt Smith's income cost explanation of the exchange value of the commodity. Marx sees Smith's adoption of this explanation of the exchange value of the commodity as excusable while Ricardo's is not. This because, for Marx, Smith adopts an alternative explanation of the exchange value of the commodity from the outset since he recognises that the formation of a general rate of profit results in the labour time expended in the production of the commodity deviating from the labour time commanded. In contrast, Ricardo begins with a labour time expended explanation of the exchange value of the commodity when discussing the relationship between the 'natural' and 'market' price of the commodity, then, in the process of this discussion, he inexplicably adopts an income cost explanation of the exchange value of the commodity in the manner of Smith, without any apparent recognition of the problem that requires Smith to adopt his alternative income cost explanation.[26] Ricardo does not see that in capitalism producers need to expend more/less labour time than they command in the form of the exchange values of their commodities to be able to appropriate an economy-wide average rate of profit. If producers expend more/less labour time than that required by the technical conditions of reproducing the bulk of commodities of a certain type, they will appropriate a smaller/larger rate of profit than the average rate appropriated by these producers—those producing the bulk of the commodities in the sector.

A third problem with Ricardo's explanation of the magnitude of the exchange value of the commodity is he sees changes in the money wage rate also having a bearing on this magnitude, with its impact depending on the labour intensity of production of the commodity. Ricardo's purpose in bringing into his analysis the impact of changes in the money wage rate on the magnitude of the exchange value of the commodity is, as noted above, to refute Smith's contention that changes in the gold wage rate result in an increase in the aggregate gold price level. For Ricardo, changes in the gold wage rate cause the gold prices of some commodities to rise and others to fall, depending on the labour intensities of production of the commodities relative to the production of gold. What Ricardo overlooks in his criticism of Smith is that changes in the gold wage rate are themselves the product of changes in the aggregate gold price level, and their impact on relative gold prices of commodities cannot be ascertained without reference to the economy-wide productivity of labour and its consequences for trend movements in the economy-wide rate of profit.

A last problem of note with Ricardo's explanation of the magnitude of the exchange value of the commodity is it requires him, like Smith, to deny that the current magnitudes of the exchange values of means of production have a bearing on the magnitude of the exchange value of the commodity produced with these. This follows from his embodied

[26] See Marx (1969a, p. 211).

cost explanation of the exchange value of the commodity and his failure to see that the purpose of the exchange value of the commodity is to facilitate the reproduction of the commodity by enabling the producer to repurchase the means of production used up in the production of the commodity. Ricardo does not see that the exchange values of commodities are set by producers with reference to the current prices of means of production and not to their historic prices.

4.5 Money and Its Functions

4.5.1 Money

Ricardo begins his analysis of money in the context of his search for an invariable standard of the exchange values of commodities. As noted above, he argues that as a produced commodity money can never be a perfect measure of the exchange values of commodities because its own value is subject to variation. Moreover, the methods used in its production, i.e., the ratio of material inputs to labour, do not consistently approximate the average methods used in the economic system.[27] However, as also noted above, Ricardo satisfies himself that gold can be assumed to be a good approximation of such an invariable standard, and can therefore justifiably assumed to be this standard.[28]

Like Smith, Ricardo (1973, p. 93) sees money emerging in the context of the development of the process of exchange as a result of traders attempting to overcome the inconveniences of barter. He argues,

> The nations of the world must have been early convinced that there was no standard of value in nature to which they might unerringly refer, and therefore chose a medium which on the whole appeared to them less variable than any other commodity.

Although Ricardo admits to commodity money, viz., gold and silver, being replaced by convertible and inconvertible pieces of paper when money is used to facilitate the exchange of commodities, he argues

[27] See Ricardo (1973, pp. 27–29).

[28] See Ricardo (1973, p. 29).

> A currency is in its most perfect state when it consists wholly of paper money, but of paper of an equal value with the gold which it professes to represent. (Ricardo, 1973, p. 244)

That is to say, for Ricardo money must ultimately assume the form of a commodity. As such, he can justifiably be classified as a 'metallist'; someone that sees money as a metal even though it can be replaced by tokens of itself when facilitating the exchange of commodities for one another. Lastly, Ricardo too, like Smith, sees money as a veil in the sense that changes in the quantity of it have no bearing on the aggregate levels of output and employment.

From the perspective of Marx's analysis the problems with Ricardo's explanation of money stem from his mistaken **conception** of it. First, although Ricardo begins by conceiving of money in capitalism as whatever serves as an invariable standard of the exchange values of commodities, he subsequently conceives of it, like Smith, as whatever serves to facilitate the exchange of commodities for one another. That is to say, like Smith, Ricardo's conception of money presumes the process of exchange that characterises capitalism is the exchange of commodities for one another and not the exchange of commodities for money as the representative of general exchangeable worth. Second, his conception of money as whatever serves to facilitate the exchange of commodities requires Ricardo, like Smith, to conceive of money as an intrinsically valueless token of the commodities whose exchange for one another it facilitates, and in the final instance a token of their values. This in turn causes him to see money as a token of labour time and not the embodiment of (socially necessary) labour time. Third, and following from the preceding, his conception of money requires him to deny that money is a commodity, notwithstanding his view that gold is the invariable standard of the exchange values of commodities for he was searching. Indeed, to the extent he sees gold as money it is as a valueless token of the commodities whose exchange it is used to facilitate. Lastly, also like Smith, Ricardo conceives of money representing particular exchange value, i.e., the quantity of another commodity it exchanges for, and not general exchange value, i.e., the quantity of any and all other commodities it commands.

Although, like Marx, Ricardo sees money **emerging** prior to the emergence of capitalism as a numéraire commodity, gold, that reduces the exchange values of commodities to equivalence and facilitates their circulation as a means of circulation,[29] unlike Marx, Ricardo sees gold becoming money as distinct from a particular commodity when it comes to be used as a valueless token of the commodities whose exchange for one another it facilitates. The problem in this regard is, as I have noted above, this requires Ricardo to conceive of the numéraire commodity becoming a valueless token of the commodities whose exchange it is used to facilitate while continuing to be a produced commodity.

Although from the perspective of Marx's analysis Ricardo also correctly sees money assuming in the first instance the **form** of whatever is used as the numéraire commodity to facilitate the exchange of commodities for one another, he does not see this form in capitalism becoming what is used by producers to denote the exchange values of their commodities as general exchange values. Ricardo does not see that money assumes the form of gold in capitalism because it is used by producers to denote the exchange values of their commodities as general exchange values and not because it is used as a numéraire commodity by capitalist traders to facilitate the exchange of commodities for one another.

Lastly, Ricardo's conception of money as the numéraire commodity that is used to facilitate the exchange of commodities for one another requires him to deny money is a **veil**, having no bearing on the reproduction of commodities in the sense that changes in the money prices of commodities have no bearing on their reproduction. However, once it is accepted, as Ricardo appears to do, that the form of money mutates from a commodity into inconvertible fiat currency, the logic of his analysis requires him to conceive of money becoming an intrinsically valueless token of commodities and, therefore, a veil. It requires him, like Smith, to deny changes in its exchange value have any bearing on the reproduction of all commodities whose exchange for one another it facilitates. Indeed, for Ricardo, as for Smith, what matters in this regard is the commodity exchange values or relative prices of commodities. It is the changes in these magnitudes that Ricardo sees as having a bearing on the reproduction of commodities. This is not to say that Ricardo sees money as a veil when he no longer conceives of it as a commodity, but rather that he sees it as a veil because he does not see it coming to represent general exchange value in capitalism and the exchange value of the commodity as its money exchange value.

[29] See Marx (1970, p. 171).

4.5.2 Functions of Money

Like Smith, and most other Classical economists, Ricardo sees the primary and defining function of money as that of medium of exchange even though, also like Smith, he formally refers to this function as its medium of circulation function.[30] Money, as a medium of exchange, facilitates the exchange of commodities for one another in accordance with their exchange values. Ricardo sees the medium of exchange in the first instance as the commodity chosen as the numeraire commodity, and in particular gold, and subsequently, with the development of the process of exchange, convertible and inconvertible fiat currency. For Ricardo, whatever is chosen as a numéraire commodity should be subject to the least variation in its exchange value among all commodities.[31] Lastly, although like Smith and other Classical economists, Ricardo pays scant attention to money's other functions, there is no reason to suppose he is unaware of these functions. Indeed, the logic of his analysis suggests he can conceive of the numéraire commodity being used to settle debts as well as held as a store of value, but not as money. I will return to this point below.

Given that Ricardo adopts Smith's explanation of the functions performed by money, including the primacy Smith attaches to its medium of exchange function, the problems with Ricardo's explanation of these functions from the perspective of Marx's analysis are much the same as those outlined above with respect to Smith's explanation of these functions.

The basic problem with Ricardo's explanation of the functions of money is, as with that of Smith, and, indeed, all other approaches, his neglect of its **measure** of the exchange values of commodities function. Although Ricardo gives the impression his search for an 'invariable measure' of the exchange values of commodities is a search for money as the measure of the exchange values of commodities,[32] this search is in effect a search for an invariable commodity standard of commodities as measures of the exchange values of one another. It needs recalling that for Ricardo the exchange value of the commodity is the quantity of another commodity it commands in the process of exchange. This means that the measure of its exchange value is the commodity it commands in the

[30] See Ricardo (1973, pp. 83–84).

[31] See Ricardo (1973, pp. 28–29).

[32] See Ricardo (1973, pp. 28–29).

process of exchange, and his search for an invariable measure of exchange value can only be a search for an invariable standard of commodities as measures of the exchange values of one another; a search for an invariable numéraire commodity. Ricardo's search for an invariable standard (numéraire) commodity cannot be construed as a search for money since this would require interpreting him explaining the exchange value of the commodity as its money exchange value and not its commodity exchange value.

For Marx, Ricardo's neglect of money's measure of exchange value function causes him, like Smith, to have a mistaken understanding of money's **means of circulation** function. Since Ricardo does not see producers using money to denote the exchange values of their commodities as general exchange values prior to putting them into the process of circulation, he cannot logically conceive of money being used to facilitate their circulation with determinate money prices.[33] Since Ricardo, like most other Classical economists, sees commodities put into exchange for one another without determinate money prices, he must see what facilitates their exchange for one another as a **medium of exchange**, and this function of money as its primary and defining function. Moreover, although Ricardo sees money assuming the form of a commodity in the performance of its function as medium of exchange, the logic of his analysis requires him, like Smith, to see its form as ideally inconvertible fiat currency. It is this form that is ideally suited to functioning as an intrinsically valueless token of the commodities whose exchange for one another it facilitates.

Lastly, insofar as Ricardo sees money as an intrinsically valueless token of the commodities whose exchange for one another it facilitates, he must deny it is held as a **store of value**. Whatever performs this function should possess value outside of the process of exchange and represent a certain magnitude of general exchange value. Money as an intrinsically valueless token of the commodities whose exchange for one another it facilitates only possesses value and represents a certain magnitude of exchange value in the context of the performance of this function. Which means that for Ricardo, as for Smith, when money assumes the form of an intrinsically valueless token of the commodities whose exchange for one another it

[33] See Marx (1969b, p. 200).

facilitates, something else is required to perform the function of store of value. For Ricardo this can be gold, but not as money.

4.6 Value of Money

Like Smith, Ricardo does not clearly distinguish between the value and exchange value of money, frequently conflating the two.[34] However, the logic of his analysis, as well as textual evidence, suggests that his work contains such a distinction, and allows for an interpretation of his explanation of the value of money as distinct from its exchange value.

To begin with, Ricardo's analysis suggests, like Smith, he distinguishes between different money forms when explaining the value (and exchange value) of money. It suggests he distinguishes between produced and non-produced money forms; between, on the one hand, commodity money, and, on the other hand, both convertible and inconvertible fiat currency. Ricardo conceives of the value of money when it is a commodity, gold, as the labour time used in its production, in the same way as the value of any commodity and the value of convertible fiat currency as the value of the quantity of gold this currency notionally represents. He implicitly conceives of the value of inconvertible fiat currency as the values of all the commodities comprising the net product whose exchange for one another it facilitates. When elaborating his doctrine of comparative advantage Ricardo conceives of gold possessing value as both a commodity and an intrinsically valueless token of the commodities whose exchange for one another it facilitates, suggesting that its value as a commodity deviates from its value as money with the former acting as an anchor of the latter.

These conceptions have implications for how Ricardo implicitly sees the measure of the value of money. They suggest that whatever form money assumes he sees the measure of its value, like the measure of an ordinary commodity, as a certain quantity of labour time. When money is a commodity, it is the labour time used in its production and when money is inconvertible fiat currency it is the labour time used in the production of all commodities whose exchange for one another it facilitates.

Ricardo's conception of the value of money also has implications for how he sees money acquiring value historically, and how this value is

[34] See Ricardo (1973, p. 88).

formed. It implies he sees money as a commodity acquiring value in the first instance when, like any other commodity, it is produced by the expenditure of labour time, and this value is formed, like the value of any commodity, in the process of its production. It also implies he sees money acquiring value as convertible or inconvertible fiat currency when it is used to facilitate the exchange of commodities for one another, and its value is formed in this process, *after* the formation of its exchange value.

Lastly, Ricardo's explanation of the magnitude of value of money follows from the preceding. When money is a commodity he explains the magnitude of its value by the relative quantity of labour time required for its production. He argues,

> Any improvement in the facility of working the mines, by which the precious metals may be produced with less quantity of labour, will sink the value of money generally. (Ricardo, 1973, p. 90)

Ricardo explains the value of money as convertible fiat currency by its face value, and ultimately by the value of the commodity it replaces in the process of circulation. He explains the magnitude of value of money as inconvertible fiat currency by the values of the commodities whose exchange for one another it facilitates. Ricardo (1973, p. 91) argues,

> Whenever the current of money is forcibly stopped, and when money is prevented from settling at its just level, there are no limits to the possible variations of the exchange. The effects are similar to those which follow when a paper money, not exchangeable for specie at the will of the holder, is forced into circulation.[35]

The problems with Ricardo's explanation of the value of money begin with its **conception**. First, like Smith, Ricardo's implicit conception of money as an intrinsically valueless token of gold or the commodities whose exchange it facilitates logically prevents him from being interpreted as conceiving of the value of gold as the value of a particular commodity *as well as* money, where the former exerts a gravitation pull on the latter. Gold cannot logically be an intrinsically valueless token of itself or the commodities whose exchange it facilitates. Ricardo's neglect of money's

[35] See also Ricardo (1973, p. 151).

function as measure of the exchange values of commodities prevents him from seeing gold possessing value as both a commodity and as money since as measure gold is only required to have an existence in the minds of producers. Second, Ricardo sees the value of money as the quantity of labour time expended in the production of all commodities it commands, and not, as for Marx, a certain quantity of socially necessary labour time required for the production of all commodities that money comes to embody when it is used as a measure of the exchange values of their commodities by all producers. Lastly, Ricardo's conception of the value of money as the value it acquires in the performance of its function as medium of exchange requires him to conceive of this value as the value of the aggregate quantity of money used to facilitate the exchange of all commodities for one another, and the value of this money as the aggregate labour time expended in the production of these commodities. Ricardo's neglect of money's function as measure prevents him from seeing the value of money as the quantity of socially necessary labour time a *unit* of it comes to embody when money is used by all producers to denote the exchange values of their commodities.

The problem with Ricardo's implicit conception of the **measure** of the value of money follows from the problems with his conception of the value of money. One problem with his conception of the measure of the value of money in this regard is that Ricardo's conception of the value of money requires him to see this measure as a certain quantity of the labour time actually expended in the production of the commodities whose exchange for one another it is used to facilitate and not a certain quantity of the socially necessary labour time required to produce all commodities that money comes to embody when it is used as a measure of the exchange values of commodities. That is, he does not see the measure of the value of money, like the measure of the values of commodities, are the transformed *form* of the labour time actually expended in the production of all commodities. Again, the source of the problem in this regard is Ricardo's neglect of money's measure of exchange value function. This prevents him from seeing money coming to embody a certain quantity of socially necessary labour time when it is used to denote the general exchange values of all commodities, with this labour time becoming the measure of the value of money at the same time and in the same context it becomes the measure of the values of all commodities. A second problem with Ricardo's conception of the measure of the value of money is that he sees it as the measure of the aggregate quantity of money used to facilitate the exchange of all commodities and not a unit of money. This follows naturally enough from his conception of the value of money as the value of the aggregate quantity of money used to facilitate the exchange of all commodities for one another and not a unit of the value of what is used to measure the exchange values of commodities.

Although in accordance with his view of the emergence of money Ricardo sees gold **acquiring** value historically as a numéraire commodity when it is used to facilitate the exchange of commodities for one another by reducing their exchange values in terms of one another to a common denominator, his conception of money as an intrinsically valueless token of the commodities whose exchange for one another it facilitates requires him to see gold acquiring value as money historically when it comes to be used as a medium of exchange. That is, his conception of money requires Ricardo to see gold acquiring value as money historically when it comes to be used as an intrinsically valueless token of the commodities whose exchange for one another it facilitates. The source of the problem with Ricardo's analysis in this regard is his conception of money as whatever is used to facilitate the exchange of commodities for one another. This precludes him from seeing something becoming money whether or not it has intrinsic worth. It precludes him from seeing money acquiring value historically as a numéraire commodity and this commodity subsequently possessing value as both a commodity and money when it comes to be used by producers to denote the general exchangeable worth of their commodities with a view to facilitating their reproduction.

Ricardo's neglect of money's function as measure of the exchange values of commodities also prevents him from seeing the value of money **formed** *prior* to it being put into the process of circulation to circulate commodities possessing determinate money prices, when money is used to denote the exchange value of the commodity as its general exchange value. It requires him instead to see the value of money formed in the process of exchange, when it is used to facilitate the exchange of commodities for one another in accordance with their gold or commodity exchange values. To the extent Ricardo sees gold as money, he is ignoring the fact that it too is a produced commodity with intrinsic worth, like the commodities whose exchange for one another it is supposed to be facilitating.

The problems with Ricardo's explanation of the **magnitude** of the value of money follow from the preceding. To begin with, Ricardo tends to explain the magnitude of value of money when it is a commodity, gold, as the magnitude of the value of a commodity and not also as money. Second, when he distinguishes between the value of gold as a commodity and as money he explains the magnitude of the latter as the magnitude of something that is intrinsically valueless even though it is a produced commodity like the commodities whose exchange for one another it is used to facilitate. Hence, his need to explain the value of money as an intrinsically valueless token of gold or of the commodities whose exchange it facilitates. Third, insofar as Ricardo explains the magnitude of the value of money as the magnitude of intrinsically valueless tokens of the commodities whose exchange it facilitates, he must be explaining it as the magnitude of value of the aggregate quantity of money used to facilitate the exchange of a certain aggregate quantity of commodities, and not the value of a unit of money. Fourth, and related to the preceding, the logic of his analysis requires Ricardo to explain the magnitude of the value of money by the magnitude of its exchange value and not, as for Marx, *vice versa*. This is because, as noted above, Ricardo sees the magnitude of the value of money as the values of all commodities commanded by all money used to facilitate their exchange for one another. Which means, a change in the quantity of money in relation to the quantity of commodities whose exchange for one another the money is used to facilitate, i.e., a change in the exchange value of money, must logically result in a change in the quantity of the values of commodities money commands in the process of facilitating the exchange of commodities for one another. That is, a change in the exchange value of money must logically result in a change in the magnitude of the value of money. Lastly, Ricardo's conception of the value of the commodity as its *relative*, and not *absolute*, value precludes him from seeing changes in the economy-wide productivity of labour having a bearing on the magnitude of value of money. It precludes him from seeing, for example, on increase in the economy-wide productivity of labour exerting upward pressure on the magnitude of value of money (and corresponding downward pressure on the aggregate money price level).

4.7 Exchange Value of Money

Ricardo, like most other Classical economists, pays far more attention to the explanation of the exchange value of money than to its value, on occasion conflating the two. As with his explanation of the value of money, he distinguishes between the different forms which money assumes when explaining its exchange value. He conceives of the exchange value of money when it is a commodity such as gold or silver in the manner of any commodity, as the quantity of another commodity it commands in the process of exchange. He conceives of the exchange value of convertible tokens of gold and silver as the quantities of the latter these paper tokens notionally represent in the process of facilitating the exchange of commodities for one another. He conceives of the exchange value of money when it is inconvertible fiat currency as the quantity of commodities whose exchange for one another it facilitates.[36]

Although Ricardo does not consider the implication of these conceptions of the exchange values of the different forms of money for an understanding of their corresponding measures, these can be deduced from the logic of his analysis. This logic implies he sees the measure of the exchange value of money when it is a commodity as any commodity it commands in the process of exchange and the measure of the exchange value of inconvertible fiat currency as the commodities whose exchange for one another that it facilitates.

Since Ricardo is similarly unclear about how money acquires exchange value historically and how this exchange value is formed, these too have to be deduced from the logic of his analysis. The latter implies he sees money acquiring exchange value historically as a particular commodity, i.e., gold, when it begins to be widely accepted as the standard of all commodities as measures of the exchange values of one another, and he sees inconvertible fiat currency acquiring exchange value as money when it is used as a medium of exchange to facilitate the exchange of commodities for one another. The logic of Ricardo's analysis also suggests he sees the exchange value of money as a commodity formed in the process of its exchange with other commodities, and its exchange value as inconvertible fiat currency formed in the process of its use to facilitate the exchange of commodities for one another.

Lastly, Ricardo pays most attention to the determination of the magnitude of the exchange value of money, especially as gold, in the context of explaining his *doctrine of comparative advantage*. When elaborating the latter, Ricardo begins by explaining the magnitude of the exchange value of gold by the magnitude of its value in the manner of any commodity,[37]

[36] See Ricardo (1973, p. 91).

[37] See Ricardo (1973, pp. 46–47).

and then shifts to its explanation by the quantity of it relative to the quantity of commodities whose exchange for one another it facilitates.[38] He sees the magnitude of the exchange values of convertible tokens of commodity money determined by their face value, and by the quantity of these tokens in relation to the quantity of commodities whose exchange they facilitate when they are inconvertible fiat currency.[39]

The problems with Ricardo's explanation of the exchange value of money from the perspective of Marx's analysis follow from the problems noted above with his conception of money and explanation of its value, and are in many ways similar to the problems noted above with Smith's explanation of the exchange value of money.

To begin with, Ricardo tends to **conceive** of the exchange value of money when it has the form of a commodity as its exchange value as a commodity and not also as money. Thus, when he conceives of the exchange value of gold as money he tends to conceive of its exchange value as a particular commodity and not also as money, with the exception being his conception of the exchange value of gold in the context of its flow between countries when elaborating his doctrine of comparative advantage. The reason for this neglect is that to conceive of the exchange value of gold as money requires him to conceive of its exchange value as the exchange value of an intrinsically valueless token of the commodities whose exchange for one another it facilitates. Second, when Ricardo conceives of the exchange value of money as an intrinsically valueless token of the commodities whose exchange for one another it facilitates, it requires him to conceive of this exchange value as that of the aggregate quantity of money used for this purpose and not a unit of money, and given by the aggregate quantity of commodities whose exchange for one another this aggregate quantity of money facilitates, not the quantity of any commodity with a determinate price whose circulation it facilitates. This is because Ricardo sees money acquiring exchangeable worth as money when it is used to perform the function of medium of exchange and not when it is used as a measure of the exchange value of the commodity.

The problems with Ricardo's conception of the **measure** of the exchange value of money follow from his conception of its exchange value. Firstly,

[38] See Ricardo (1973, pp. 86–87).

[39] See Ricardo (1973, p. 91).

when he conceives of the measure of the exchange value of money as gold, Ricardo tends to see this as the measure of its exchange value as a commodity and, as such, any and all commodities it exchanges with. Second, when Ricardo conceives of the exchange value of money as the exchange value of what facilitates the exchange of all commodities for one another, like Smith, he necessarily conceives of what is being measured as the aggregate quantity of money used to facilitate the exchange of commodities for one another and this measure as the aggregate quantity of commodities whose exchange for one another money facilitates. The problem for Ricardo in this regard, as for Smith, is the aggregation of heterogeneous commodities. It should be apparent from what was argued above in the context of the problems with Ricardo's conception of the exchange value of money that the source of the problem with his conception of its measure is his neglect of money's measure of exchange value of commodities function. This prevents Ricardo from conceiving of the measure of the exchange value of money as the measure of the exchange value of a unit of money, and its measure as any and every commodity with a determinate money price.

Although Ricardo sees gold **acquiring** exchange value historically as a numéraire commodity that is used to reduce the exchange values of commodities to a common denominator, his conception of money as a valueless token of the commodities whose exchange for one another it facilitates requires him to see gold acquiring exchange value as money historically when it comes to be used as an intrinsically valueless token of the commodities whose exchange for one another it facilitates. Again, the source of the problem with Ricardo's analysis in this regard is his conception of money as an intrinsically valueless token of the commodities whose exchange for one another it facilitates. This prevents Ricardo from conceiving of money acquiring exchange value historically as a particular commodity, the numeraire commodity, and then acquiring exchange value as money in addition to its exchange value as a commodity with the emergence of capitalism and the use in the first instance of the numéraire commodity as a measure of the exchange values of commodities.

Ricardo's neglect of money's measure of exchange value function also precludes him from seeing the exchange value of money **formed** *prior* to it and commodities being put into circulation. Ricardo certainly sees the exchange value of gold formed in the context of the formation of the exchange values of all commodities, but this is in the context of the formation of their numéraire commodity exchange values not their money exchange values. Even then, he sees the gold exchange values of commodities formed in the context of the exchange of gold for all other commodities and not *prior* to it.

The problems with Ricardo's explanation of the **magnitude** of the exchange value of money begin with his explanation of the magnitude of the exchange value of money as a particular commodity, gold. The problem in this respect is his confusion of the explanation of the magnitude of the exchange value of gold as a commodity and as money. Ricardo sees the magnitude of the exchange value of gold determined by the magnitude of its value as a commodity in the first instance, and then abandons this explanation when elaborating his doctrine of *comparative advantage*, arguing that changes in the magnitude of the exchange value of gold result from trade-related inflows and outflows of gold.[40] For Marx, the source of Ricardo's confused explanation of the magnitude of the exchange value of gold when expounding his doctrine of comparative advantage is his conflation of the explanations of the magnitude of the exchange value of gold as a commodity and as money. That is, Ricardo ends up explaining the magnitude of the exchange value of gold in his doctrine of comparative advantage as the magnitude of the exchange value of gold as a valueless token of the commodities whose international exchange for one another it facilitates even though gold is a commodity with intrinsic value.

Second, Ricardo's explanation of the magnitude of the exchange value of money requires him to explain this magnitude as the magnitude of the exchange value of the aggregate quantity of money used to facilitate the exchange of commodities comprising the net product for one another, in an analogous way to his explanation of the magnitude of value of money. As such it precludes him from explaining the magnitude of the exchange value of money as the quantity of any commodity with a determinate money price that a unit of money commands.

Third, Ricardo's explanation of the magnitude of value of money precludes him from explaining this magnitude by the magnitude of its value. It will be recalled that the logic of Ricardo's explanation of the magnitude of value of money requires him to explain it by the magnitude of its exchange value. This means, that even if Ricardo can be interpreted as seeing changes in the economy-wide productivity of labour and raw

[40] See Ricardo (1973, p. 174).

material prices having a bearing on the magnitude of value of money, he cannot be interpreted as seeing them having a bearing on the magnitude of its exchange value.

A fourth problem with Ricardo's explanation of the magnitude of the exchange value of money is that it requires him, also like Smith, to deny the impact on this magnitude of excess aggregate demand, unless the latter corresponds to an excess quantity of money used to facilitate the exchange of commodities for one another.

A last, and related, problem with Ricardo's explanation of the magnitude of the exchange value of money is that, like all those adopting the CQTM, it requires him to conceive of the quantity of money used to facilitate the exchange of commodities for one another as exogenously determined, i.e., independent of the quantity and money prices of the commodities whose exchange for one another it is used to facilitate. This follows logically from his implicit concept of money, like those adopting the CQTM, as whatever is used to facilitate the exchange of commodities for one another where the commodities being exchanged are put into the process of exchange for one another without determinate money prices.

4.8 Money Price of the Commodity

Ricardo mostly conceives of the money price of a commodity as the quantity of gold or even tokens of gold a commodity commands, although his acceptance that money can assume the form of inconvertible fiat currency suggests that he does not exclude the possibility of conceiving of the money price of the commodity as the quantity of inconvertible fiat currency that it commands. Insofar as Ricardo conceives of the measure of the money price of the commodity, it is as a certain quantity of gold, with no indication of his conception of the measure of the money price of the commodity when money assumes the form of inconvertible fiat currency.

The logic of Ricardo's analysis suggests he sees commodities acquiring gold prices historically when gold is used as the numéraire commodity, with the implication being they acquire gold prices *after* they acquire exchange values in terms of one another. It also suggests he sees commodities acquiring fiat currency prices when this form of money is used to facilitate the exchange of commodities for one another. The logic of his analysis also suggest Ricardo sees money prices formed in the process of exchange, either in the exchange of commodities for gold or their exchange for one another mediated by inconvertible fiat currency.

When explaining the magnitude of the money price of the commodity, Ricardo focuses his attention on the determination of the magnitude of its gold price. He explains this magnitude by the value of the commodity relative to that of gold, i.e., by the relative quantity of actual labour time used in their production. As noted above, he explains the general money price level, or exchange value of money, by the quantity of money used to facilitate the exchange of commodities for one another relative to the quantity of these commodities, whatever form money assumes.

From the perspective of Marx's analysis, the problems with Ricardo's explanation of the money price of the commodity begin with its **conception**. First, the logic of Ricardo's analysis prevents him, like Smith, from conceiving of the money price of the commodity as its money exchange value. Instead, it requires him to conceive of it as its gold or commodity exchange value where money is a token of gold or the commodities whose exchange for one another it is used to facilitate. Second, and related to this, Ricardo is not able to conceive of the money price of a commodity as its commodity money price, notwithstanding his conception of the money prices of commodities as their gold prices. This follows from Ricardo's conception of money as an intrinsically valueless token of the commodities whose exchange for one another it facilitates. It is a conception of money that logically precludes him from conceiving of gold as money. Which means that when Ricardo conceives of the money price of the commodity as its gold price, he is not conceiving of it as the money price of the commodity but rather its numéraire commodity exchange value where gold is the numéraire commodity that reduces the exchange values of commodities to equivalence. Third, Ricardo is not able to conceive of the money price of the commodity as the form assumed by its value. This is because, as noted above, Ricardo conceives of the value of the commodity in a way that precludes him seeing any link between it and money. Lastly, Ricardo's conception of the money price of the commodity precludes him, like Smith, from conceiving of the relative price of the commodity as its money price relative to the money price of another commodity and, correspondingly, the aggregate money price level as the aggregate of the money prices of all commodities. Instead, as for Smith, it requires him to conceive of the relative money price of the commodity as its gold exchange value, where money is a token of gold, and the aggregate money price level as conceived of above; the aggregate quantity of money used to facilitate the exchange of all commodities for one another relative to the quantity of these commodities as a cluster.

It follows from his conception of the money price of the commodity that Ricardo is unable to conceive of its **measure** as a certain quantity of money. In fact, his conception of the money price of the commodity, as its commodity exchange value where money is a token of the commodities being exchanged for one another, requires him to conceive of its measure, like the measure of the exchange value of the commodity, as any commodity that is exchanged for another. The difference in the case of the measure of the money price of the commodity is that money is seen as a token of the commodities as measures of the exchange values of one another. Insofar as Ricardo sees gold as the measure of the money price of a commodity, it is as a particular commodity, albeit the standard of all commodities as measures of the exchange values of one another. A further problem with Ricardo's conception of the measure of the money price of the commodity is that he is not able to see it as the form assumed by the measure of the value of the commodity. The problem in this regard, as I have argued above, is that Ricardo does not see the labour time that is the measure of the value of the commodity as a transformed form of the labour time expended in the production of commodities, i.e., the socially necessary labour time, with this transformation taking place in the context of the use of money to set the money price of the commodity and resulting in the money price assuming the form of the value of the commodity.

Although Ricardo sees commodities **acquiring** gold prices historically when gold comes to be used as a numéraire commodity to facilitate the exchange of commodities for one another by reducing their exchange values to a common denominator, his conception of money precludes him seeing these prices as money prices. Instead, his conception of money requires him, like Smith, to see commodities acquiring gold prices as money prices historically when gold comes to be used as an intrinsically valueless token of the commodities whose exchange for one another it is used to facilitate. What Ricardo is not able to see is that commodities acquire money prices as gold prices when gold is used as a numéraire commodity to reduce the exchange values of commodities to equivalence prior to the emergence of capitalism, and money prices continue to have the form of gold prices when gold is used by producers as a measure of the general exchange values of their commodities in the early phases of capitalism.

Ricardo's conception of money and corresponding neglect of its function as the measure of the exchange values of commodities also prevents him, like Smith, from seeing the money price of the commodity **formed** *prior* to the commodity being put into the process of circulation. It prevents him from seeing the formation of the money price of the commodity taking place when money is used by all producers to denote the general exchange values of their commodities *prior* to putting them into the process of circulation. In fact, Ricardo's neglect of money's function as measure requires him, like Smith, to see the money price of the commodity formed in the process of the exchange of commodities for one another facilitated by money, i.e., in the context of the formation of the exchange values of commodities in terms of one another.

Lastly, the problems with Ricardo's explanation of the **magnitude** of the money price of the commodity follow from his conception of the money price of the commodity. This conception prevents Ricardo, like Smith, from explaining the magnitude of the money price of the commodity as magnitude of its money exchange value. As for Smith, this is because to explain the money price of the commodity as its money exchange value would require Ricardo to conceive of money possessing value in itself and not as a token of commodities with values whose exchange for one another it is used to facilitate. Instead, the logic of Ricardo's analysis requires him to explain the magnitude of the money price of the commodity as the magnitude of its commodity exchange value, where money is a token of the commodities being exchanged for one another and in the final instance a token of the labour time expended in the production of all commodities. Second, also like Smith, Ricardo is unable to explain the magnitude of the money price of the commodity as its commodity money price. This is because, as argued above, Ricardo, like Smith, must logically deny money can assume a commodity form. Which means Ricardo's explanation of the magnitude of the gold price of a commodity is not an explanation of the magnitude of its money price but rather an explanation of the magnitude of its gold exchange value where gold is the standard of all commodities as measures of the exchange values of one another—the numéraire commodity. Third, Ricardo's conception of the money price of the commodity also prevents him from seeing changes in the magnitude of the relative money price of the commodity taking place in the context of changes in the aggregate money price level as well as independently of the latter. It causes him, instead, to see changes in the former taking place independently of changes in the latter. This is because his conception of the money price of the commodity prevents him from explaining the magnitude of the relative money price of the commodity as the magnitude of its money price relative to the magnitude of the money price of another commodity, and the aggregate money price level as the weighted average of the money prices of all commodities. Instead, it causes him to explain the magnitude of the relative money price of a commodity as the quantity of another commodity it commands in the process of exchange with money a token of labour time, and the aggregate money price level as the quantity of money used to facilitate the exchange of commodities for one another relative to the quantity of these commodities. As I argued above, Ricardo explains the relative money price of the commodity by the quantity of labour time directly expended in its production relative to that directly expended in the production of other commodities. He explains the aggregate money price level as the exogenously given quantity of money relative to the cluster of commodities comprising the net product whose exchange for one another it facilitates, without any reason to suppose the factors determining changes in the relative money prices of commodities have a bearing on the aggregate money price level. Of note in this regard is his implicit denial that changes in the economy-wide productivity of labour have a bearing on the aggregate money price level notwithstanding his argument that changes in the relative productivity of labour have a bearing on the relative money price of the commodity.

From the perspective of Marx's analysis the source of the problems with Ricardo's explanation of the money price of the commodity is, as with Smith, his conception of the value of the commodity and its link to money. Although, unlike Smith, Ricardo conceives of the source of the value of the commodity as the expenditure of labour time in the production of the commodity, he does not see this labour time linked to money. Specifically, he does not see this labour time as the transformed form of the labour time actually expended in the production of the commodity, where the transformation results from the use by producers of money to denote the exchange values of their commodities as general exchange values, i.e., as money prices, prior to putting the commodities into the process of circulation. It is this conception of the value of the commodity that causes Ricardo to have a mistaken conception of money, as an intrinsically valueless token of labour time, and a corresponding mistaken conception and explanation of the money price of the commodity, as its commodity exchange value with money a token of labour time. The most obvious manifestation of Ricardo's mistaken conception and explanation of the money price of the commodity is that it requires him to explain changes in the relative money prices of commodities taking place independently of changes in the aggregate money price level, with changes in the economy-wide productivity of labour seen as having no bearing on the latter in spite of changes in the relative productivity of labour seen as having a bearing on the former.

References

Marx, K. (1969a). *Theories of surplus value: Part II* (R. Simpson, Trans.). Lawrence & Wishart.

Marx, K. (1969b). *Theories of surplus value: Part II* (E. Burns, Trans.). Lawrence & Wishart.

Marx, K. (1970). *A contribution to the critique of political economy* (S. W. Ryazanskaya, Trans.). Progress.

Marx, K. (1972). *Theories of surplus value: Part III* (translated from German by J. Cohen & S. W. Ryazanskaya). Lawrence & Wishart.

Marx, K. (1976). *Capital, volume I* (B. Fowkes, Trans.). Penguin Books.

Marx, K. (1978). *Capital, volume II* (D. Fernbach, Trans.). Penguin Books.

Ricardo, D. (1973). *The principles of political economy and taxation.* J. M. Dent & Sons (Originally published in 1817).

Schumpeter, J. A. (2006). *History of economic analysis.* George Allen & Unwin (Originally published in 1954).

Sraffa, P. (ed.). (1951). *The works and correspondence of David Ricardo, Volume I: On the principles of political economy and taxation.* Cambridge University Press.

CHAPTER 5

Sraffa's Explanation of Money Price

5.1 Introduction

Even though Sraffa does not leave behind an explanation of the money price of the commodity, his explanation of price in his *Production of Commodities by Means of Commodities* (*PCMC*) can be extended to provide such an explanation, especially since, as I will argue below, he does not see any reason to suppose money cannot be brought into this analysis.[1] Given this, it is curious Sraffians have been reluctant to extend his explanation of price to include the money price of the commodity. In what follows I will extend what I see as the logic of Sraffa's analysis, particularly that in his *PCMC*, to provide such an explanation. My purpose in doing so is to show that this logic requires him to have a conception of money and explanation of money price which is similar to that found in the works of Smith and Ricardo. This should not really be a surprise since Sraffa sees himself building on the foundations left by these two Classical economists, especially Ricardo.[2]

[1] See for example Sraffa (1960, p. 48).

[2] See Sraffa (1960, p. v).

H. Nicholas, *Explorations in Marx's Theory of Price—Why Marx Is Still Relevant for Understanding the Modern Economy*,
https://doi.org/10.1057/978-1-137-56564-8_5

5.2 Object and Approach

Sraffa's *PCMC* is the culmination of his lifelong concern with the theory of price, which he sees as necessarily underpinning any meaningful explanation of economic phenomena.[3] The theory of price he presents in *PCMC* is an input cost theory of price in the manner of Ricardo (and Marx), but where the inputs are commodities, not labour time.[4] As the sub-title of PCMC suggests, Sraffa sees his alternative theory of price providing the foundations for a critique of orthodox Neoclassical theory.

When explaining prices in *PCMC*, Sraffa begins by abstracting in the first instance from capital, money, and supply–demand imbalances, and later only brings capital back into his analysis.[5] This is because for Sraffa bringing money and supply–demand imbalances into his analysis is unnecessary given its limited purpose; the explanation of the exchange value of the commodity and criticism of the Neoclassical marginal productivity explanation of the return to capital.

From the perspective of Marx's analysis, the **focus** of Sraffa's analysis, i.e., the explanation of the magnitude of the exchange value of the commodity, is too narrow. It is even more narrow than that of Ricardo, who Marx criticises for the same reason (see Chapter 4). This narrow focus causes Sraffa to have a fundamentally distorted conception of the nature of economic systems of production in general, and capitalism in particular. It causes him to conceive of all systems of production, including capitalism, as characterised by the production of exchangeable commodity outputs with exchangeable commodity inputs. That is, it causes, or rather allows, Sraffa to ignore the labour input in the explanation of production in general, and, therefore, also in capitalism. This

[3] See Kurz (2012, p. 1553).

[4] A number of Sraffians contend that an important concern of Sraffa is also to explain the surplus product (net product) and its distribution (see Blankenburg et al., 2012, p. 1272). I will discuss Sraffa's explanation of the net product in Nicholas (forthcoming) but note here that it is essentially a by-product of his attempt to develop a commodity theory of price.

[5] There has been some debate within Sraffian circles as to whether or not Sraffa conceives of the prices to be explained as equilibrium prices assuming balance of supply and demand, with a few (most notably Sinha, 2012) denying he made such an assumption. I will return to this issue in the discussion of Sraffa's *PCMC* in Nicholas (forthcoming) but note here that I take his point of departure when explaining prices to be the assumption of balance in keeping with the majority of sympathetic interpreters of his work (see Blankenburg et al., 2012; Kurz, 2012; Roncaglia, 1978).

in turn causes him to ignore the social dimension of economic systems, including capitalism.

The problem with Sraffa's method of abstraction from the perspective of Marx's approach is, like most other approaches, that its purpose is not to permit him to capture the essence of what is being abstracted from, but rather to make its study more manageable. Consequently, it leads to a distorted understanding of what is abstracted from when this is brought back into the analysis. When Sraffa abstracts from the surplus product in the first instance, he conceives of the economic system as a subsistence economy where commodities are produced by means of commodities, such that when he brings the surplus product into the analysis it is conceived of as arising from the productivity of commodity means of production, and even the productivity of an artificially constructed commodity input—the *Standard commodity*. Similarly, when Sraffa abstracts from capital in the first instance, he conceives of the produced inputs into production as exchangeable commodity inputs such that when he brings capital into the analysis he conceives of it in the manner of Neoclassicals, as a collection of long-lasting commodity inputs that are lent and borrowed.

Although Sraffa also abstracts from money and supply–demand imbalances in the first instance, as noted above, he does not subsequently bring them into the analysis. However, the manner of his abstraction from them provides certain clues as to how they need to be conceived of when they are brought back into the analysis. The manner in which Sraffa abstracts from money suggests that when it is brought back into the analysis it is to be conceived of as a token of the values of the commodities whose exchange it facilitates. A corollary of this is that the economic system needs to be conceptualised in the manner of the Classical (and Neoclassical) economists as one characterised by a real-monetary dichotomy. In notes he makes when preparing a critical review of Hayek (1931), Sraffa alludes to the existence of such a dichotomy as well as his own concern with real as opposed to monetary phenomena. Lastly, when Sraffa abstracts from supply–demand imbalances he does so in a way that requires him to see trend or equilibrium prices pertaining to supply–demand balance as centres of gravity around which market prices fluctuate in the context of supply–demand imbalances.[6] He does not see

[6] See Roncaglia (1978), Blankenburg et al. (2012), Kurz (2012).

the trend prices as average of the market prices, and the forces causing the market prices to deviate from their trend prices having a bearing on the trend prices.

5.3 Sraffa's Economics as Ideology

From the perspective of Marx's analysis, Sraffa, like the PKs and Neoclassicals, adopts an ideological stance in the sense that it too is founded on a denial of the source of profits as the expenditure of surplus labour time. Indeed, the unavoidable conclusion of *PCMC* is that the source of profits is, as for the Neoclassicals, the productivity of the commodity inputs used in the production of the commodity. Some Sraffians, together with a few Marxists, suggest Sraffa's purpose in *PCMC* is not to undermine the labour theory of value explanations of prices and profits in the works of Ricardo and Marx but to resurrect them in a more logically sound form. A number of Marxists even cite Sraffa's well-known sympathy for Marx's transformation procedure as evidence for his purpose in this regard.[7] However, these defenders of Sraffa do not explain why he adopts what is essentially a Neoclassical conception of capital and corresponding explanation of profit if his purpose is to resurrect the explanations of profit in the works of Ricardo and Marx.

Whatever Sraffa's purpose in writing *PCMC*, it is apparent that the manner in which he presents his arguments in this work has provided fertile ground for his followers to join in the modern tendency towards the mathematisation of economic arguments. Kurz (2011, p. 102) remarks:

> It is telling that apart from Maurice Dobb Sraffa discussed his work typically only with mathematicians; in the late 1920s with Frank Ramsey and in the 1940s and 1950s with Abram S. Besicovitch and Alister Watson.

This unfortunate legacy of Sraffa's work is perhaps most clearly evidenced in the so-called capital controversies, which resulted in a profusion of mathematical arguments but little or no attention to the elephant in the room; the conception of capital and explanation of profit.

[7] See for example Bellofiore (2014).

5.4 Production and Value of the Commodity

5.4.1 Production

Sraffa conceives of the production of goods in all economic systems as the production of commodities, i.e., the production of goods for exchange. He sees this production undertaken by a producer with the aid of produced and non-produced material inputs. The produced inputs comprise means of production and 'subsistence' commodities required to sustain labour at a certain basic standard of living. The non-produced material inputs comprise 'natural resources', including land and mineral deposits.[8] Distinguishing between subsistence and surplus product economic systems, Sraffa tacitly sees all produced and non-produced commodities owned by labour in the former economic system but not in the latter. He tacitly sees the producer in a surplus product economic system borrowing long-lasting inputs or capital goods from the capitalist and renting non-produced inputs from their owners.

Although Sraffa sees labour as a factor of production in the production of commodities, viz., the sole factor in a subsistence economy and one of three factors in a surplus product or capitalist economy setting, he denies that the labour input has a 'quantitative dimension' in either economy, other than the commodities appropriated by it in the form of an income.[9] Sraffa also implicitly sees the incomes appropriated by labour in a subsistence economy comprising subsistence commodities (wheat and pigs), and those appropriated as incomes by all factor owners in a surplus product economy as 'luxury' commodities. He sees the wage goods appropriated by labour in a surplus product economy comprising both subsistence wage goods and luxuries, with the quantity of the latter determined by the struggle between labour and the owner of capital over the surplus product—the net product.

Sraffa conceives of the process of production in both the subsistence and surplus production systems as the productive expenditure of produced material inputs, scrupulously avoiding any reference to the expenditure of labour time by the labour input. For Sraffa the process of production is the production of commodities by means of commodities and not the production of commodities with the aid of the labour

[8] See Sraffa (1960, p. 74).

[9] See Kurz and Salvadori (2005, p. 418).

input. Sraffa argues that the labour input needs to be excluded from the analysis since, unlike commodity inputs, it leaves no 'residue' behind.[10]

Lastly, as already alluded to above, Sraffa sees the commodities produced in both subsistence and surplus product systems as produced for exchange and comprising commodities commanded as incomes and means of production, where the commodities commanded as incomes do not include means of production. Of note in this regard is, that unlike Smith, Sraffa denies what is produced excludes means of production, but like Smith he sees the net product excluding means of production.

From the perspective of Marx's analysis, the problem with Sraffa's explanation of production begins with its **conception**, and his tacit denial of its social nature. This denial stems from his denial that all economic systems are based on the cooperative expenditure of social labour time in the production of the required goods and services. In fact, Sraffa explicitly eliminates labour as an input into production in all economic systems and replaces it with the wage goods required to sustain labour, or what he refers to as subsistence wage goods. As noted above, the formal reason Sraffa gives for conceptualising inputs into production excluding labour is that it has no quantitative dimension and leaves no residue unlike commodity inputs. Hence, for him the labour input needs to be replaced by a certain quantity of commodities, subsistence commodities, as part of the commodity inputs used in the production of commodities in all modes of production, with subsistence commodities being distinguished from luxury commodities appropriated by labour in surplus product economies. Accordingly, for Sraffa, it is only the subsistence commodity component of the wage that constitutes inputs into production in surplus product economies, even though labour is also seen as appropriating luxury commodities as part of their incomes. The obvious problem is the dividing line between subsistence and luxury goods.

Like Smith, Sraffa is unclear about the nature of the **producer**. He is unclear whether the producer is to be conceived of as existing in a subsistence economy, and whether the producer is an entrepreneur or manager in a surplus product economy. Sraffa's conception of a subsistence economy suggests the producer can only be labour. Hence, when he sees labour replaced by subsistence goods in this economy, the producer effectively disappears. Sraffa conceives of the producer in a surplus

[10] See Kurz and Salvadori (2005, p. 418).

product economic system in the first instance as an entrepreneur that owns the capital advanced at the outset of production and appropriates a profit in relation to the value of this outlay. However, he subsequently conceives of the producer as in effect a manager that borrows means of production (or the money needed to buy the means of production) and hires labour to produce an output of a certain value allowing incomes to be paid to both labour and the owner of capital for their use in production. As I will argue below, it is this latter conception of the producer as a manager that underpins Sraffa's commodity theory of price in a surplus product economy, i.e., in capitalism.

A related problem with Sraffa's explanation of production is that he sees the producer purchasing **commodity inputs** in all modes of production, and denies labour power is the most important commodity input purchased in capitalism. Sraffa does not see that the goods constituting the means of sustenance of labour and means of production in pre-capitalist systems are not systematically produced for exchange and, therefore, do not possess exchange values. He does not see that even when on the odd occasion these products possess exchange values in these systems, their magnitudes are not such that they facilitate the reproduction of these products. The products that sustain labour power and constitute the means of production only become commodities, only possess exchange value, in capitalism. It is only in capitalism that products are systematically produced for exchange. It is only in capitalism that labour power becomes a commodity that can be bought and sold like any other commodity.

Sraffa is also unclear why the wages paid to workers in capitalism are used to purchase luxury goods while those paid to workers for the supply of the **labour** input in this system are used to purchase subsistence goods. Even leaving aside the fact that subsistence wage goods cannot be conceived of as constituting direct inputs into production, Sraffa provides no justification for his treatment of subsistence wage goods being on *a par* with means of production as inputs into the production of commodities. Of course, Sraffa's purpose in conceiving of subsistence wage goods as inputs into production is his desire to replace labour as an input with produced commodities in the process of production, much as his purpose in drawing a distinction between subsistence and luxury wage commodities is his desire to explain profit by a struggle between labour and the owners of capital over the net product.

Sraffa's elimination of labour as an input into the production of commodities stems from his mistaken understanding of this input and the process of production in which it is used. It is a conception of the labour input that is found in the works of Smith and Keynes. As such Sraffa not see that the labour input is a commodity, labour power, that also has a quantitative dimension like any other commodity, and the expenditure of labour power is over certain discrete periods of time. He does not see the residue this expenditure leaves behind is the transformed form of the commodity inputs, i.e., the commodity output. This is analogous to the use of electricity in the production of a car leaving behind the car as the residue of the use of electricity. Eliminating labour as an input into production means Sraffa is unable to explain the active element in the process of production, the element that is responsible for the transformation of the material inputs into social use values.

Lastly, Sraffa sees all **outputs**, whether in subsistence or surplus economic systems, as produced for exchange. Like Smith, Sraffa does not see that in pre-capitalist systems only certain commodities acquire the form of exchange values, those comprising an excess of what is needed for the reproduction of the system, and these exchange values do not typically facilitate the reproduction of these commodities. Additionally, although like Smith, Sraffa sees the net product excluding means of production, unlike Smith he sees it also excluding subsistence wage goods, without providing any rationale why this should be the case. In excluding means of production from the net product, Sraffa is conceiving of the capitalist system as one of simple reproduction, and, in conceiving of wages as divided into subsistence and luxury wages, he is tacitly seeing wages paid for the inputs provided by workers as necessary for their basic sustenance. Sraffa provides little or no justification for these crucial assumptions.

5.4.2 *Value of the Commodity*

Although Sraffa, like Smith, formally conceives of commodities only possessing exchange values, it is apparent that he too implicitly conceives of them possessing values. The value of the commodity for Sraffa is the *quantity of commodity means of production* required to produce it, where all means of production possess exchange values.[11] Sraffa sees

[11] See Bellofiore (2012, p. 1389), Porta (2012, p. 1375).

all commodities in a subsistence economic setting as 'basics', in the sense that they are used in their own production as well as those of other commodities. This suggests he sees the value of the commodity in this sort of economy as the relative quantity of any commodity, including itself, used in its production. Sraffa sees all commodities in a surplus product economy comprising basics and 'non-basics' or 'luxury' commodities. Non-basics or luxuries are commodities appropriated as incomes, including wages. They are only used as means of production in their own production or that of other luxuries.[12] This suggests Sraffa sees the value of the commodity in a surplus economy setting as the relative quantity of basics used directly and indirectly in the production of the commodity. Some confusion is caused by Sraffa's consideration of the prices of commodities from what he refers to as "their cost-of-production aspect",[13] giving the impression that like Smith he sees the value of the commodity as its commodity income costs of production. However, the emphasis he places at the very outset of *PCMC* on the methods of production in the explanation of the exchange value of the commodity belies this.[14]

In accordance with his conception of the value of a commodity, as the quantity of commodity means of production used to produce a commodity, Sraffa sees the measure of the value of the commodity as a certain quantity of these commodities reduced to equivalence by a numéraire commodity. He sees the numéraire commodity in a subsistence economy setting as any arbitrarily chosen commodity,[15] and in a surplus product economy as a cluster or composite of basic commodities produced in fixed ratios to one another and having correspondingly fixed exchange ratios to one another, the so-called *Standard commodity*, or, more specifically, a unit of the Standard commodity.[16] Although Sraffa is somewhat vague about the production of the Standard commodity, the implication of his analysis is that he sees it produced in a sub-system of the actual system in which the surplus product in this sub-system comprises the same (basic) commodities as the means of production used in their

[12] See Sraffa (1960, pp. 7–8).

[13] See Sraffa (1960, p. 34).

[14] See Sraffa (1960, p. 3).

[15] See Sraffa (1960, p. 18).

[16] See Sraffa (1960, p. 20).

production.[17] He refers to this sub-system as the *Standard system* and conceives of a unit of the Standard commodity which functions as the measure of the exchange value of the commodity in a surplus product economy as "the quantity of it that would form the net product of a Standard system employing the whole annual labour of the actual system" (1960, p. 20), referring to this unit as the Standard net product. The importance of the Standard commodity construct for Sraffa is that it allows the numéraire commodity to be conceived of as invariant to factors causing changes in the exchange values of commodities whose exchange values it is used to measure. It warrants remarking here that a number of Sraffians do not see the importance Sraffa accords to the Standard commodity as an invariable measure of the exchange values of commodities. Consequently, they interpret him conceiving of the measure in a surplus product economy in the manner of his measure in a subsistence economy setting; as an arbitrarily chosen numéraire.[18]

Even more than most other economists and approaches considered in the present work, Sraffa is unclear about how a commodity acquires value historically or how this value is formed. However, as with other economists and approaches these can be deduced from his analysis. This suggests he sees commodities acquiring values historically when they are produced with commodity means of production possessing exchange values, and these values are formed in the process of production, in the context of the productive consumption of commodity means of production.

Lastly, Sraffa sees the magnitude of value primarily determined by the relative quantity of the means of production used to produce a commodity. In the case of a surplus product economy (capitalism) this requires him to also conceive of *the productivity of the means of production* used in the production of all commodities to explain the surplus product. Sraffa argues that changes in the productivity of non-basic commodities when they are used as means of production will only have a bearing on the (relative) value of the commodity produced with them. An increase in the productivity of these means of production will cause the relative values of these commodities to fall. In contrast, changes in the productivity of basic commodities as means of production will impact on the (relative) values of

[17] See Sraffa (1960, p. 21).

[18] See for example Hahnel (2017, p. 10).

all commodities, with the nature of the impact depending on the relative quantity of the basics used in the production of the commodity.[19]

From the perspective of Marx's analysis, the problems with Sraffa's explanation of the value of the commodity, as with all other approaches, begins with his implicit **conception** of its value. First, Sraffa's implicit conception of the value of the commodity, as the quantity of commodity inputs required to produce a commodity, requires him to reduce all inputs to commodity inputs. To do this Sraffa makes a number of dubious assumptions. Most importantly, he assumes it is meaningful to substitute the labour input with a certain quantity of commodities consumed by labour, those constituting what he refers to as subsistence wage goods, and, in the case of a surplus economy, to distinguish these from non-subsistence or luxury wage goods, which comprise the other component of the wage goods consumed by labour. Sraffa sees the luxury wage goods appropriated by labour as constituting its share of the surplus product. I noted above that Sraffa's justification for replacing the labour input with subsistence wage goods is that the labour input has no quantitative dimension and leaves no residue after its use in production. I argued that this justification by Sraffa stems from his mistaken conception of the labour input, a conception found in the works of Smith and Keynes, i.e., the labour input purchased with the wage. What requires adding here is that Sraffa provides no indication of the criteria he uses to distinguish between subsistence and luxury wage goods, or explain how labour is able to share in the surplus product.[20] Second, Sraffa's implicit conception of the value of the commodity also requires him to assume it is meaningful to distinguish between basic and non-basic commodities as means of production, conceiving of the former as means of production that enter either directly or indirectly into the production of all commodities and are only produced by themselves. It should be apparent that this distinction between basic and non-basic commodities is required to avoid conceiving of the economic system as a sort of corn economy in the manner of Smith. Although critics have focused on the meaning of basics entering

[19] See Sraffa (1960, pp. 7–8).

[20] I will deal with Sraffa's argument that labour is able to share in the surplus product in Nicholas (forthcoming), simply noting here that it has important implications for understanding the formation of the general rate of profit and the driving force underlying technological change.

the production of all commodities indirectly,[21] the more fundamental problem is surely his assumption that it is possible to conceive of means of production that are only produced by themselves. Third, Sraffa's implicit conception of the value of the commodity requires him to reduce the commodity inputs used to produce commodities to comparable magnitudes. For this purpose he adopts a numéraire commodity, without providing any justification for the particular numéraire commodity used apart from its analytical usefulness. Specifically, he adopts an arbitrarily chosen numéraire commodity to arrive at determinate magnitudes of exchange values of commodities produced and exchanged in a subsistence economy setting, and an artificial construct, the Standard net product, to do the same in a surplus product setting. Lastly, Sraffa's implicit conception of the value of the commodity requires him to conceive of this value as the *relative* value of the commodity and not, more fundamentally, its *absolute* value. This is because for Sraffa to conceive of the value of the commodity as its absolute value would require him to conceive of the latter as the particular commodities used to produce a commodity, and provide a rationale for the particular commodities chosen.

It needs emphasising that the source of the problem with Sraffa's implicit conception of the value of the commodity is his attempt to bypass the labour theory of value. It is this that requires him to substitute the labour input with commodities consumed by labour, and in the process make an arbitrary distinction between subsistence and luxury commodities consumed by labour. It is also this that requires him to distinguish between basic and non-basic commodities, conceiving of basics in a way that tacitly sees them replacing labour time as the common element in the production of all commodities.

The problem with Sraffa's conception of the **measure** of the value of the commodity is that he needs to see it as a certain quantity of either an *arbitrarily chosen* commodity means of production or an *artificially constructed* composite of basic commodities. Sraffa notes the problem with the arbitrarily chosen commodity is that its own exchange value is impacted on by the same forces as those impacting on the exchange values of the commodity means of production it is being used to measure making it impossible to detect the source of the change in the exchange

[21] See Nicholas (2011, p. 146).

values of the commodity means of production it is used to measure.[22] However, he does not appear to be aware of the problem with his Standard commodity construct. Namely, its artificial nature. Indeed, Sraffa even contends the Standard commodity could be adopted as a money of account "without too great a stretch of the imagination" (1960, p. 48). It is difficult to fathom how a unit of the Standard commodity, as the quantity of it that would form the net product of a Standard system employing the whole annual product of the actual system, could possibly be conceived of as a money of account in a real world setting. I will return to this point below when discussing the implications of Sraffa's analysis for his conception of money.

Although Sraffa's conception of the value of the commodity suggests he sees commodities **acquiring values** historically with the development of exchange in the manner of Smith, it also suggests he sees them acquiring values when they are produced with the same basic commodity means of production. The obvious questions this raises are why and how commodities can be seen as acquiring values historically when they come to be produced with the same basic commodity means of production, and what these basic commodities might be.

Although Sraffa cannot be criticised in the manner of Smith for seeing the values of commodities **formed** before the process of production, he can be criticised for seeing the values of commodities formed in the context of the productive consumption of commodity means of production, without any recognition that the entity responsible for the productive consumption of the commodity inputs is labour power; the productive consumption of commodity means of production taking place in the context of the expenditure of labour time by labour. Moreover, like Smith and Ricardo, Sraffa too can be criticised for not seeing the value of the commodity in capitalism formed with reference to money, in the context of the use of money to denote the general exchange values of commodities.

The fundamental problem with Sraffa's explanation of the **magnitude** of value of the commodity from the perspective of Marx's analysis is it requires him to deny the quantity of labour time expended in the production of the commodity has any bearing on the magnitude of its value. Following from what was argued above, this requires him to replace

[22] See Sraffa (1960, p. 18).

the labour input in both the subsistence and surplus product economic settings with a 'subsistence' basket of commodities required to sustain labour, and conceive of these commodities being distinct from the luxury commodities appropriated by labour in a surplus product setting. As I argued above, Sraffa provides no justification for conceiving of the labour input in this way, apart from the vague contention in his unpublished notes that the labour input has no quantitative dimension and leaves no residue as a result of its use in production (see above).

A second problem with Sraffa's explanation of the magnitude of value, and one that follows logically from his attempt to replace the labour input with commodities, is it requires him to explain changes in the value of the commodity in a surplus product economic setting by changes in the productivity of the means of production and, in the final instance, the productivity of his Standard commodity with respect to its own production, i.e., its production with decreasing quantities of itself. Sraffa argues that the productivity of the means of production in the Standard system, the sub-system in which the Standard commodity is produced, corresponds to the productivity of the means of production in the actual system as a result of appropriate price adjustments in the actual system.[23,24] He sees these adjustments as those causing the rate of profit in the actual system to correspond to the rate of profit in the Standard sub-system. Of note in this regard is that Sraffa is also tacitly assuming that the productivity of the means of production in all sectors of the actual economy are the same, and equal to the productivity of the means of production in the Standard sub-system. The problem with Sraffa's explanation in this regard is that it requires him to assume physical outputs, including those used as inputs, can be continuously produced with smaller quantities of physical inputs. This only makes sense if the reduced quantity of physical inputs used to produce a given quantity of physical outputs corresponds to a reduced quantity of wage goods used in their production as a result of a reduction in the quantity of labour time required for their production, something that would also allow for differences in productivity between sectors.

A last problem with Sraffa's explanation of the magnitude of value of the commodity is that he sees the value of the commodity as its *embodied*

[23] See Kurz and Salvadori (2005, p. 418).

[24] See Sraffa (1960, p. 23).

costs of production and not the costs *required* for the reproduction of the commodity. This, in turn, requires him to conceive of the value transferred from the means of production to the value of the commodity as the layered quantities of the means of production used in the production of the commodity. What Sraffa must deny in this regard is that the value transferred to the commodity from the means of production is the value of what is needed to repurchase the means of production. This is because to conceive of the value transferred as what is needed to reproduce the commodity requires Sraffa to deny that the value of the commodity is the means of production used in its production.

5.5 Exchange and Exchange Value of the Commodity

5.5.1 Exchange

Like the Classics, Sraffa conceives of the process of exchange as essentially one commodity for another, i.e., (C-C'), and sees exchange as general and widespread in all modes of production, which, in the case of Sraffa's *PCMC*, is his 'subsistence' and 'surplus product' modes of production. Where he differs from the Classics is in seeing the commodities exchanged including the commodity means of production, and the process of exchange facilitating the reproduction of the commodity by enabling the producer to purchase the commodity means of production and subsistence wage goods required to reproduce the commodity. It should be recalled here that for both Smith and Ricardo exchange facilitates the reproduction of the commodity insofar as it enables owners of factor inputs to purchase the consumption goods they need to satisfy their consumption requirements, and, therefore, the commodities exchanged exclude the means of production.

The problem with Sraffa's explanation of the process of exchange from the perspective of Marx's approach begins with his **conception** of this process. First, although Sraffa sees the purpose of exchange as the reproduction of the commodity, he sees what producers acquire in the process of exchange when they sell their products is a particular commodity, not something that represents general exchange value. He does not see that for producers to be able to reproduce their commodities what they acquire in exchange for their commodities should permit them to repurchase all the required commodity inputs, including labour power.

An arbitrarily chosen numéraire commodity, let alone Sraffa's artificially constructed Standard commodity, cannot realistically be seen as serving this purpose. Neither of these can be conceived of as representing general exchange value. A second problem with Sraffa's conception of the process of exchange is that he tacitly sees his artificially constructed Standard commodity among the commodities being exchanged for one another. As I noted above, although Sraffa does not see a problem with conceiving of the Standard commodity having a real existence, his justification for doing so suggests it cannot possibly be conceived of as constituting a particular commodity, or even a cluster of the means of production, that is exchanged for another particular commodity. Specifically, Sraffa sees a unit of the Standard commodity having no bodily existence but instead representing "a fraction of each asset and each liability" in a joint product economic system (1960, p. 48).

Sraffa does not see that the process of exchange facilitating the reproduction of the commodity is unique to capitalism, **emerging** with the emergence of capitalism. The exchange of products for one another to meet the consumption needs of the exchanging parties takes place in pre-capitalist economic systems, but not their exchange for something representing general exchange value to facilitate their reproduction. The latter form of exchange is unique to capitalism.

Lastly, although Sraffa does not conceive of the process of exchange as one of **barter**, he tacitly sees commodities put into the process of exchange for one another without determinate money prices. That is to say, even if he is interpreted as seeing money facilitating the exchange of the commodities for one another he cannot be interpreted as seeing commodities put into the process of exchange with determinate money prices. This follows from his conception of the process of exchange as one particular commodity for another. I will return to this point below when expanding on the implications of Sraffa's analysis for his understanding of money.

5.5.2 *Exchange Value of the Commodity*

Sraffa conceives of the exchange value of a commodity as the quantity of another commodity it commands in the process of exchange. He sees the commodities being exchanged as the measures of the exchange values of one another, with one of these commodities the standard of all commodities as measures of the exchange values of one another.

He conceives of this commodity as a numéraire commodity whose own exchange value is taken to be unity. Sraffa conceives of the numéraire commodity in a subsistence production economy as any arbitrarily chosen commodity,[25] and in a surplus production economy as an artificially constructed Standard commodity.[26]

The logic of Sraffa's explanation of the exchange values of commodities suggests he sees them acquiring exchange values historically with the development of exchange, at the same time as, or even before, they acquire values. It should be recalled that Sraffa implicitly sees commodities acquiring values when they begin to be produced with commodity means of production that possess exchange values. The logic of Sraffa's explanation of the exchange values of commodities also suggests he sees the exchange value of the commodity formed in the process of exchange. It was argued above Sraffa tacitly sees the process of exchange as in effect one of barter, with commodities acquiring determinate magnitudes of exchange values in the process of exchange.

Lastly, Sraffa sees the magnitude of exchange value that needs explaining in the first instance as its *trend* magnitude in the manner of the Classical economists and Marx, and explains this magnitude primarily by the magnitude of the value of the commodity as the commodity means of production used to produce the commodity output in both subsistence and surplus product economies. He also sees changes in the numéraire wage rate having a bearing on the magnitude of the exchange values of commodities, but argues this impact is indeterminate due to the different methods of production adopted in the production of the various layers of means of production required to produce the commodities.[27]

From the perspective of Marx's analysis, the problems with Sraffa's explanation of the exchange value of the commodity begin with its **conception**. The basic problem in this regard is that Sraffa sees the exchange value of the commodity as the quantity of another particular commodity it commands in the process of exchange, and not the quantity of something that represents general exchange value prior to it being put into the process of circulation. Sraffa does not see that the exchange

[25] See Sraffa (1960, p. 5).

[26] See Sraffa (1960, p. 34).

[27] See Sraffa (1960, pp. 14–15).

value of the commodity must assume the form of something that represents general exchange value prior to it being put into the process of circulation if the purpose of its exchange value is to facilitate its reproduction. There is no reason to suppose that the exchange value of the commodity as its numéraire exchange value serves this purpose, especially since the numéraire for Sraffa is either an arbitrarily chosen commodity or, in a surplus product setting, an artificial construct.

Sraffa also appears to ignore the fact that the logic of his analysis suggests the commodity commanded in the process of exchange in a surplus product economy must necessarily be what is paid as incomes in the process of production. Formally, this requires him conceiving of it as a luxury commodity or cluster of luxury commodities. Conceiving of the exchange value of the commodity as its Standard commodity exchange value in a surplus product economy requires him to conceive of the incomes appropriated in the process of production assuming the form of the Standard commodity, that is, the form of an artificially constructed commodity.

The problem with Sraffa's concept of the **measure** of the exchange value of the commodity follows from the problem with his conception of the exchange value of the commodity. That is, he sees the measure of the exchange value of the commodity as any commodity it commands in the process of exchange, with an arbitrarily chosen numéraire or a unit of his Standard commodity (the Standard net product) as the standard of all commodities as measures of the exchange values of one another. What Sraffa does not see is that if the purpose of the exchange value of the commodity is to facilitate the reproduction of the commodity, its measure should be what is used to denote its general exchange value, enabling the producer to repurchase all the inputs (including the labour input) used up in the process of producing the commodity. As I have argued above, an arbitrarily chosen or an artificially constructed Standard commodity cannot be conceived of as something that represents general exchange value in the sense of being used to purchase any and all commodities and pay wages. To conceive of the numéraire commodity as representing general exchange value requires conceiving of its as money. I will deal with the problems of doing so below in the framework of Sraffa's analysis when considering the implications for this analysis of bringing money into it. Lastly, the logic of Sraffa's analysis causes him to implicitly see the measure of the exchange value of the commodity as the same as the measure of its value and not the form of the latter. This follows logically from Sraffa's conflation of the value with the exchange value of the commodity.

Sraffa's conception of the value of the commodity prevents him from seeing commodities **acquiring** exchange values historically *after* they acquire values. This is because to see commodities acquiring exchange values historically *after* they acquire values would require him to see the means of production acquiring exchange values historically *prior* to the outputs produced with these means of production. It should be recalled here that for Sraffa the value of a commodity is the commodity means of production used in its production where the latter have exchange values. Sraffa's conception of the exchange value of the commodity, as the quantity of another commodity commanded by it in the process of exchange, also prevents him from seeing its exchange value **formed** *prior to* the commodity being put into the process of exchange by the producer. Conceiving of the process of exchange as one commodity for another and the exchange value of the commodity as the quantity of one commodity commanded by another in the process of exchange, requires Sraffa to conceive of the exchange value of the commodity formed in the process of exchange.

The problem with Sraffa's explanation of the **magnitude** of the exchange value of the commodity follows from the preceding. To begin with, like Smith and Ricardo, Sraffa does not see the magnitude of the exchange value that needs explaining in the first instance as the magnitude of its general exchange value or *money exchange* value, not its *commodity exchange value* or relative price. It could be argued, as Sraffa appears to do so, that his explanation of the exchange value of the commodity as its Standard commodity exchange value in a surplus product economic setting is in effect the explanation of its money exchange value. However, as I will argue below, this requires him to see an artificial construct, the Standard commodity, as money.

An important consequence of Sraffa's explanation of the magnitude of the exchange value of the commodity in a surplus product economic setting is that it requires him to conceive of wages in a way that allows their exclusion from the *cost price* of the commodity on which a profit mark-up is levied. That is, it requires Sraffa to distinguish between subsistence and luxury wages, conceiving of the former as part of the means of production and the latter paid *post factum* as a share of the annual net product—not advanced from capital.[28] This allows Sraffa to conceive of the unit costs on which the profit mark-up is based as the unit means of production (MP) and not the unit means of production and wage costs (MP + wL). That is, it requires him to conceive of the exchange value of the commodity as;

$$EV_i = (MP_i \times (1 + r)) + wL_i \tag{5.1}$$

where EV_i is the numéraire exchange value of the average commodity produced in sector *i*, MP_i is the numéraire quantity of the means of production used to produce the average commodity in the sector, *r* is the numéraire rate of interest, *w* the numéraire wage rate, and L_i is the quantity of labour that is employed in sector i to produce an average commodity of the type produced in the sector. Most importantly, it allows Sraffa to avoid having to tacitly see unit costs as unit wage costs determined by unit labour costs. The problem is, of course, that to avoid this conclusion Sraffa has to make an arbitrary distinction between subsistence and luxury wage goods, and assume that the former comprise basic commodities akin to other basic commodities. As I argued above, not only is the dividing line between subsistence and luxury commodities murky, Sraffa offers no justification for why he sees luxury wages paid *post factum* out of the net product. It should be noted in this context that Marx sees the source of wages paid to workers as their own produce and part of the capital outlaid.

A related consequence of Sraffa's explanation of the magnitude of the exchange value of the commodity is that it requires him to abstract from changes in the productivity of labour when explaining unit wage costs. He does this by assuming the net product and the total quantity of labour employed are given. This leaves only changes in the numéraire wage share and corresponding changes in the numéraire wage rate to explain changes in unit labour costs (wL). Sraffa does not see that changes in the wage share result from changes in the (money) wage in relation to the productivity of labour in the production of all commodities, where the former are conditioned by the latter. More fundamentally still, he does not see that the unit (money) wage cost is determined by the quantity of the labour time expended in the production of the commodity times the (money) wage rate.

[28] See Sraffa (1960, p. 10).

A second problem with Sraffa's explanation of the magnitude of the exchange value of the commodity that warrants some attention is his contention that changes in the numéraire wage rate have an indeterminate impact on this magnitude due to the layering of means of production and differences in the labour intensity of their production. It should be apparent from the preceding that this contention is premised on Sraffa's failure to see the magnitudes of the exchange values of commodities set by producers prior to putting their commodities into the process of circulation, with the purpose of facilitating their reproduction. What matters in this context is not the historic exchange values of the means of production but their current repurchase prices. This is not to say that the numéraire wage rate has a determinate impact on the magnitude of the exchange value of the commodity contrary to the argument advanced by Sraffa, but rather that his argument is premised on a mistaken conception and explanation of the magnitude of the exchange value of the commodity.

A last, and related, problem with Sraffa's explanation of the magnitude of the exchange value of the commodity is it requires him to see this magnitude determined by the costs *actually incurred* in the production of the commodity, i.e., the means of production used in its production, and not the costs that *need to be incurred*. This prevents Sraffa from seeing the current prices of the means of production required for the reproduction of the commodity as having a bearing on the magnitude of the exchange value of the commodity. Instead, it requires him to the means of production that have been directly and indirectly used in the production of the commodity having a bearing on this magnitude.

Before concluding this section, it warrants remarking that a number of Sraffians argue Sraffa's *dated labour analysis* undermines Marx's labour theory explanation of the exchange value of commodities.[29] These Sraffians do not see that the only thing Sraffa's concept of dated labour has in common with Marx's concept of labour time is the word *labour*. Sraffa conceives of dated labour as the quantity of the total workforce that can be commanded by the net product when the wage share changes, assuming that the wage share employs the entire labour force. He emphasises the fact that this quantity can increase "without limit" as the wage share falls (1960, p. 32). Since Sraffa is fully aware that for Marx the aggregate quantity of labour commanded equals the aggregate quantity

[29] See for example Steedman (1977), Hodgson (1982).

of labour expended, the target of his dated labour analysis is clearly not Marx but rather those adopting income cost explanations of prices in which labour is seen as a factor input.

5.6 Money and Its Functions

5.6.1 Money

Sraffa refers to money on only a couple of occasions in his *PCMC*. This requires anyone seeking to derive his understanding of money to also look to his other published and unpublished writings, including the collection of his notes and correspondences housed at the University of Cambridge, England, and referred to as the *Sraffa Papers* (SP).

Sraffa formally conceives of money in his *PCMC* as the numéraire commodity, and in particular his artificially constructed Standard commodity in a surplus product economic setting, which he insists has a real-world existence.[30] He implicitly sees the purpose of money being to facilitate the exchange of commodities for one another in a way that enables their reproduction. Conceiving of money as the numéraire commodity requires Sraffa to see money emerging with the development of the process of exchange when one commodity among those being exchanged is 'chosen' as the numéraire commodity. The economic system he implicitly sees money emerging in is what he refers to as a 'subsistence production' system, which could be interpreted as a pre-capitalist economic system. Insofar as Sraffa sees money as a numéraire commodity he sees it necessarily assuming the form of a commodity. This does not, however, preclude him from being interpreted as conceiving of intrinsically valueless tokens of the numéraire commodity being used as a means of circulation to circulate commodities in accordance with their numéraire money prices. Lastly, interpreting Sraffa conceiving of money as a numéraire commodity requires interpreting him denying money is a 'veil'. Changes in the numéraire prices of commodities are in effect changes in their relative prices, something that must logically impact on their reproduction.

[30] Sraffa argues (1960, p. 48) "…a Standard commodity….can be adopted as a money of account without too great stretch of the imagination provided that the unit is conceived as representing, like a share in a company, a fraction of each asset and of each liability, the latter in the shape of an obligation to deliver without payment certain quantities of particular commodities".

From the perspective of Marx's analysis, the problems with Sraffa's implicit understanding of money begin with its **conception**. The problem with his conception of money, as a numéraire commodity, is that it requires Sraffa to conceive of money as an arbitrarily chosen or artificially constructed numéraire commodity that is used as a money of account to facilitate the reproduction of commodities. While particular commodities have been used as numéraire commodities to facilitate the exchange of commodities for one another in pre-capitalist economic systems, they have not been arbitrarily chosen commodities let alone artificial constructs. Rather, they have been among the most frequently traded commodities, typically assuming the form of metals, and used to facilitate trade for the purposes of enhancing the satisfaction of those exchanging their commodities with one another, not to facilitate the reproduction of these commodities. In any case, there is no reason to believe that facilitating the exchange of commodities for one another would facilitate their reproduction. For Marx, although commodities that were used as numéraire commodities in pre-capitalist economic systems have also been used in capitalism by producers to facilitate the reproduction of their commodities, they have been used as measures of the exchange values of commodities and not as numéraire commodities. That is, they have been used by capitalist producers to denote the general exchange values of their commodities and not to reduce the exchange values of their commodities with other commodities to equivalence. The commodities used as measures of the exchange values of commodities by capitalist producers are neither arbitrarily chosen nor artificial constructs.

To avoid interpreting Sraffa conceiving of money as an arbitrarily chosen or artificially constructed numéraire commodity requires interpreting him conceiving of money in the manner of Smith and Ricardo, as an intrinsically valueless token of the commodities being exchanged for one another. Although this avoids having to interpret Sraffa conceiving of money as a commodity, and worse still as an arbitrarily chosen or artificially constructed commodity, it does not avoid having to interpret him conceiving of money being in the final instance a token these—a token of the numéraire commodity (see below). Moreover, it presumes the process of exchange in capitalism is characterised by the exchange of commodities for one another, albeit mediated by money, and that money represents particular exchangeable worth and not general exchangeable worth.

Interpreting Sraffa conceiving of money as a token of the commodities whose exchange for one another it facilitates, requires interpreting him denying it **emerges** historically as a numéraire commodity. Instead, it requires him seeing money emerging with capitalism as credit money resting on an inconvertible fiat currency base. It also requires interpreting him seeing money emerging to facilitate the exchange of commodities for one another and not their reproduction. As argued above, there is no reason to suppose that the exchange of commodities for one another in accordance with the relative quantities of means of production required for their production serves to facilitate their reproduction.

Interpreting Sraffa conceiving of money as whatever facilitates the exchange of commodities for one another requires interpreting him denying money assumes the **form** of a commodity unless the commodity can be assumed to function as an intrinsically valueless token of the commodities whose exchange for one another it facilitates. This means that Sraffa cannot logically be interpreted as conceiving of money having assumed the form of gold, let alone assuming that of an arbitrarily chosen or artificially constructed numéraire commodity. Instead, it requires Sraffa to be interpreted as seeing money as necessarily assuming the form of credit money.

Lastly, interpreting Sraffa conceiving of money as an intrinsically valueless token of the commodities whose exchange for one another it facilitates requires interpreting him seeing money as a **veil** in the manner of the Classical (and Neoclassical) economists. This is because it precludes him from seeing money as the representative of general exchange value that is used by capitalist producers to denote the exchange values of their commodities as general exchange values with a view to facilitating their reproduction. This in turn precludes Sraffa, like the Classical (and Neoclassical) economists, from seeing changes in the value and exchange value of money as well as changes in the money prices of commodities having a bearing on their reproduction. Of note in this context is Sraffa's criticism of what he sees as Hayek's attempt to bring money into the explanation of equilibrium prices, seeing this attempt as contrary to the 'standard approach' which denies money has any role to play in the explanation of trend relative prices—an approach Sraffa appears to be sympathetic to.[31]

[31] See Sraffa (1932, p. 53).

5.6.2 *Functions of Money*

Sraffa's implicit conception of money, as a token of the numéraire commodity, suggests that like most Classical (and Neoclassical) economists he sees the primary and defining function of money as its medium of exchange function. He sees it becoming a token of the numéraire commodity when it facilitates the exchange of commodities for one another in accordance with the magnitudes of their numéraire exchange values. Moreover, although there can be no doubt he sees money performing functions apart from that of medium, e.g., settlement of debts and store of value,[32] there is nothing in his published and unpublished writings to suggest he sees these as more important than money's medium of exchange function. This has not, however, prevented a number of Sraffa's followers from interpreting him attaching primacy to these other functions in an attempt to hitch him to the Post-Keynesian wagon.[33]

From the perspective of Marx's analysis, the fundamental problem with Sraffa's implicit understanding of the functions of money is that the logic of his analysis does not allow him to see money functioning as the **measure** of the exchange values of commodities, let alone it being money's primary and defining function. This is because, like the Classical (and Neoclassical) economists, Sraffa sees the measure of the exchange value of the commodity as the commodity it is being exchanged for, with one commodity, the numéraire commodity, assigned the role of the standard of all commodities as measures of the exchange values of one another. For Smith the standard commodity is corn, for Ricardo it is gold, and for Sraffa it is an arbitrarily chosen or artificially constructed commodity (the Standard commodity). The numéraire commodity reduces the exchange values of commodities to equivalence while the measure of the exchange values of commodities denotes the exchange values of commodities as general exchange values.

Interpreting Sraffa conceiving of money as a token of the numéraire commodity that facilitates the exchange of commodities for one another requires interpreting him attaching primacy to money's function as **medium of exchange** in the manner of Smith and Ricardo, and to see

[32] See Sraffa (1932, p. 43).

[33] See for example Hodgson (1981) and Deleplace (2014) placing emphasis on what they see as the implied store of value function in Sraffa's work.

whatever is used for this purpose as money. This precludes the Standard commodity being conceived of as money of account, contrary to Sraffa's assertions in *PCMC*. Rather, it requires Sraffa to be interpreted as conceiving of money as a valueless token of the Standard commodity in a surplus product economic system, and representing a certain magnitude of the Standard commodity when money is used to facilitate the exchange of commodities for one another according to their Standard commodity values.

Lastly, interpreting Sraffa conceiving of money as an intrinsically valueless token of the numéraire commodity precludes interpreting him conceiving of money as a **store of value**. What functions as a store of value should in principle possess value and represent a certain quantity of general exchange value. Money as a token of the numéraire commodity only possesses value and represents a certain magnitude of exchange value in the process of exchange, i.e., in the context of its use as medium of exchange. Outside of this process it possesses neither of these. This means that, like Smith and Ricardo, Sraffa should be interpreted as conceiving of what is held as a store of value as something other than money. In the case of Smith and Ricardo one could plausibly conceive of this as the numéraire commodity, but not in the case of Sraffa's artificially constructed Standard commodity.

5.7 Value of Money

When extending the logic of Sraffa's *PCMC* to elicit his explanation of the value of money, a distinction needs to be drawn in the manner of all other approaches between different forms of money. As noted above, in his *PCMC* Sraffa suggests that, at least in the first instance, money assumes the form of a commodity, the numéraire commodity, and possesses value like any other produced commodity, viz., the means of production used to produce the commodity. Although, as also noted above, Sraffa does not formally consider other forms of money, his analysis does not preclude him being interpreted as conceiving of money assuming non-commodity forms; the forms of a convertible token of the numéraire commodity and an inconvertible token of commodities whose exchange for one another it is used to facilitate. In the case of a convertible token of the numéraire commodity, its value is logically given by the value of the quantity of the numéraire commodity its face value indicates that it commands. In the case of an inconvertible token of commodities whose exchange for one another it facilitates, its value must logically be seen as given by the values of the commodities whose exchange for one another it facilitates. To the extent that Sraffa can be interpreted as seeing the numéraire commodity as money performing the function of a medium of exchange, he can be interpreted as seeing its value as a commodity deviating from its value as money, with the former acting as the *anchor* of the latter.

The implication of Sraffa's conception of the value of money as the numéraire commodity and a token of the commodities whose exchange for one another it facilitates is that its measure is a certain quantity of the numéraire commodity. Specifically, it is a certain quantity of an arbitrarily chosen numeraire commodity in a subsistence product economic setting and a certain quantity of the artificially constructed Standard commodity in a surplus product economic setting.

Sraffa's conception of money as a numéraire commodity requires him to be interpreted as seeing it acquiring value historically in the manner of all commodities, i.e., when it comes to be produced with commodity means of production, and its value formed, like the value of any commodity, in the process of its production. Interpreting Sraffa conceiving of money as a token of the commodities whose exchange for one another it facilitates requires interpreting him seeing money acquiring value when it comes to be used to facilitate the exchange of commodities for one another, and its value formed in the process of exchange, when it is used as a medium of exchange.

Lastly, the logic of Sraffa's analysis suggests he sees the magnitude of value of money as the numéraire commodity determined by the quantity of the means of production used to produce it, and as a token of the numéraire commodity, whatever form it assumes, by the quantity of means of production used to produce the commodities whose exchange for one another it facilitates. To the extent Sraffa is interpreted as seeing the numéraire commodity as both a particular commodity and what is used to facilitate the exchange of commodities for one another, he can be interpreted as seeing the magnitude of the value of the numéraire commodity acting as an *anchor* of its magnitude as a token of the numéraire commodity, with the latter gravitating towards the former whenever there are deviations between them.

The problems with Sraffa's implicit explanation of the value of money begin with its implicit **conception**. Firstly, once it is accepted that Sraffa needs to be interpreted as conceiving of money as an intrinsically valueless token of the commodities whose exchange for one another it is used to facilitate, he cannot be interpreted as conceiving of money as commodity having value as both a particular commodity and as an intrinsically valueless token of commodities. This is because to do so would require Sraffa to be interpreted as conceiving of money as the numéraire commodity that has value but functions as an intrinsically valueless token of commodities. Secondly, interpreting Sraffa conceiving of money as a token of the commodities whose exchange for one another it facilitates requires interpreting him, like Smith and Ricardo, conceiving of the value of money as the value of the aggregate quantity of money used to facilitate the exchange of commodities comprising the net product and given by the aggregate value of these commodities. That is to say, it requires interpreting Sraffa, like Smith and Ricardo, denying that the value of money being explained is the value of a unit of money that is given by the value of the commodity it comes to embody when it is used to denote the general exchange values of commodities. Lastly, Sraffa's implicit conception of the value of money as the values of commodities whose exchange for one another it facilitates, presumes it is meaningful to conceive of the latter as commodity means of production that are reduced to equivalence in terms of an arbitrarily chosen or artificially constructed commodity. As I have remarked on above it requires a considerable stretch of the imagination to conceive of the values of commodities in this manner.

The problem with Sraffa's implicit conception of the **measure** of the value of money follows from the problems with his conception of the value of money. Specifically, this conception requires Sraffa to be interpreted as conceiving of the measure of the value of money as the measure of the aggregate quantity of money used to facilitate the exchange of commodities comprising the net product for one another, and this measure as a certain aggregate quantity of an arbitrarily chosen or artificially constructed numérarire commodity. As such, it requires interpreting him conflating the measure of the value of money with the measure of its exchange value (see below).

Whether Sraffa is interpreted as conceiving of money as a numéraire commodity or a token of the numéraire commodity, he cannot logically be interpreted as seeing money **acquiring** value historically as gold. Instead, he must logically be interpreted as seeing money acquiring value historically when an arbitrarily chosen or artificially constructed commodity comes to be used as the numéraire commodity or when something is used to facilitate the exchange of commodities for one another.

Interpreting Sraffa conceiving of money as whatever is used to facilitate the exchange of commodities for one another precludes him from being interpreted as seeing money **formed** *prior* to it being put into the process of circulation to circulated commodities with determinate money prices. Interpreting Sraffa conceiving of money as a numéraire commodity allows him to be interpreted as conceiving of its value formed prior to it being put into the process of circulation, but requires him to be interpreted as seeing the numéraire commodity as an arbitrarily chosen or artificially constructed commodity whose value is formed in the process of its production.

The problems with Sraffa's implicit explanation of the **magnitude** of value of money follow from the preceding. First, insofar as Sraffa is interpreted as conceiving of money as a numéraire commodity, he must be interpreted as explaining the magnitude of its value like the magnitude of any commodity and not its value as money. Insofar as Sraffa is interpreted as conceiving of money as something that facilitates the exchange of commodities for one another, he can only be interpreted as seeing the magnitude of its value as money deviating from the magnitude of its value as a commodity if he can be interpreted as conceiving of the numéraire commodity as a valueless token of the commodities whose exchange for one another it is used to facilitate and, in the final instance, if he can be interpreted as conceiving of the numéraire commodity as a valueless token of itself.

Second, insofar as Sraffa is interpreted as conceiving of money as a token of the commodities whose exchange for one another it facilitates, he must be interpreted as seeing the magnitude of its value determined by the magnitude of its exchange value, and not *vice versa*. This is because he must be interpreted as seeing the value of money determined by the values of all the commodities whose exchange for one another it facilitates. Which means that a change in the quantity of money used to facilitate the commodities relative to the quantity of commodities whose exchange for one another money facilitates will cause a change in the magnitude of the value of money.

Lastly, Sraffa's conception of the value of the commodity as its *relative*, not *absolute*, value, precludes him from being interpreted as seeing changes in the values of commodities impacting on the magnitude of the value of money. Specifically, it precludes him from seeing changes in the economy-wide productivity of the means of production having a bearing on the magnitude of the value of money, in much the same way Ricardo's conception of the value of the commodity precludes him from seeing changes in the economy-wide productivity of labour having a bearing on the magnitude of value of money.

5.8 Exchange Value of Money

Insofar as Sraffa is interpreted as seeing money assuming the form of a numéraire commodity, he needs to be interpreted as conceiving of its exchange value as the quantity of another commodity it commands in the process of exchange in the manner of the conception of the exchange value of any commodity. Insofar as Sraffa is interpreted as seeing money assuming the form of a token of the commodities whose exchange for one another it facilitates, he needs to be interpreted as conceiving of its exchange value as the aggregate quantity of commodities commanded by money in the process of facilitating this exchange. These interpretations of Sraffa's conceptions of the exchange value of money have corresponding implications for interpretations of his conception of their measures. Interpreting Sraffa conceiving of money as a numéraire commodity requires interpreting him conceiving of the measure of its exchange value as a certain quantity of any commodity with a determinate numéraire price it is used to purchase, while interpreting him conceiving of money as a token of the commodities whose exchange for one another it is used to facilitate requires interpreting him conceiving of the measure of its exchange value as a certain quantity of all commodities whose exchange for one another it facilitates.

Interpreting Sraffa conceiving of money as a numéraire commodity requires interpreting him seeing it acquiring exchangeable worth historically when it comes to be used to denote the exchange values of commodities in terms of itself, and its exchange value formed, like the exchange value of any commodity, in the process of its exchange with other commodities. Interpreting Sraffa conceiving of money as a token of the numéraire commodity requires interpreting him seeing money acquiring exchange value historically when it comes to be used as a medium of exchange, and its exchange value formed in the context of its use to facilitate the exchange of commodities for one another, at the same time as the formation of its value.

Lastly, interpreting Sraffa conceiving of money as a numéraire commodity requires interpreting him explaining its magnitude like any other commodity; by the magnitude of its value. Interpreting Sraffa conceiving of money as a token of the numeraire commodity requires interpreting him explaining this magnitude in the manner of the CQTM; by the quantity of commodities whose exchange for one another money is used to facilitate relative to the quantity of money used to facilitate their exchange for one another. As with adherents of the CQTM, Sraffa needs to be interpreted as seeing the quantity of money put into the process of exchange as exogenously determined, i.e., independent of the money prices and quantities of commodities put into the process of circulation.

The problems with the implied explanation of the exchange value of money arising from Sraffa's work begin with its **conception**. Firstly, and analogously to what was argued above with regard to the interpretation of Sraffa's explanation of the value of money, once it is accepted that Sraffa needs to be interpreted as conceiving of money as a token of the commodities whose exchange for one another it facilitates, he cannot be interpreted as conceiving of money as a commodity possessing exchange value as both a commodity and money. Second, interpreting Sraffa conceiving of money as a token of the commodities whose exchange for one another it facilitates precludes him being interpreted as conceiving of the exchange value of money as the quantity of any commodity with a determinate money price that a unit of it is used to purchase. Instead, as noted above, it requires interpreting him conceiving of the exchange value of money as the exchange value of the aggregate quantity of money used to facilitate the exchange of all commodities and given by the aggregate of all commodities whose exchange for one another it facilitates. Lastly, whether Sraffa is interpreted as conceiving of money as a numéraire commodity or a token of all commodities whose exchange for one another it facilitates, he cannot be interpreted as conceiving of its exchange value as the form assumed by its value. This follows from the interpretations of Sraffa conceiving of the value and exchange value of money, whatever form it assumes, as a certain quantity of the numéraire commodity.

The problems with Sraffa's implicit conception of the **measure** of the exchange value of money follow from the problems noted above with his implicit conception of the exchange value of money. To begin with, Sraffa cannot be interpreted as seeing the quantity of money whose exchange value is being measured as a *unit* of money since this would require him being interpreted as seeing money acquiring general exchangeable worth when it is used to measure the general exchangeable worth of commodities. Second, and related to this, Sraffa cannot be interpreted as seeing this measure as a certain quantity of a commodity having a determinate money price since, again, this would require interpreting him seeing money used as a measure of the exchange values of their commodities by capitalist producers. Third, Sraffa cannot be interpreted as seeing the measure of the exchange value of money as the form of the measure of its value. This follows logically from it not being possible to interpret Sraffa conceiving of the exchange value of the commodity as the form assumed by its value.

Interpreting Sraffa conceiving of the numéraire commodity acquiring exchange value as money historically money as an intrinsically valueless token of the commodities whose exchange for one another it facilitates requires interpreting him denying money **acquires** exchange value historically as a numéraire commodity since it would require interpreting him conceiving of the numéraire commodity as intrinsically valueless even though it is a produced commodity. The source of the problem in this regard is that interpreting Sraffa seeing money as a valueless token of the numéraire commodity requires interpreting him seeing money emerging as a valueless token of the numéraire commodity and not the numéraire commodity itself.

Interpreting Sraffa conceiving of money as a token of the numéraire commodity prevents him from being interpreted as seeing the exchange value of money **formed** prior to money being put into the process of circulation to circulate commodities with determinate money prices. This in turn precludes Sraffa from being interpreted as seeing the quantity of money put into the process of circulation as *endogenously* determined, i.e., determined by the quantity and money prices of commodities put into the process of circulation.

The problems with Sraffa's implicit explanation of the **magnitude** of the exchange value of money follow from the preceding. To begin with, insofar as Sraffa is interpreted as conceiving of money as a token of the numéraire commodity, he cannot be interpreted as explaining the magnitude of the exchange value of money as the magnitude of its exchange value as a commodity. This means that insofar as he is interpreted as explaining the magnitude of the exchange value of money as the magnitude of the exchange value of gold it must be as a valueless token of his Standard commodity.

Second, interpreting Sraffa conceiving of money as a token of the numéraire commodity precludes him from being interpreted as explaining the magnitude of the exchange value of money by the magnitude of its value. In fact, as noted above, it requires interpreting him explaining the magnitude of the value of money by the magnitude of its exchange value. This logically precludes Sraffa being interpreted as explaining the magnitude of the exchange value of money by the productivity of the Standard commodity. More fundamentally, it requires interpreting Sraffa seeing changes in the magnitude of the exchange value of money divorced from changes in the conditions of production of all commodities or even changes in the exchange values of raw materials.

Lastly, interpreting Sraffa conceiving of money as a token of the numéraire commodity, a token of the commodities whose exchange for one another it facilitates, requires interpreting him, like Smith and Ricardo, denying that changes in aggregate excess demand have a bearing on the magnitude of the exchange value of money unless they correspond to changes in the excess quantity of money used to facilitate the exchange of commodities for one another.

5.9 Money Price of the Commodity

Although Sraffa does not explain the money price of the commodity this explanation can be deduced from his explicit and implicit explanations of the exchange values of the commodity and money outlined above. These explanations suggest he sees the money price of a commodity as its numéraire commodity exchange value for a given value of money. This in turn suggests Sraffa sees the measure of the money price of the commodity as any other commodity denominated in terms of money as a token of the numéraire commodity.

His implicit conception of the money price of the commodity requires Sraffa to be interpreted as seeing commodities acquiring money prices historically when an intrinsically valueless token of the numéraire commodity is used to facilitate their exchange for one another, after they have acquired exchange values with respect to one another. That is, it suggests he sees commodities acquiring money prices historically after they acquire relative prices. Sraffa's implicit conception of the money price of the commodity also suggests he sees money prices formed in the process of the exchange of commodities for one another, when money is used to facilitate this exchange.

Lastly, it follows from his implicit conception of the money price of the commodity that Sraffa should be interpreted as seeing the magnitude of the money price of the commodity determined by the magnitude of its numéraire exchange value for a given value of money. As I have argued above, Sraffa sees the magnitude of numéraire commodity exchange value of the commodity determined by the magnitude of its value, and implicitly sees the magnitude of the value of money determined by its exchange value.

The problem with Sraffa's implicit explanation of the money price of the commodity begins with its implicit **conception**. First, like Smith and Ricardo, Sraffa cannot be interpreted as conceiving of the money price of the commodity as its money exchange value. This is because, like Smith and Ricardo, Sraffa sees commodities being exchanged with one another and not with money as the representative of general exchangeable worth. Second, and related to the preceding, Sraffa cannot be interpreted as conceiving of the money price of the commodity as its numéraire commodity price since this would require him to be interpreted as conceiving of the numéraire commodity as money, and denying money is a token of the numéraire commodity. Third, Sraffa also cannot be interpreted as conceiving of the money price of the commodity as the form assumed by its value in the manner of Marx. This is because, as argued above, he cannot be interpreted as conceiving of an intrinsic link between money and the value of the commodity, one that is created when producers use money to denote the general exchange values of their commodities. Lastly, Sraffa's implicit conception of the money price of the commodity precludes him, like Smith and Ricardo, from conceiving of the relative money price of the commodity as its money price relative to that of another commodity, and the aggregate money price level as the aggregate money prices of all individual commodities. Instead, it requires him to be interpreted as conceiving of the relative money price of the commodity as its numéraire commodity (Standard commodity) exchange value with money a token of the numéraire commodity, and the aggregate money price level as the aggregate quantity of money used to facilitate the exchange of commodities for one another relative to the quantity of these commodities as a cluster.

Sraffa's implicit conception of the money price of the commodity precludes him from being interpreted as conceiving of the **measure** of the money price of the commodity as a certain quantity of money, since this would require him to be interpreted as conceiving of money used to denote the exchange values of commodities as general exchange values. Instead, as argued above, it requires him to conceive of money as a token of the numéraire commodity as a standard of commodities as measures of the exchange values of one another.

Interpreting Sraffa conceiving of money as an intrinsically valueless token of the numéraire commodity requires him to be interpreted as seeing commodities **acquiring** money prices historically with the emergence of capitalism when money comes to acquire the form of credit money. This follows from the necessary denial that Sraffa sees money emerging as a numéraire commodity prior to the emergence of capitalism and mutating into a measure of exchange value with the emergence of capitalism.

Interpreting Sraffa conceiving of money as a token of the numéraire commodity also precludes him being interpreted as seeing money prices **formed** *prior* to money being put into the process of circulation to circulate commodities with determinate money prices. This is because, as argued above, interpreting Sraffa conceiving of money in this manner, i.e., as a token of the numéraire commodity, requires interpreting him conceiving of money's primary and defining function as that of medium of exchange and the money prices of commodities formed in the context of money's performance of this function in the process of exchange.

Lastly, the problems with Sraffa's implicit explanation of the **magnitude** of the money price of the commodity follow from the problems noted with his implicit conception of it and, as is to be expected, parallel those noted with respect to the explanations of the magnitude of money price in the works of Smith and Ricardo. To begin with, like Smith and Ricardo, Sraffa's implicit conception of the money price of the commodity prevents him from being interpreted as explaining its magnitude as the magnitude of its money exchange value. Instead, it requires him to explain this magnitude as the magnitude of its numéraire commodity exchange value, with money a token of the numéraire commodity. This in turn requires Sraffa to be interpreted as seeing changes in the magnitude of value of the commodity having a bearing on the magnitude of the money price of the commodity *via* its impact on the magnitude of its numéraire commodity exchange value, and not directly.

Second, Sraffa's implicit conception of the money price of the commodity precludes him from being interpreted as explaining changes in the relative money prices of commodities taking place in the context of changes in the aggregate money price level. This is because it requires him, in the manner of Smith and Ricardo, to conceive of the relative money price of the commodity as its numéraire commodity price where money is a token of the numéraire commodity, and the aggregate money price level as the exogenously determined quantity of money used to facilitate the exchange of commodities for one another relative to the quantity of these commodities, not the aggregate of the money prices of individual commodities. Accordingly, as for Smith and Ricardo, Sraffa cannot be interpreted as seeing the factors having a bearing on changes in the relative price level having a bearing on changes in the aggregate money prices of all commodities, and *vice versa*.

Lastly, and most importantly from the perspective of Marx's analysis, Sraffa's implicit explanation of the magnitude of the money price of the commodity requires him denying that changes in the productivity of labour have any bearing on it and, therefore, on either the relative money prices of commodities or the aggregate money price level. This, of course, follows from Sraffa's conception of the value of the commodity that seeks to bypass the labour theory of value in the manner of Smith but in a way that does not fall foul of the logical problems besetting the latter's concept of value.

From the perspective of Marx's analysis the source of the problems with Sraffa's implicit explanation of the money price of the commodity, like that of Smith and Ricardo, is his conception of the value of the commodity and its link with money. Sraffa's conception of the value of the commodity, as the quantity of the numéraire commodity used directly and indirectly in its production, requires him to deny the productivity of labour has any bearing on this value and prevents him from seeing it formed in the context of the use of money to denote the general exchange value of the commodity. This in turn causes Sraffa to have a mistaken implicit conception of money and corresponding mistaken conception and explanation of the money price of the commodity. The most obvious manifestation of the problematic nature of this implied conception and explanation of the money price of the commodity in Sraffa's work is that it requires him to explain changes in the relative money prices of commodities taking place independently of changes in the aggregate money price level, and to deny changes in the productivity of labour having a bearing on changes in either.

References

Bellofiore, R. (2012). The "tiresome objector" and old moor: A renewal of the debate on Marx after Sraffa based on the unpublished material at the Wren library. *Cambridge Journal of Economics, 36*(6), 1385–1399.

Bellofiore, R. (2014) 'The Loneliness of the Long Distance Thinker: Sraffa, Marx, and the Critique of Economic Theory' in Bellofiore, R. and Carter, S. (eds.), pp. 198–240.

Bellofiore, R., & Carter, S. (Eds.). (2014). *Towards a New Understanding of Sraffa: Insights from Archival Research*. Palgrave Macmillan.

Blankenburg, S., Arena, R. and Wilkinson, F. (2012). 'Piero Sraffa and "the true object of economics": The role of the unpublished manuscripts', *Cambridge Journal of Economics*, 36(6), 1267–90.

Deleplace, G. (2014). 'The essentiality of money in the Sraffa papers' in Bellofiore, R. and Carter, S. (eds.), pp. 139–66.

Hahnel, R. (2017). *Radical Political Economy: Sraffa versus Marx*. Routledge.

Hayek, F. A. (1931). *Prices and Production*. Augustus M. Kelly.

Hodgson, G. (1981). Money and the Sraffa system. *Australian Economic Papers, 20*(36), 83–95.

Hodgson, G. (1982). *Capitalism, Value and Exploitation: A Radical Theory*. Martin Robertson.

Kurz, H. D. (2011). Keynes, Sraffa and the latter's "secret skepticism." In H. D. Kurz & N. Salvadori (Eds.), *Revisiting Classical Economics: Studies in Long-period Analysis* (pp. 102–122). Routledge.

Kurz, H. D. (2012). Don't treat too ill my Piero! Interpreting Sraffa's papers. *Cambridge Journal of Economics, 36*(6), 1535–1569.

Kurz, H. D., & Salvadori, N. (2005). Representing the production and circulation of commodities in material terms: On Sraffa's objectivism. *Review of Political Economy, 17*(3), 413–441.

Nicholas, H. (2011). *Marx's Theory of Price and its Modern Rivals*. Palgrave Macmillan.

Roncaglia, A. (1978). *Sraffa and the Theory of Prices, translated from Italian by Kregel, J.A.* John Wiley & Sons.

Porta, P. L. (2012). Piero Sraffa's early views on classical political economy. *Cambridge Journal of Economics, 36*(6), 1357–1383.

Sinha, A. (2012). Listen to Sraffa's silences: A new interpretation of Sraffa's "Production of Commodities." *Cambridge Journal of Economics, 36*(6), 1323–1339.

Sraffa, P. (1932). Dr. Hayek on money and capital. *Economic Journal, 42*(165), 42–53.

Sraffa, P. (1960). *Production of Commodities by Means of Commodities*. Cambridge University Press.

Steedman, I. (1977). *Marx after Sraffa*. New Left Books.

CHAPTER 6

Post-Keynesian Explanations of Money Price

6.1 Introduction

The Post-Keynesian (PK) school emerged in the mid-1970s as a collection of disparate approaches with a common antipathy towards Neoclassical economics that subsequently morphed into a coherent body of economic thought comprising several distinctive strands.[1] It is generally acknowledged the foundations of the school are the writings of J.M. Keynes, especially his *General Theory*, and those of M. Kalecki between 1933 and 1970, as well as selected writings of certain of the disciples of Keynes and Kalecki including J. Robinson, N. Kaldor, P. Davidson, and H. Minsky. There has been an on-going debate among PKs as to who should and shouldn't be included in the PK fold.[2] Of particular importance for the present work is whether or not Sraffa and Austrians should be included under the PK umbrella. In what follows I will adopt my practice in Nicholas (2011) and exclude them from the PK fold, considering the work of Sraffa in a separate chapter (viz., Chapter 5) and those of Austrians in the context of a consideration of the Neoclassical school (viz., Chapter 8).

[1] See Dunn (2000, 2008), Nicholas (2011, 2014) for an elaboration of these strands.

[2] See Dunn (2000, 2008) for an elaboration of this debate.

H. Nicholas, *Explorations in Marx's Theory of Price—Why Marx Is Still Relevant for Understanding the Modern Economy*,
https://doi.org/10.1057/978-1-137-56564-8_6

6.2 Object and Approach

The focus of PK economics is aggregate output and employment, with aggregate demand seen as the fundamental driver of these *via* its impact on investment.[3] Considerable attention is also accorded to income distribution and its bearing on aggregate demand.[4] PKs draw a distinction between short and long periods of time when explaining economic phenomena, with most modern PKs seeing this distinction analogous to that between cyclical and trend movements in these phenomena and focusing on the short period.[5] When explaining economic phenomena PKs emphasise; the behaviour of entrepreneurs and their propensity to invest, the behaviour of capitalists and their desire for liquidity, and the behaviour of individuals with respect to their propensity to consume. It is in the context of their explanation of aggregate output and employment that PKs locate their explanation of the money prices of commodities. As I will expand on below, PKs see aggregate demand having no direct impact on the aggregate money price level, only an indirect one *via* its impact on the money wage rate when unemployment falls to very low levels.

PKs argue that when explaining economic phenomena, including the prices of commodities, it is epistemologically inappropriate to abstract from phenomena such as production, capital, money, and aggregate supply–demand imbalances. They argue that abstraction from production in the first instance causes the economy being studied to be conceived of as a barter economy in the manner of Neoclassical economists.[6] Individuals exchanging products in such economies are seen as in effect hunter-gatherers. Following Keynes, PKs further argue that to conceive of the economy as production-based while abstracting from capital and money is to explain it as essentially a cooperative economic system in which factors of production are rewarded by dividing up the output of their cooperative efforts in agreed proportions.[7] Lastly, also following

[3] J.E. King (2015, p. xiv) states that "Stripped down to its bare essentials, Post Keynesian economics rests on the principle of effective demand; in capitalist economies output and employment are normally constrained by aggregate demand".

[4] See Eichner (1979), Holt and Pressman (2001).

[5] See Eichner (1979).

[6] See King (2015).

[7] See Rotheim (1981).

Keynes, PKs argue that including money in such an economic system, and seeing it facilitating exchange in the manner of the Classical economists (such as Marx), is to explain 'a neutral economy' where factors are paid in money instead of commodities "provided that all of them accept the money merely as a temporary convenience, with a view to spending the whole of it forthwith on purchasing such part of current output as they chose" (Rotheim, 1981, pp. 575–576). For most PKs, as for Keynes, such an economy is also a cooperative economy but one where money is in effect a veil. Instead, what is required is the conception of the capitalist system as one characterised by the ubiquitous use of money and credit for the purposes of expanding money wealth in the form of money capital; a conception of the economic system that Keynes refers to as "an entrepreneurial" economic system.[8]

From the perspective of Marx's analysis, the problem with the PK objective of analysis is that it stems from the narrow initial purpose of Keynes (and Kalecki), i.e., the justification of activist fiscal and monetary policies with a view to boosting aggregate demand and ending the protracted economic stagnation and chronic unemployment gripping the advanced countries in the 1930s. This focus causes PKs to have a distorted view of the dynamics of the economic system as a whole, including the movement of prices. It causes them to focus on phenomenal forms created by competition, the forms that are manifest in the cyclical movement of the system.

The problem with the PK failure to abstract from capital, money, and supply–demand imbalances in the first instance is it causes them to have a superficial understanding of these and, therefore, the essence of the observed cyclical phenomena. It causes PKs to see capital as an expanding sum of money and not an expanding sum of value that assumes the forms of money and commodities in its circuit.[9] It causes PKs to mistakenly conceive of money as value and, correspondingly, commodities as intrinsically valueless entities that only acquire values in their exchange with

[8] King (2015, p. 6) notes that in an early draft of *General Theory* Keynes used Marx's representation of the capitalist circulation process to explain why money matters and the purpose of the production process is the generation and appropriation of a money profit.

[9] See Nicholas (forthcoming) for an elaboration of this point.

money. Lastly, the failure of PKs to abstract from supply–demand imbalances causes, or even requires, them to conceive of the phenomena to be explained in the first instance as cyclical and not trend phenomena, tacitly denying the latter are averages of the former.

6.3 Post-Keynesian Economics as Ideology

From the perspective of Marx's analysis, PKs can be seen as adopting the viewpoint of the entrepreneur as a manager, notwithstanding the apparent radical tenor of some of the adherents of the approach, particularly in respect of their focus on income distribution. Keynes even conceives of entrepreneurs as akin to workers who contribute to the net product. He argues; "It is preferable to regard labour, including, of course, the personal services of the entrepreneur and his assistants, as the sole factor of production …" (1973, pp. 213–214). Consequently most PKs, like Keynes, are reluctant to attribute economic ruptures to the drive of entrepreneurs to accumulate, seeing these instead as the result of shortfalls in aggregate demand due to increases in income inequality or the speculative behaviour of money capitalists. The current attention paid by PKs to 'global financial cycles' being one of the manifestations of this latter tendency. Another is the attention paid to the problem of 'financialisation'. Even when it is accepted that the behaviour of productive capitalists may also have a role to play in the cyclical movement of the system, this role is downplayed. For example, Dow (1991, pp. 191–192) argues:

> The instability of capitalism arises from the motive of monetary accumulation: the desire of producers and financial investors to amass wealth for its own sake. It must be said that this motivation is more muted for producers, particularly owner-managers. But for the large publicly owned corporations the goals of management must be tempered by the desire for increased profits on the part of the shareholders.

As with other approaches, it is readily apparent there has also been an increasing tendency for adherents of the PK approach to adopt mathematical presentations of their arguments and econometric analyses in support of these. This is in spite of many PKs recognising the importance of concrete historical analyses of time-series and cross-section data to take into account continuing changes in the institutional environment and information provided by 'outliers'. King suggests this tendency towards mathematical presentations of arguments and econometric analyses is at least "in part a question of career advancement (or sheer survival) with PKs using econometrics as a form of rhetoric to demonstrate that they are technically as competent as mainstream economists" (2015, p.41). However, there are good reasons to believe this drift towards mathematics and econometric analyses is, as for Neoclassicals, more likely the product of attempts to mask the obvious theoretical flaws in their analyses. I will elaborate on certain of these flaws below and others in Nicholas (forthcoming).

6.4 Production and Value of the Commodity

6.4.1 Production

PKs conceive of the production of commodities in capitalism as undertaken by the entrepreneur with the aid of both 'prime' and 'non-prime' inputs. Prime inputs are non-produced inputs that enter either directly or indirectly into the production of all commodities. They comprise the labour input and natural resources or raw materials. PKs are vague about what is to be included in the labour input, with most of them denying, in opposition to Keynes, that it includes the personal services of entrepreneurs and their assistants. Most PKs follow Keynes in denying capital can be treated as a factor of production in the manner of labour (and natural resources). Robinson argues Keynes's purpose in placing emphasis on labour services as the sole factor input is to argue it is misleading to treat capital as a factor of production on the same footing as labour.[10] PKs see non-prime inputs comprising intermediate commodities and the depreciation charges required to replace fixed capital, but differ with one another over whether the depreciation charges are part of costs or part of the mark-up on costs.[11]

PKs conceive of the process of production as in essence money- or credit-based, involving the outlay of money with a view to producing commodities of a greater money value than the money outlaid. Wray (2010, p. 5) describes the process as follows:

[10] Robinson (1968).

[11] I will expand on this in Nicholas (forthcoming).

> *...the production process itself begins with money on the expectation of ending up with more money (M-C-C'-M'). Not only is production required to result in sales for money, but it must begin with money. Production is thoroughly monetary. It cannot begin with commodities, because the commodities must have been produced for sale for money. Analysis must also therefore begin with money.*

PKs also conceive of the process of production involving 'forward contracting', with the most important of these contracts being the purchase of labour services at the outset of production when money is paid to labour for the future delivery of their services. Davidson (1978b, p. 58) argues:

> *Production takes time, and hence in a market-oriented economy most production transactions along the non-integrated chain of firms involve forward contracts. For example, the hiring of factor* inputs *(especially labour) and the purchase of materials for the production of goods will normally require forward contracting if the production process is to be planned efficiently.*

From the perspective of Marx's analysis the problems with the PK explanation of production begin with its **conception.** Like all other approaches, PKs do not recognise the social nature of the production process as one involving the cooperative expenditure of labour time in this process. The clearest manifestation of this in a capitalist setting is their conception of natural resources as a prime input alongside labour.

Following Keynes, PKs see the **entrepreneur** as a manager and not the owner of the firm. It is a conception of the entrepreneur that causes most PKs to implicitly, if not explicitly, conceive of capitalism as 'managerial capitalism'.[12] In fact, PKs see entrepreneurs as workers with specialised skills, who appropriate *profits* in the form of a wage. The owners of the firms, 'the capitalists', are conceived of as rentiers who appropriate *interest* in proportion to the capital they 'lend' to the entrepreneurs. That is to say, the shareholders of companies are seen as rentiers who lend money to the entrepreneurs in return for interest that assumes the form of a *dividend*. PKs do not see that the value of the share held by shareholders changes with the profits appropriated by the firm, unlike the value

[12] Galbraith (1967), Wood (1975).

of money that represents interest-bearing capital.[13] PKs tacitly see the wages of entrepreneurs, like the wages of ordinary workers, determined in the labour market,[14] although it is accepted that the remuneration of entrepreneurs is in many cases not commensurate with implied skill differentials. What PKs do not see in this regard is that those they refer to as entrepreneurs are the senior managers in capitalist firms whose wages are deductions from the profits belonging to the owners of the firm, i.e., the owners of capital, and result from the expenditure of labour time by workers when they add use value to the product.[15] Consequently, like Neoclassicals, PKs are unable to explain the formation and movement of the general rate of profit as distinct from the rate of interest. In fact, PKs deny, and indeed must deny, the existence of a general rate of profit in capitalist economies. As I will argue below, the PK conception of the entrepreneur as a manager and corresponding denial of the formation of a general rate of profit, stems in large part from Keynes' attempt to bypass Marx's labour theory of value explanation of price, requiring him to explain profits as corresponding to the labour time expended by the entrepreneur as a worker with specialised skills.

PKs are also unclear about the nature of the **prime inputs** into production, and in particular the labour input. What PKs, like most other approaches, do not see is the labour input purchased by the producer with the wage is not certain specific labour services but labour power as a commodity whose price is determined like any other commodity by its value. PKs do not see the money wage paid by the producer to obtain this labour power is linked to the prices of wage goods, and more generally the aggregate money price level. It is not independent of these. I will return to this point below. For those PKs conceiving of prime inputs including natural resources the question is why these are conceived of as prime inputs in the manner of the labour input when, unlike the labour input, they cannot be argued to directly enter the production of all commodities.

PKs conceive of the essence of the **process of production** as involving the expenditure of money, notwithstanding the importance they accord to the labour input. For PKs there would be no production of commodities without the expenditure of money at the start of the production

[13] See Nicholas (forthcoming) for an elaboration of this point.

[14] See Robinson (1971, p. 30).

[15] See Nicholas (forthcoming) for a further discussion of this point.

process. PKs do not see that the characteristic of all modes of production, including capitalism, is the expenditure of labour time. What differs in capitalism is that the process of production is facilitated by the outlay of money on all inputs, including the labour input. This should not be taken to mean, however, that the essence of the production process in capitalism is the expenditure of money and not labour time. As I will argue below, the PK conception of the production process is largely attributable to their explanation of the price of the commodity in capitalism as the money required for its production. For PKs, it is money, and not labour time, that is the source of the value of the commodity.

Lastly, like the Classical economists, PKs ignore the **commodities produced** to replace what is used up in the production of the commodity. This is because their focus is on the commodities purchased with the incomes received in the context of the production of the commodities and not the commodities that are required to reproduce the system as a whole. What PKs are ignoring here is the production of the commodities purchased with the revenues appropriated by firms that do not correspond to the incomes appropriated.

6.4.2 Value of the Commodity

Like most other economists, PKs do not formally distinguish between the value and exchange value of the commodity, although when explaining the exchange values of commodities they too implicitly distinguish between them. Specifically, PKs implicitly see the value of the commodity as the money outlaid by a price leader or monopoly producer on the means of production and labour inputs required to undertake production, and the exchange value of the commodity as the quantity of money the commodity commands in the process of circulation. Following Keynes, PKs conceive of the measure of the value of the commodity as the quantity of money needed to purchase a unit of labour—the unit money wage.[16]

Given that PKs do not formally distinguish between the value and exchange value of the commodity, it is hardly surprising they pay no attention to how commodities acquire values historically, or how they are formed in the context of the reproduction of commodities. However,

[16] See Robinson in Eichner (ed.) (1979, pp. xiii–xiv), Wray (2010, p. 4).

as with other approaches that are similarly vague in this regard, these can be deduced from their conceptions of production and explanation of the exchange value of the commodity. These suggest PKs see commodities acquiring values historically with the emergence of wage labour, and the values of commodities formed prior to their production, in the context of the wage bargaining process.

Lastly, PKs implicitly explain the magnitude of the value of the commodity by the quantity of money that is outlaid on the labour and means of production used in its production. PKs see the means of production comprising fixed capital and intermediate commodities (i.e., those that are deemed to be non-long lasting). There are differences between PKs regarding the treatment of fixed capital, and in particular the depreciation charges pertaining to it. Most PKs follow Robinson in seeing these charges as part of the profit mark-up on costs, arguing that these magnitudes cannot be known *a priori*.[17] A few PKs, those referred to as adopting a 'full cost' approach, see depreciation charges as part of the means of production on which the profit mark-up is levied. They argue that entrepreneurs typically add a depreciation charge to their general unit costs when setting prices.[18] PKs see the money wage determined independently of the money prices of wage goods and, more generally, independently of the aggregate money price level.[19] Although the consensus among PKs is that the profit mark-up on costs does not correspond to an economy-wide average rate of profit, there is considerable disagreement between them regarding its actual determination. Some PKs, following Kalecki, see the profit mark-up in different sectors determined by the relative monopoly power of firms in these sectors. Others see it determined by the particular goals companies set themselves (e.g., refinancing needs).[20] A few, those adopting a Sraffian approach, see it corresponding to an economy-wide average rate of profit.[21] Since the profit mark-up is on money costs, the focus of PKs in the explanation of the magnitude of value of the commodity is on the explanation of these money costs. Moreover, since the means of production are themselves

[17] See Robinson (1971, pp. 30–31).

[18] See Lee (1994).

[19] See Moore (1979, p. 125).

[20] See Lavoie (2001, pp. 25–26).

[21] See Lavoie (2001, pp. 26–27).

commodities, the emphasis in the final instance is on money wage costs and in particular the money wage rate.

When explaining the magnitude of money wage costs most PKs follow Keynes in distinguishing between short and long periods of time in the manner of his mentor, Alfred Marshall, focusing in the first instance, and indeed for the most part, on the short period. The short period is a period of time during which changes in the productivity of labour are seen as limited and having an indeterminate impact on the value of the commodity. This is because the short period is assumed to be a period of time during which the quantity of long-lasting inputs and, therefore, all other inputs including labour used in the production of commodities, can be assumed to be fixed. Since this implies the quantity of aggregate output over this period can also be assumed to be relatively fixed, it suggests changes in the productivity of labour over the period are limited, initially rising and subsequently falling as argued by Marshall. This allows PKs, like Keynes, to conceive of changes in the magnitude of value determined solely by changes in the money wage rate over the short period,[22] only bringing in changes in the productivity of labour over the long period, by way of offsetting the impact of changes in the money wage rate.

The problems with the PK explanation of the value of the commodity from the perspective of Marx's analysis begin with their implicit **conception** of its value as the money incomes appropriated in the process of the production of the commodity, where money commands a certain quantity of the labour input. The first problem with this conception of the value of the commodity from the perspective of Marx's analysis is that it causes PKs to lose sight of the *source of the value of the commodity*, seeing this source as a certain quantity of money, viz., the money appropriated as incomes in the process of the production of the commodity. It causes them to lose sight of labour, and in particular the expenditure of labour time as socially necessary labour time, as the source of the value of the commodity. It is pertinent to note in this context Marx's comments on Malthus's similar conception of the value of the commodity to that of PKs;

> *In other words: the value of a commodity is equal to the sum of money which the purchaser must pay, and this sum is best estimated in terms of the amount of ordinary labour which can be bought with it. But what determines the*

[22] See Keynes (1973, p. 249).

> *sum of money is, naturally, not explained. It is the quite ordinary idea of the matter that is prevalent in everyday life. A mere triviality expressed in high-flown language. In other words, it means nothing more than that cost-price and value are identical, a confusion which, in the case of Adam Smith, and still more in the case of Ricardo, contradicts their real analysis, but which Malthus elevates into a law. It is the conception of value held by the philistine who, being a captive of competition, only knows the outward appearance of value.* (1972, p. 32)

A second problem with the PK conception of the value of the commodity, and one that follows from the preceding problem, is it causes them to conflate the value of the commodity with its exchange value. This is because the money commanded by the commodity must logically equal the money commanded as incomes in the production of the commodity, i.e., the money outlaid to purchase the labour input and the money profit mark-up on unit costs.

The problems with the PK conception of the **measure** of the value of the commodity follow from the problems with its conception. Most importantly in this regard is that the conflation of the value of the commodity with its exchange value causes PKs to correspondingly conflate their respective measures. It causes PKs to implicitly conceive of the measure of the value of the commodity as a certain quantity of money, which is also the measure of the exchange value or money price of the commodity (see below).

The PK conception of the value of the commodity causes PKs to implicitly see commodities **acquiring** values (money incomes) historically at the same time, not before, they acquire exchange values. In fact, the PK conception of the value of the commodity requires them to see commodities acquiring values historically with capitalism and the use of money to pay wages. From the perspective of Marx's analysis, what PKs do not see is that products acquire values when they are produced in the context of a division of labour, prior to the appearance of money and money wage labour. They do not see the money exchange value of the commodity is the form the value of the commodity assumes when its reproduction is facilitated by money-based exchange, and that money wage labour is the form the labour input assumes in this context (see below).

The PK conception of the value of the commodity also causes them to see the value of the commodity **formed** prior to production, in the context of the outlay of money borrowed from capitalists to purchase the means of production and the labour input. PKs do not see that the values of commodities in capitalism are formed after their production, and not prior to, or even in, the process of their production. They do not see that they are formed in the context of the use of money by producers to denote the general exchange values of their commodities just prior to putting them into the process of circulation, and not the use of money to purchase the means of production and/or the labour input. I will return to this point below when considering the PK explanation of the money price of the commodity against a backdrop of their explanation of the functions of money.

The problems with the PK explanation of the **magnitude** of value of the commodity follow from the above. To begin with, the PK conflation of the value of the commodity with its exchange value causes them to conflate the explanation of the magnitude of the value of the commodity with that of its exchange value. This is manifest in PK explanations of both primarily by the money wage rate.

Second, their explanation of the magnitude of the value (exchange value) of the commodity requires PKs to abstract from changes in the productivity of labour to permit a focus on changes in the money wage rate when explaining changes in unit money costs by changes in unit money wage costs. For PKs unit money wage costs are determined by the quantity of the labour input multiplied by the money wage rate. Assuming the labour input to be fixed allows PKs to see changes in unit money wage costs resulting from changes in the money wage rate. Following Keynes, PKs justify this assumption by adopting Alfred Marshall's distinction between different periods of time, and focusing on the short period, arguing this is the most relevant period for policy makers to focus on. As noted above, Marshall's short period is a period of time over which the quantity of the capital input is assumed to be given. Since PKs see factor inputs used in fixed proportions to one another, the assumption of a fixed quantity of capital used in the process of production over this period translates into a fixed quantity of both the labour employed and aggregate output produced, allowing PKs to justify the assumption of a given productivity of labour over this period. When PKs bring the impact of changes in the productivity of labour into their explanation of the magnitude of values of commodities over the long period, they see these as offsetting the impact of increases in the money wage rate on this magnitude. What PKs do not see is that the productivity of labour pertains to the quantity of labour time expended in the production of any commodity. This can, and typically does, change without any change in the quantity of labour employed.

Third, the PK explanation of the magnitude of the value of the commodity by the money wage rate requires them to conceive of changes in the values of commodities as changes in their economy-wide relative values that take place in the context of changes in their absolute values. However, the implication of the changes in the wage rate for changes in the relative values of commodities causes PKs to tacitly deny this impact. That is, it causes them to deny the consequences of changes in the money wage rate for changes in relative magnitudes of values of all commodities while admitting to their impact on the absolute magnitudes of values of all commodities. This denial is required for PKs to avoid conceiving of increases in the absolute values of all commodities accompanied by continuous increases in the relative values (and, therefore, prices) of commodities produced in sectors having more labour-intensive production techniques, unless it is assumed that there are continuous increases in profit rates in sectors producing commodities with less labour-intensive techniques.

Lastly, the PK embodied money wage cost explanation of the magnitude of the value of the commodity requires them to conceive of the value transferred from the commodity means of production to the commodity output as the layered money wage cost of producing the means of production used directly and indirectly in the production of the commodity, and not the money outlaid on the means of production. What PKs do not see in this regard is that when producers set the money prices of their commodities they take into account the money needed to repurchase of the means of production (and labour power) and not what has been outlaid in the purchase of the means of production.

Keynes' Labour Theory of Value

In the *General Theory* Keynes gives the impression he distinguishes between the value and exchange value of the commodity, conceiving of the former as the labour required for the production of the commodity where this labour includes that expended by the entrepreneur. He argues:

> *I sympathise, therefore, with the pre-classical doctrine that everything is produced by labour, aided by what used to be called art and is now called technique, by natural resources which are free or cost a rent according to their scarcity or abundance, and by the results of past labour, embodied in assets,*

> *which also command a price according to their scarcity or abundance. It is preferable to regard labour, including of course, the personal services of the entrepreneur and his assistants, as the sole factor of* production… (Keynes, 1973, pp. 213–214)

This conception of the value of the commodity implies Keynes sees; the measure of the value of the commodity as a certain quantity of labour that includes the labour of the entrepreneur, commodities acquiring values historically when they are produced with the use of labour, these values formed at the outset of production, and the magnitude of the value of the commodity fundamentally determined by the quantity of labour used in its production where this labour includes the labour of the entrepreneur.

Keynes' purpose in conceiving of the labour expended in the production of the commodity including the labour of the entrepreneur would seem to be to avoid having a vacuous explanation of profit, as simply a mark-up on wage costs. The consequence of him including the labour of the entrepreneur as part of the labour expended in the production of the commodity, however, is that it requires him to conceive of profits as the wages of the entrepreneur, where these wages too are determined in the labour market and reduced to equivalence with those of ordinary workers in the same way as the wages of skilled labour—as multiples of the wages of ordinary workers. PKs have understandably been reluctant to explicitly embrace Keynes' explanation of the magnitude of the value (price of production) of the commodity, even over the long period. The price of this reluctance has been a vacuous explanation of profit and implicit adoption of what is in effect a monetary theory of value.

6.5 Exchange and Exchange Value of the Commodity

6.5.1 Exchange

PKs deny that it is meaningful to conceive of the process of exchange as the exchange of commodities for one another, i.e., C–C', even when this exchange is mediated by money, i.e., C-M-C'.[23] Instead, for PKs the

[23] Martin (2014, p. 10) quotes a leading anthropologist of money, George Dalton, arguing that "Barter in the strict sense of moneyless market exchange, has never been a

process of exchange needs to be conceived of as M-C-M', where M' is a greater sum of money than M.[24] For Keynes it is this process of exchange that characterises the capitalist economy. For many PKs it is this process of exchange as one additionally involving credit and 'forward contracting' that characterises the modern capitalist economy.[25] Most PKs see the process of money- or credit-based exchange facilitating the reproduction of the commodity in the context of the expansion of money wealth. They see this process as characteristic of the capitalist mode of production, but accept that the exchange of commodities for one another can be found in pre-capitalist economic systems.

The problems with the PK explanations of exchange from the perspective of Marx's analysis begin with their **conception** of this process. Although PKs see the process of exchange as the exchange of the commodity for money, they do not see that the money commanded by the commodity in the process of exchange represents general exchange value, or that money comes to represent general exchange value because of its use by producers to denote the general exchange values of their commodities prior to putting them into circulation. Instead, PKs see the money acquired in the process of exchange as what represents command over the labour input, that comes to represent command over the labour input in the context of the wage bargain. There is no reason to suppose what is used to purchase the labour input represents general exchange value. I will return to this point below in the context of a consideration of the PK conception of money.

PKs also do not see the **purpose** of exchange as facilitating the reproduction of the commodity. Instead, they see its purpose as the recovery (and expansion) of the quantity of money outlaid to undertake the production of the commodity. They do not see the exchange of the commodity that facilitates the reproduction of the commodity is C-M and M-C', where C-M is the sale of the commodity for money and M-C' the use of money to repurchase the commodities needed to reproduce the commodity inputs, including labour power. It is not M-C-M' or even

quantitatively important or dominant mode of transaction in any past or present economic system about which we have hard information".

[24] See Rotheim (1981), Wray (2010).

[25] See Davidson (1978b).

M-C and C'-M' *per se*. PKs do not see, except formally, that the augmentation of money wealth takes place in the context of the expansion of material wealth.

PKs who place emphasis on credit mediating the process of exchange do not see the essential nature of the exchange process is the transfer of ownership of the commodity between contracting parties. This transfer is not a characteristic of credit-based transactions *per se*. Commodities bought on credit remain the property of the seller until the payment of money to settle the outstanding debt cements the transfer.

PKs cannot admit to money based exchange **emerging** prior to the emergence of capitalism since, as I will elaborate on below, it requires them to accept that money assumes a commodity form prior to its assumption of a credit form, and that the nature of the process of money-based exchange changes with the emergence of capitalism.

Lastly, although PKs deny the process of exchange in a capitalist economy can be conceived of as in essence one of **barter**, they base this denial on the necessity for the commodity to be exchanged for money and not other commodities. PKs do not see that the reason the process of exchange in capitalism cannot be conceived of as one of barter is because producers set the money prices of their commodities before putting them into circulation to be exchanged for money and not other commodities. Indeed, this *lacuna* in PK analyses means there is in principle nothing to stop adherents of the approach seeing money prices formed in the process of the exchange of commodities in the manner of Classical and Neoclassical approaches.

6.5.2 *Exchange Value of the Commodity*

PKs conceive of the exchange value of the commodity as the quantity of money commanded by it in the process of exchange. That is to say, they conceive of the exchange value of the commodity as its money exchange value or money price, and not, as for Classical and Neoclassical economists, its commodity exchange value or relative price. As noted above, PKs see the purpose of the money price of the commodity the recovery of the money outlaid by producers along with the appropriation of a profit. They emphasise, in opposition to Neoclassical economists, that this purpose is not to provide market signals to producers and consumers.[26] Since, as argued above, PKs follow Keynes in seeing the quantity of money a commodity commands in the process of exchange representing a certain quantity of labour, they also follow him implicitly, if not explicitly, in seeing the measure of the exchange value of the commodity as the quantity of money that is used to purchase a unit of labour; the unit money wage.[27]

Although PKs pay little, if any, attention to how commodities acquire exchange values historically, this can be deduced from their conceptions of the process of exchange and exchange value of the commodity. These suggest they see commodities acquiring exchange values historically when money is used to purchase the labour input. PKs are generally more forthcoming about the formation of the exchange values of commodities, seeing this taking place prior to commodities being put into the process of circulation, and even prior to the process of production.[28] It warrants remarking in this context that Keynes tacitly sees the exchange value (money price) of the commodity formed in the process of its circulation, referring to what is formed before this as the "supply price" of the commodity.[29]

Lastly, in keeping with their explanation of the magnitude of the value of the commodity, PKs distinguish between short and long periods as well as absolute and relative magnitudes when explaining the magnitude of the exchange value of the commodity. As noted above, the basis for the distinction between the two time periods is the assumed relative fixity of long-lasting means of production over each period; its perfect fixity over the short period and variability over the long period. The absolute magnitude of the exchange value of a commodity refers to its money exchange value *per se* while its relative exchange value refers to its money exchange value relative to that of another commodity. Focusing in the first instance on the short period, PKs explain changes in the magnitude of the absolute exchange value of the commodity over this period by changes in the money wage rate, and changes in the relative exchange value of the commodity by changes in the relative demand for the commodity. Extending this analysis to the long period, PKs explain changes in the

[26] See Kaldor (1985).

[27] See Robinson (1979), Wray (2010).

[28] See for example Lee (2003, p. 285).

[29] See Keynes (1973, pp. 25, 68, 328).

magnitudes of the absolute exchange value of the commodity by changes in the money wage rate offset to a certain extent by changes in the economy-wide productivity of labour. They explain changes in the relative exchange values of commodities over this period by changes in relative profit mark-ups in different sectors. It warrants remarking here, however, that PKs are not particularly forthcoming when it comes to the explanations of changes in the relative exchange values of commodities over either the short or long periods.

Some confusion is caused by the various PK conceptions of costs on which the profit mark-up is based. As noted above, some PKs see the costs as prime costs, comprising the money outlaid on labour and raw materials, while others see the costs comprising all direct inputs into production, including the costs of intermediate inputs and depreciation charges but excluding raw materials unless they represent direct inputs into the production process.[30]

The problems with the PK analysis of the exchange value of the commodity from the perspective of Marx's analysis begin with its **conception**. Although, from the perspective of Marx's analysis, PKs correctly conceive of the exchange value of the commodity as its money and not commodity exchange value, i.e., its money price, unlike Marx, they do not see that the money price of the commodity as can assume a commodity form. PKs are not able to conceive of money prices of commodities being, for example, gold prices. I will expand on this below. Second, PKs do not see the money price of the commodity indicating the general exchange value of the commodity. In fact, their conception of money causes them to implicitly see money prices indicating the particular exchange value of the commodity; the quantity of the labour input it can be used to purchase. Lastly, PKs do not see the money price of the commodity as *the form* which the value of the commodity assumes. This is because, as argued above, they collapse the value of the commodity into its exchange value. Keynes' conception of the value of the commodity, as the quantity of money commanded as incomes by owners of factor inputs used in the production of the commodity, does not overcome this conflation. It will be recalled Keynes conceives of the labour input as including the

[30] Lee (1999, p. 144) argues the inclusion of raw materials in prime costs in PK explanations of the magnitude of the exchange value of a commodity is a legacy of Kalecki's explanation of this magnitude.

labour of the entrepreneur, and profit as the wage appropriated by the entrepreneur.

The problems with the PK conception of the **measure** of the exchange value of the commodity from the perspective of Marx's analysis follow from the problems noted above with its conception. For one thing, their conception of the value of the commodity precludes PKs from conceiving of the measure of its exchange value as the *form* of the measure of its value. Rather, their conflation of the value of the commodity with its exchange value causes PKs to conflate their respective measures, these being a certain quantity of money. Moreover, the PK conception of the exchange value of the commodity precludes them from conceiving of its measure as representing general exchangeable worth in the sense of being what is used by the producer to purchase any and all commodities. Rather, the measure of the exchange value of the commodity is implicitly seen by PKs as representing particular exchangeable worth, viz., what is used to purchase a certain quantity of the labour input.

Although PKs see commodities **acquiring** exchange values or money prices historically with the emergence of the capitalist mode of production, they mistakenly see this as due to the emergence of money wage labour *per se*. They do not see it as more fundamentally when large numbers of producers use money to denote the general exchange values of their commodities with a view to being able to repurchase all the commodity inputs, including labour power, required for the reproduction of their commodities. PKs also do not see that the precondition of commodities acquiring exchange values historically is that the products of labour possess values, i.e., commodities are produced in the context of a division of labour.

PKs do not see is that the exchange values of commodities are **formed** after the production of commodities, prior to them being put into the process of circulation. Again, this is because PKs do not see the exchange values of commodities formed when money is used by producers to denote the general exchange values of their commodities before putting them into the process of circulation. Instead, they see the exchange values of commodities formed when producers outlay money to hire factors of production, in particular the labour factor of production.

The problems with the PK explanation of the **magnitude** of the exchange value of the commodity follow from the above. To begin with, the PK explanation of the magnitude of the money exchange value of the commodity requires them to see changes in the money wage rate having a bearing on only the *absolute* money exchange value of the commodity, not also its *relative* money exchange value, in the same way it requires them to see changes in the money wage rate only having a bearing on the *absolute* values of commodities and not also their *relative* values. This is because for PKs to see changes in the money wage rate having a bearing on the relative money exchange values of commodities requires them seeing the money exchange values of commodities produced with relatively more labour-intensive techniques rising continuously relative to those produced with relatively less labour-intensive techniques in the context of continuous increases in the money wage rate and alongside corresponding increases in the money exchange values of all commodities. Instead, PKs explain the relative money exchange values of commodities in the manner of their explanation of the relative values of commodities; by relative demand over the short period and relative profit margins over the long period.

Second, PKs need to assume that changes in the money exchange values of commodities do not have a bearing on changes in the money wage rate to avoid a circuitous explanation of the former by the latter. PKs justify this assumption by arguing that workers bargain for money and not real wages. However, this requires PKs denying that over the long period workers bargain to maintain living standards.

Third, and following from their explanation of the magnitude of the value of the commodity, the PK explanation of the magnitude of the exchange value of the commodity requires them to abstract from the productivity of labour when explaining this magnitude in the first instance, i.e., when explaining this magnitude over the short period. To repeat what was argued above, this abstraction is premised on a mistaken conception of the productivity of labour; the quantity of output produced by a given quantity of labour employed. Once it is accepted that the productivity of labour is more correctly defined as the quantity of the output produced with the expenditure of a given quantity of labour time there is no reason to suppose that a given quantity of labour employed implies a given productivity of labour.

Lastly, their embodied money income cost explanation of the magnitude of the exchange value of the commodity prevents PKs from seeing the current exchange values of means of production having a bearing on this magnitude. Instead, it requires them to conceive of what has a bearing on the magnitude of the exchange value of the commodity as the exchange values of the layered means of production used in its production where these are determined by their respective values. Aside from there being no reason to suppose the magnitude of the exchange values of the layered means of production is determinate, there is also no reason to suppose the magnitude of their embodied values is determinate, especially given the divergences in the technical conditions of production required to produce the various layers of means of production.

6.6 Money and Its Functions

6.6.1 Money

PKs conceive of money as a token of debt that is used to purchase the inputs used in the production of the commodity, especially the labour input. The wage contract being typically regarded as the most ubiquitous of all debt contracts.[31] For a few PKs (neo-Chartalists) money is conceived of as a token of debt that is used to pay taxes.[32] All PKs see the token of debt as credit-money, with fiat currency issued by the state forming the base of the entire credit-money system.[33] Most PKs see credit-money emerging with credit-based exchange and giving rise to uncertainty, i.e., the uncertainty that naturally arises with debt contracts.[34] Neo-Chartalists see credit money emerging with the payment of taxes. Lastly, all PKs, including neo-Chartalists, deny money is a commodity,[35] and that it is a veil in the sense it has no bearing on the reproduction of the commodity.[36]

From the perspective of Marx's analysis the problems with the PK explanation of money begins with its **conception**. Their conception of money implies PKs see it as an intrinsically valueless token of the labour input, and for neo-Chartalists an intrinsically valueless token of taxes, that represents a particular magnitude of exchange value. Crucially, this conception presumes the labour input (and taxes) is (are) quantifiable. As I argued above, there is little reason to see the labour input, and

[31] See Davidson (1978a, 1978b), Arestis and Eichner (1988).

[32] See Wray (2007).

[33] See Wray (1992, 2007).

[34] See Dow (2001), Moore (1979), Lavoie (2014).

[35] See Martin (2014).

[36] See Davidson (1978b, 1980), Rotheim (1981).

no reason whatsoever to see taxes, as quantifiable. The PK conception of money precludes them from seeing it representing general exchange value, a defining characteristic of money. There is no reason to see something that is a token of the labour input or taxes as representing general exchange value.

Their conception of money prevents PKs from seeing money **emerging** historically with the development of the process of exchange of commodities for one another and the use of one of the commodities being exchanged as a numéraire commodity. That is to say, it requires PKs, including neo-Chartalists, to deny money emerges historically as a commodity, and in particular gold. The problem for PKs is that to admit money emerges as a commodity would not only require them to admit money emerges prior to the emergence of capitalism but also that it emerges prior to the emergence of credit-based transactions. It would require them to deny that money is necessarily credit money.

Their conception of money also prevents PKs from seeing money assuming the **form** of a commodity in capitalism. That is to say, it requires them to deny money ever assumed the form of gold or any other precious metal in capitalism. The reason given by PKs is that commodities are not used by capitalist producers to purchase labour and the other inputs required for the production of their commodities, or used by labour to purchase their means of sustenance. However, the inconvenient fact is that for PKs to see money as a commodity requires them to conceive of it as a numéraire commodity whose exchange value is unity. PKs do not see that money can assume any form provided that it is what is used by producers to denote the exchange values of their commodities as general exchange values.

Lastly, although PKs correctly reject the notion of money as a **veil**, they implicitly base this rejection on the contention that money is value and commodities have no value unless money is used to purchase the inputs required for their production. What PKs do not see is that money should not be seen as a veil because it is used by producers to denote the exchange values of their commodities as general exchange values with a view to facilitating their reproduction.

6.6.2 *Functions*

Most PKs see money's primary and defining function as the denominator and settler of debts, with whatever is designated as money of account by the state serving to denominate and settle these debts and denominate the exchange values of commodities.[37] Money is also seen as a store of value in the sense of being a means of holding wealth and not a repository of the means of purchase and payment.[38] Keynes sees the store of value function as a first approximation to his concept of 'liquidity preference'. He sees the decision to hold money as a store by individuals and businesses taken with respect to the reward for parting with liquidity, this reward being interest.[39] PKs see whatever functions as the settler of debts and a store of value serving as a means of purchase and medium of circulation.

From the perspective of Marx's analysis, the major problem with the PK conception of the functions performed by money is their neglect of money's **measure** of exchange value function, and corresponding primacy they attach to money's function as **means of purchase** and, in the context of this function, its function as the **denominator and settler of debts**. What PKs do not see in this regard is that credit-based transactions, and, therefore, money's function as the denominator and settler of debts, presupposes its function as measure of the exchange values of commodities. They do not see the use of money to purchase means of production and the labour input presupposes money has been used by producers of all commodities, including means of production and wage goods, to denote the money prices of these commodities.

A number of PKs, following Keynes in his *Treatise*, place particular emphasis on money's function as **money of account**, with some PKs even seeing it akin to money's function as 'measure of value'.[40] What is not recognised by these PKs, and indeed Keynes in his *Treatise*, is that whatever is used as money of account presupposes its prior use as means of purchase, and this in turn the prior use of money as measure of the exchange value of commodities. In fact, whatever is used as money of account must logically be what is used to purchase inputs and this in turn whatever is used as measure of the exchange values of commodities or a token of this measure.

[37] See Keynes (2011 [1930], p. 3), Davidson (1978a, p. 152), Cardim de Carvalho (1995, p. 20).

[38] See Rotheim (1981, pp. 579–580).

[39] See Keynes (1973, p. 174).

[40] See, for example, Ingham (2004).

A last problem of note with the PK conception of the functions of money is their conception of its function as a **store of value**. The problem in this regard is their confusion of money as a store of value with money capital, or, more specifically, the confusion of money with interest-bearing capital. This confusion arises from PKs tacitly seeing all depositors of money with commercial banks holding deposits as interest-bearing capital and not simply hoards or reserves of means of purchase and payment on which interest is paid. Which means PKs do not distinguish between those depositing money with banks and the use by banks of these deposits as interest-bearing capital. It is the banks (and other financial institutions) that lend money with a view to obtaining a return on this lending, not the depositors with these banks.

6.7 Value of Money

Their conception of money requires PKs to see its value as the quantity of the labour it purchases.[41] This in turn implies they see the measure of the value of money as the quantity labour commanded by it. Although PKs do not formally consider how money acquires value historically or how this value is formed, they can be deduced from their conception of the value of money and explanation of its magnitude. These imply PKs see money acquiring value historically when producers begin to use it to purchase the labour input, and this value formed and reformed in the context of the wage bargain. Lastly, and following logically from the preceding, PKs explain the magnitude of the value of money by the money wage rate, with particular attention paid to the institutional environment governing the bargaining strength of labour.[42]

The problems with the PK explanation of the value of money begin with its implicit **conception**. First, their implicit conception of the value of a commodity requires PKs to deny the value of money is related to the values of the commodities purchased with money. Consequently, their conception of the value of money causes them, more than any other approach, to lose sight of the source of its value. This source being the value of the commodity. It needs recalling in this context that for PKs the value of the commodity is the quantity of money commanded

[41] See Davidson (1978a, pp. 152–153).

[42] See Davidson (1978a, pp. 152–153).

as incomes in the production of the commodity. Which means that for PKs to conceive of the value of money as the value of the commodities commanded by money would require them to see the value of money given by the quantity of money it commands. Second, the implicit PK conception of the value of money, as the quantity of labour it commands, requires labour to be quantifiable. As I have argued above, the PK conception of the labour input does not lend itself to quantification. Third, their conception of the value of money requires PKs to conceive of its value as the value of all money used to purchase all labour, and not the value of an individual unit of money used to purchase the labour input.

The problems with the implicit PK conception of the **measure** of the value of money follow from the problems with their implicit conception of the value of money. Most obviously it requires PKs to conceive of the money whose value is to be measured as the aggregate quantity of money used to purchase all labour in economy-wide wage bargains, and not the labour time required to produce the commodity whose exchange value money is used to measure. Second, it requires PKs to conceive of the labour input as homogeneous, allowing for all labour commanded by money in wage bargains to be aggregated. The problem in this regard, as noted above, is that there is no reason to suppose the labour input is even quantifiable.

The PK conception of money prevents them from seeing it **acquiring** value historically as a numéraire commodity prior to the emergence of capitalism. Consequently, it requires them to deny money acquires value historically as gold when gold is used as a numéraire commodity to facilitate the exchange of commodities for one another prior to the emergence of capitalism and the emergence of credit based transactions. Instead, as noted above, the PK concept of money requires them to see it acquiring value with the emergence of capitalism and the use of tokens of debt to purchase the labour input.

The PK neglect of money's function as measure of the exchange values of commodities prevents them from seeing its value in capitalism **formed** in the context of its use by capitalist producers of money to denote the exchange values of their commodities as general exchange values, prior to its use in the process of circulation to circulate commodities with money prices. Instead, it causes PKs see the value of money formed independently of the production of commodities, in the process of economy-wide wage bargains.

The problems with the PK explanation of the **magnitude** of value of money follow from the preceding. First, for PKs to explain the magnitude of value of money by the quantity of the labour input commanded by it in the context of the wage bargain requires the quantification of the labour input. As argued above, this is precluded in PK analyses by their conception of the labour input. Second, the explanation of the magnitude of the value of money as the quantity of the labour input commanded by money in the context of the wage bargain causes PKs to see this magnitude divorced from the magnitude of value of the commodity. Third, and following from the preceding, the implicit PK explanation of the magnitude of the value of money requires them to tacitly deny changes in the productivity of labour and money prices of raw materials have a bearing it. PKs provide no reason to suppose that changes in the productivity of labour or raw material prices have any bearing on the wage bargain.

6.8 Exchange Value of Money

PKs are not clear about the conception of the exchange value of money and its corresponding measure. They implicitly conceive of the exchange value of money as the aggregate money prices of all commodities, or aggregate money price level, tacitly seeing its measure as an aggregate cluster of commodities. Money is implicitly seen as acquiring general exchange value historically, and this exchange value formed and reformed, when it is used to denominate debt contracts involving labour and other inputs. When explaining the magnitude of the exchange value of money, and in keeping with their explanations of the magnitude of the exchange value of the commodity, PKs follow Keynes in focusing on the short period, arguing that the magnitude of the exchange value of money, or the aggregate money price level, is determined over this period by the magnitude of the values of commodities, i.e., by the money wage rate in the context of a diminishing marginal productivity of labour.[43] Also following Keynes, PKs see the aggregate money price level over the long period determined by the money wage rate allowing for economy-wide increases in the productivity of labour.[44] Increases in the economy-wide productivity of labour are seen as offsetting the impact of increases in

[43] See Keynes (1973, pp. 301–303), Moore (1979, pp. 124–125).

[44] See Keynes (1973, p. 308), Moore (1979, p. 131), Smithin (2003, p. 188).

the money wage rate over this period. Where many PKs diverge from Keynes is in seeing the quantity of money in the process of circulation as *endogenously* determined in the sense of being dependent on the demand for money where this comprises the transactions, precautionary and speculative demand for money. Although Keynes sees the supply of money *exogenously* determined, he does not see changes in the quantity of it put into circulation having a direct impact on the aggregate money price level in the manner of traditional or modern quantity theories. For Keynes, if the quantity of money has an impact on the aggregate money price level, it is an indirect impact, *via* its impact on the rate of interest.[45]

The problems with the PK explanation of the exchange value of money from the perspective of Marx's analysis begin with its **conception**. Like all other approaches PKs are unable to conceive of the exchange value of money as a certain quantity of any commodity with a determinate money price that it is used to purchase. This is because such a conception of the exchange value of money requires money to be seen as a measure of the exchange values of commodities in the manner of Marx. Instead, PKs conceive of the exchange value of money as the quantity of all commodities possessing money prices whose circulation a certain aggregate quantity of money facilitates.

The problem with the PK conception of the exchange value of money follows from the problem with its conception. That is, it requires PKs, like all other approaches, to deny that the **measure** of the exchange value of money is any commodity whose general exchange value it is used to denote. PKs, like all other approaches, are not able to conceive of the measure of the exchange value of money in this way for the same reason they are not able to conceive of money as the measure of the exchange value of the commodity; their neglect of money's exchange value function. Instead, their concept of the exchange value of money requires PKs to see what is being measured as the aggregate quantity of money used to circulate all commodities with determinate money prices, and the latter as the measure of the exchange value of the aggregate quantity of money used to facilitate their circulation.

The PK conception of money prevents them from seeing money **acquiring** exchange value historically as a numéraire commodity prior to

[45] See Keynes (1973, pp. 301–302).

the emergence of capitalism and the widespread production of commodities for exchange. Consequently, it requires them to deny that money acquires exchange value historically as gold, when gold comes to be used as a numéraire commodity to facilitate trade, especially international trade. Instead, as noted above, they implicitly see money acquiring exchange value historically with the emergence of capitalism and the development of credit based transactions.

Their neglect of money's function of measure of the exchange values of commodities prevents PKs from seeing the exchange value of money **formed** in the context the use of money by producers to denote the exchange values of commodities *prior* to putting them into the process of circulation. Instead, they tacitly see the exchange value of money formed in the process of the circulation of commodities with determinate money prices when money is used to facilitate this circulation, even though they see the money prices of commodities formed in the process of production.

The problems with the PK explanation of the **magnitude** of the exchange value of money follow from the preceding. First, their explanation of the magnitude of the exchange value of money by the magnitude of its value, i.e., by the money wage rate, requires PKs to assume the exchange value of money or aggregate money price level has no bearing on the money wage rate to avoid a circuitous explanation of the exchange value of money. As I argued above, this assumption might be plausible when considering the short period, but not when considering the long period. Second, the PK explanation of the magnitude of the exchange value of money by the magnitude of its value requires PKs to deny aggregate demand has a bearing on the latter except insofar as it has a bearing on the money wage rate. Most importantly, it requires them to deny aggregate demand has an impact on money profit margins. Third, their explanation of the magnitude of the exchange value of money by the magnitude of its value requires PKs to deny that changes in the economy-wide productivity of labour and raw material prices have a bearing on the magnitude of the exchange value of money, also over the long period, since there is no reason to suppose changes in these have a bearing on the money wage rate. Moreover, since the logic of the PK explanation of the money exchange value of the commodity precludes them from seeing changes in the money exchange values of means of production having a direct bearing on the money exchange values of outputs, this reinforces their necessary denial of the impact of changes in prices of raw materials on the prices of commodities produced with these.

6.9 Money Price of the Commodity

PKs conceive of the money price of a commodity as the quantity of money commanded by a unit of it, with money assumed to purchase a certain quantity of labour time. They see this price permitting the producer to recover the money outlaid in the production of the commodity and appropriate a certain money profit in relation to this outlay.[46] Most PKs, implicitly if not explicitly, see commodities acquiring money prices historically when they begin to be produced with credit-based purchases of inputs, especially wage labour, and these prices formed prior to the process of production in the context of the formation of contractual labour obligations.[47] When explaining the magnitude of the money price of the commodity, PKs focus on changes in the money price of the individual commodity in the context of changes in the aggregate money price level. In spite of the differences in PK explanations of the money prices of commodities referred to above, there is general agreement that changes in the aggregate money price level are primarily explained by changes in the money wage rate, with economy-wide changes in the productivity of labour offsetting the impact of increases in money wages over the long period. Insofar as PKs pay any attention to relative money prices, it is to explain these too in the context of a distinction between short and long periods, by the relative demand for commodities over the former period and structural shifts in sectoral rates of profit over the latter period.

The problems with the PK explanation of money prices begin with its **conception**. First, following from what was argued above in the context of the PK concept of the money exchange value of the commodity, PKs do not see the money price of the commodity as the form assumed by its value. This is because, as argued above, PKs collapse the value of the commodity into its money exchange value or money price. Second, the PK conception of the money price of the commodity causes them to see it indicating the quantity of the labour input that can be purchased with the commodity and not the quantity of any and all commodities that can be purchased with it. That is to say, PKs do not conceive of the money price of the commodity representing general exchangeable worth.

The PK conflation of the value and exchange value of the commodity prevents them from seeing the **measure** of the money price of the

[46] See Lee (1994), Lavoie (2001, 2014).

[47] See Barrère (1985–1986), Lee (2003).

commodity, i.e., the measure of its money exchange value, as the form assumed my the measure of its value. Instead, it causes them to see the measure of the money price of the commodity as the same as the measure of its value, viz., a certain quantity of money. Moreover, the PK conception of money prevents them from seeing the measure of the money price of the commodity as something that represents general exchange value, i.e., something that is used to buy any and all commodities. Instead, it causes them to conceive of this measure as something that represents a particular quantity of the labour input. What PKs ignore in this regard is that money's function as a means of purchase, even as a means of purchase of the labour input, presupposes it functions as a measure of the exchange values of commodities.

The PK conception of money prevents them from seeing commodities **acquiring** money prices historically prior to capitalism, when what emerges as the numéraire commodity is used to reduce the commodity exchange values of commodities to a common denominator. That is to say, it prevents PKs from seeing commodities acquiring money prices historically as gold prices prior to the emergence of capitalism, and continuing to possess gold prices in the early phases of capitalism prior to the emergence of credit money on an inconvertible fiat currency base.

The PK neglect of money's function as measure of the exchange values of commodities not only prevents them from seeing the value and exchange value of money **formed** in capitalism in the context of the use of money by producers to denote the exchange values of their commodities as general exchange values, it prevents them from seeing the money prices of commodities formed in the same context. PKs do not see that the purchase and sale of commodities on credit presupposes the commodities have been put into the process of circulation with determinate money prices as a result of producers using money as a measure of the exchange values of their commodities. Instead, it requires PKs to see money prices formed in the process of production and the use of money by producers as money of account.

The problems with the PK explanation of the **magnitude** of the money price of the commodity from the perspective of Marx's analysis follow from the problems noted above with respect to the PK conception of the money price of the commodity and their explanation of the magnitude of money exchange value of the commodity in section 6.5.2. To begin with, and following from what was argued above, PKs see changes in the magnitude of values of commodities only having a bearing on the *absolute* magnitudes of the money prices of commodities and not also their *relative* magnitudes. This is to avoid having to conceive of the magnitudes of money prices of commodities produced in labour-intensive sectors rising continuously relative to those produced with less labour-intensive techniques in the context of a continuous increase in the money wage rate. Second, and following from the preceding, their explanation of the magnitude of the money price of the commodity requires PKs to see changes in the relative money prices of commodities taking place independently of changes in the aggregate money price level. PKs do not see that while changes in the relative money prices of commodities may at times take place independently of changes in the aggregate money price level the latter should in principle always be accompanied by the former. They do not see the major force impacting on the aggregate money price level should in principle be seen as having a bearing on the money prices of commodities relative to one another. Third, PKs do not, and cannot, see the productivity of labour having a bearing on either the relative money price of the commodity or the aggregate money price level.

From the perspective of Marx's analysis the problems with the PK explanation of the money price of the commodity, as with all other approaches, stems from their conception of the value of the commodity and its link to money. However, unlike all other approaches, the problem with the PK conception of the value of the commodity is not that they deny its intrinsic link with money, but rather that the source of value is seen as money; the money appropriated as incomes in the production of the commodity. It is this that causes PKs to have a mistaken conception of money, as a token of the labour input, and corresponding mistaken explanation of the money price of the commodity. The most obvious manifestation of the latter is that it requires PKs to explain changes in the relative money prices of commodities taking place independently of changes in the aggregate money price level in the manner of all other approaches, and deny the productivity of labour has a bearing on either.

References

Arestis, P., & Eichner, A. S. (1988). The post-Keynesian and Institutionalist theory of money and credit. *Journal of Economic Issues, 22*(4), 1003–1021.

Barrère, A. (1985–1986). Price system and money-wage system. *Journal of Post Keynesian Economics, 8*(2), 315–335.

Cardim De Carvalho, F. J. (1995–1996). The independence of central banks: A critical assessment of the arguments. *Journal of Post Keynesian Economics, 18*(2), 159–175.
Davidson, P. (1978a). *Money and the real world* (2nd ed.). Macmillan Press.
Davidson, P. (1978b). Why money matters: Lessons from a half-century of monetary theory. *Journal of Post Keynesian Economics, 1*(1), 46–70.
Davidson, P. (1980). The dual-faceted nature of the Keynesian revolution: Money and money wages in unemployment and production flow prices. *Journal of Post Keynesian Economics, 2*(3), 291–307.
Dow, S. C. (1991). The post-Keynesian school. In D. Mair & A. Miller (Eds.), *A modern guide to economic thought: An introduction to comparative schools of thought in economics* (pp. 176–206). Edward Elgar.
Dow, S. C. (2001). Post Keynesian methodology. In R. P. F. Holt & S. Pressman (Eds.) (pp. 11–20).
Dunn, S. P. (2000). Wither post Keynesianism? *Journal of Post Keynesian Economics, 22*(3), 343–364.
Dunn, S. C. (2008). *The 'Uncertain' foundations of post Keynesian economics.* Routledge.
Eichner, A. S. (Ed.). (1979). *A guide to post-Keynesian economics.* Macmillan Press.
Galbraith, J. K. (1967). *The new industrial state.* Princeton University Press.
Holt, R. P. F., & Pressman, S. (Eds.). (2001). *A new guide to post-Keynesian economics.* Routledge.
Ingham, G. K. (2004). *The nature of money.* Polity.
Kaldor, N. (1985). *Economics without equilibrium.* University College Cardiff Press.
Keynes, J. M. (1973). *The collected writings of John Maynard Keynes, Volume VII: The general theory of employment, interest and money.* Macmillan Press (originally published in 1936).
Keynes, J. M. (2011). *A treatise on money.* Martino (originally published in 1930).
King, J. E. (2015). *Advanced introduction to post Keynesian economics.* Edward Elgar.
Lavoie, M. (2001). Pricing. In R. P. F. Holt & S. Pressman (Eds.) (pp. 21–31).
Lavoie, M. (2014). *Post-Keynesian economics: New foundations.* Edward Elgar.
Lee, F. S. (1994). From post-Keynesian to historical price theory, part I: Facts, theory and empirically grounded pricing model. *Review of Political Economy, 6*(3), 303–336.
Lee, F. S. (1999). *Post Keynesian price theory.* Cambridge University Press.
Lee, F. S. (2003). Pricing and prices. In J. E. King (Ed.) (pp. 285–289).
Martin, F. (2014). *Money: The unauthorized biography—From coinage to cryptocurrencies.* Vintage.

Marx, K. (1972). *Theories of surplus value: Part III* (trans. from German by J. Cohen & S. W. Ryazanskaya. Lawrence & Wishart.

Moore, B. J. (1979). Monetary factors. In A. S. Eichner (Ed.) (pp. 120–138).

Nicholas, H. (2011). *Marx's theory of price and its modern rivals*. Palgrave Macmillan.

Nicholas, H. (2014). Problems with post Keynesian price theory: A Marxist perspective. *World Review of Political Economy, 5*(1), 78–95.

Nicholas, H. (forthcoming). *Explorations in Marx's theory of price, Volume 2: Profits and business cycles*. Palgrave Macmillan.

Robinson, J. (1968). Value and price. *Social Science Information, 7*(6), 63–72.

Robinson, J. (1971). *Economic heresies: Some old-fashioned questions in economic theory*. Macmillan Press.

Robinson, J. (1979). Foreword. In A. S. Eichner (Ed.) (pp. xi–xxi).

Rotheim, R. J. (1981). Keynes' monetary theory of value (1933). *Journal of Post Keynesian Economics, 3*(4), 568–585.

Smithin, J. (2003). Inflation. In J. E. King (Ed.) (pp. 186–191).

Wood, A. (1975). *A theory of profits*. Cambridge University Press.

Wray, L. R. (1992). Commercial banks, the central bank, and endogenous money. *Journal of Post Keynesian Economics, 14*(3), 297–310.

Wray, L. R. (2007). Endogenous money: Structuralist and horizontalist. Levy Economics Institute, Bard College, Working paper, No. 512.

Wray, L. R. (2010). Money. Levy Economics Institute, Bard College, Working paper, December, No. 647.

CHAPTER 7

Marxist Interpretations of Marx's Explanation of Money Price

7.1 Introduction

There have been a great many, and varied, interpretations of Marx's explanation of price since the publication of his *magnum opus*, *Capital*, with perhaps the majority of these being in the context of the debate surrounding the alleged flaws in his transformation procedure. In Nicholas (2011) I review some of the interpretations of Marx's theory of price by those I consider to be sympathetic to his economic writings. I argue most of them misrepresent his transformation procedure, whether or not they endorse the contention that it is fatally flawed. My concern in the present chapter is with Marxist interpretations of Marx's explanation of price that pay heed to his theory of money.

H. Nicholas, *Explorations in Marx's Theory of Price—Why Marx Is Still Relevant for Understanding the Modern Economy*, https://doi.org/10.1057/978-1-137-56564-8_7

7.2 Object and Approach

7.2.1 Object

With a few notable exceptions,[1] most Marxists have taken for granted Marx's purpose in his later economic writings, particularly *Capital*, is to explain profit in terms of the exploitation of labour.[2] This interpretation is in part due to the perception that his life's work is to aid the overthrow of the capitalist system and foster its replacement by an alternative non-exploitative one. However, there can be little doubt it is also in part a response by those sympathetic to Marx's work to what is perceived to be certain intractable problems with his explanation of price, in particular his so-called "transformation problem".[3] While there can be no denying Marx's motivation in his study of the capitalist system is to aid the overthrow of capitalism, *Capital* being the culmination of this study, it is patently obvious from even a cursory glance at this work that it did not cause him to have the sort of myopic focus on the exploitation of labour Marxists have traditionally interpreted him having. In fact, interpreting Marx's economic analysis having this focus greatly diminishes its importance as an explanation of the functioning of the capitalist system. Among other things, as I will expand on below, it leads to a distorted interpretation of his explanation of the values of the commodity and money—the foundations on which the entire edifice of his economic analysis is built.

The relevance of Marx's economic analysis for understanding capitalism has long been questioned by both those hostile and sympathetic to his work alike. An early and continuing criticism of Marx's work by those sympathetic to it is that it pertains to a competitive capitalist system while the modern economy is one dominated by monopoly corporations, something that Marx himself admitted.[4] More recently the emphasis of many of these critics has shifted to the contention that the modern economy is dominated by cognitive and/or financial capitalist corporations, with capital assuming additionally, or even primarily, the form of cognitive or

[1] See Shaikh (1977).

[2] See Sweezy (1968) and Meek (1973) as examples of traditional Marxists, and Foley (1986), Kliman (2007), and Moseley (2016) as examples of Modern Marxists interpreting Marx in this manner.

[3] See Nicholas (2011, pp. 39–40) for a discussion of Marx's alleged transformation problem.

[4] See, for example, the well-known work of Baran and Sweezy (1966).

financial capital. This contrasts with Marx's focus on an economy dominated by industrial capitalists with capital primarily assuming the form of productive capital.[5] A number of radical scholars have also criticised Marx's approach for conceiving of a single reality and not 'different realities'. The realities typically alluded to are those of women, persons of colour, and the LGBTQ community. While there can be no disputing the evolving tendencies of the capitalist system or the existence of different perceived realities, the focus of Marxist scholars on these tendencies and perceived realities has caused them to lose sight of the fundamental nature of the capitalist system they are purporting to analyse. It has caused them to abandon Marx's analysis of this system for all manner of nebulous and vacuous alternatives.

7.2.2 *Approach*

Most Marxists accept, to one degree or another, two of the three pillars I argued in Chapter 2 constitute Marx's approach to analysing the capitalist economy, viz., his materialist understanding of history and his method of abstraction, albeit with differences between Marxists regarding how Marx's writings on the capitalist economy are to be interpreted in relation to these two aspects of his method. The debates concerning the former have focused on the interpretation of Marx's concept of 'modes of production', especially how he understands the transition from the feudal to the capitalist mode of production.[6] Of greater relevance for the present work, however, is the debates among Marxists with respect to Marx's method of abstraction.

Some Marxists interpret his method of abstraction as the 'partialisation of the concrete'; the focus on certain important phenomena while ignoring others, and then gradually bringing the phenomena ignored, or abstracted from, into the analysis. Pivotal in this regard has been the interpretation of Marx's abstraction from capital, money, and supply–demand imbalances. It is not recognised, or least not so clearly recognised, that when Marx abstracts from these, his intention is to capture their essential nature. In the case of capital this essential nature is one of a sum

[5] See Hardt and Negri (2000), Moulier-Boutang (2012) on the shift of the modern economy towards cognitive capitalism, and Foster (2000), Lapavitsas (2009) on the shift of the modern economy towards finance.

[6] See Brenner (1976), Hilton (ed.) (1978).

of expanding value that assumes the form of commodities and money in the process of its expansion, value being the labour time that needs to be expended in the production of the commodity. This nature is not a certain sum of money or a certain quantity of commodities outlaid at the outset of the process of production. In the case of money this essential nature, as I will elaborate on below, is the objectification or materialisation of the socially necessary labour time expended in the production of all commodities. It is not a certain quantity of abstract labour time or the labour input commanded by money. Crucially, for Marx, money cannot be understood without reference to commodities as values. In the case of supply and demand, Marxists interpret Marx abstracting from, in the sense of ignoring, supply–demand imbalances, and then subsequently bringing these into an analysis of the system as one inherently in, or tending towards, balance. Sweezy (1968, p. 53) claims that the law of value is "essentially a theory of general equilibrium developed in the first instance with reference to simple commodity production and later on adapted to capitalism". What is not recognised in this regard is that for Marx the capitalist system is constantly tending towards and away from balance. The essence that Marx seeks to capture when abstracting from imbalances in supply and demand is the drive of capitalists to accumulate wealth in the context of a competitive battle between them, one that results in the cyclical movement of the system and periodic ruptures in it that are necessary for its continuous regeneration.

Some Marxists, most notably adherents of the TSSI approach, even explicitly deny Marx's method of analysis is one of capturing a hidden essence, at least in respect of capital, money, and supply–demand imbalances.[7] They typically downplay the importance of Marx's method of abstraction. Consequently, Marx is interpreted by them conceiving of capital as a sum of money and not value advanced to undertake production,[8] the expenditure of money on inputs into production and not the expenditure of labour time as the basis for commodities acquiring values,[9] and the production of commodities taking place in the context of continuous supply and demand imbalances in a capitalist system suggesting the

[7] See, for example, Duménil (1983–1984, p. 439), Freeman and Carchedi (1996b, p. xvi).

[8] See Bellofiore (1989, p. 12).

[9] See Kliman (2007, p. 24).

point of departure for understanding the system is that of supply–demand imbalances.[10]

Most Marxists pay little or no attention to the importance Marx accords to the critical evaluation of other explanations of the workings of the economic system, both those that are perceived to be the dominant explanations and those that are seen as having a similar orientation to that of Marx. A consequence of this neglect has been the increasing proclivity of Marxists to, wittingly or unwittingly, graft various elements of these alternate explanations of certain economic phenomena onto what they see to be the corpus of Marx's analysis when attempting to extend it or defend Marx from his critics. As I will make clear below, this is particularly evident when it comes to Marx's explanation of price. The explicit or implicit justification used for adopting these explanations is some alleged flaw or lacuna in Marx's explanation of price. While there can be no doubting there are lacuna in Marx's economic analysis, the problem with grafting bits and pieces of other approaches onto it is that it results in inconsistencies in this analysis, eliciting, somewhat inevitably, charges of redundancy.

7.3 Production and Value of the Commodity

7.3.1 Production

Marxists are generally agreed that Marx sees the production of commodities as the basis for the accumulation of wealth in capitalism. There is, however, considerable disagreement regarding his understanding of the production of commodities in capitalism. These disagreements pertain to Marx's conceptions of the capitalist producer and capital outlaid, the process of production, and the nature of the outputs produced. Many, if not most, of these disagreements originate from differences between Marxists with respect to Marx's alleged transformation problem and proposed solutions to it.[11]

The disagreements among Marxists regarding Marx's conception of the capitalist producer and capital advanced relate to whether or not the

[10] Freeman and Carchedi (1996b, p. xvi) argue "The focus of this work, like that of Marx, is not how equilibrium comes about but on why it cannot exist".

[11] See Nicholas (2011, pp. 39–40, 71–74, 77–87) for a discussion of Marx's alleged transformation problem and proposed "solutions".

producer owns the capital outlaid to undertake production, and whether or not this capital constitutes commodities or money. Some Marxists interpret Marx conceiving of the capitalist producer owning the capital outlaid, while others interpret him conceiving of the capitalist producer using borrowed capital.[12] Some Marxists interpret Marx conceiving of the capitalist producer outlaying commodity inputs, including wage goods, to undertake production,[13] while others, mostly those I refer to below as Monetary Interpretation Marxists (MIMs),[14] interpret him conceiving of the capitalist producer outlaying money, including money wages, to undertake production. There is more agreement among Marxists with respect to the production process. Most Marxists interpret Marx conceiving of the essence of this process as the expenditure of abstract labour time. Lastly, few Marxists, if any, pay attention to the nature of the outputs produced, and in particular whether or not these include the means of production.

From the perspective of Marx's analysis presented in Chapter 2, it should be readily apparent there are a number of problems with the preceding Marxist interpretations of his understanding of production. To begin with, it suggests some Marxists do not see clearly enough that for Marx the point of departure for studying capitalist production is the **capitalist producer** as the owner, not borrower, of capital. Those Marxists seeing the capitalist system shifting towards finance are particularly inclined to the latter interpretation of the capitalist producer.[15] Capitalist producers certainly borrow some capital to undertake the production of the commodity, but this does not capture the essence of the capitalist process of production and the capitalist producer. This essence is the accumulation of capital by the capitalist producer and not the financial capitalist, even though the accumulation of capital by financial capitalists accompanies the accumulation of capital by capitalist producers.[16]

[12] Among Marxistss conceiving of the producer as borrowing capital are those subscribing to a view of modern capitalism as characterised by the ascendancy of financial capital.

[13] Meek (1977), Shaikh (2016).

[14] See below for an indication of those included in this grouping.

[15] See for example Lapavitsas (2009).

[16] For Marx financial capitalists are those capitalists that use money to make money without directly engaging in production.

Some Marxists also do not see clearly enough that for Marx **capital** is a certain quantity of value that assumes the form of commodities and money in the process of its expansion and not certain quantities of either commodities or money *per se*. Marxists who interpret Marx ignoring money in his explanation of price typically interpret him conceiving of the outlay of capital as a certain quantity of commodities (means of production and wage goods), while Marxists who interpret Marx having a monetary explanation of price interpret him conceiving of the outlay of capital as a certain quantity of money.

Although Marxists generally interpret Marx seeing the processes of production in all modes of production as characterised by the expenditure of **labour time**, most do not see, or at least do not see clearly enough, the importance he accords to the nature of the labour time expended in the production of commodities in capitalism. They do not see clearly enough the importance Marx attaches to the fact this labour time is what is required for the production of goods to satisfy social demand and not what is actually expended in the production of the individual commodity. They do not see that in capitalism the latter becomes transformed into the former when producers use money to denote the general exchange values of their commodities.

Lastly, Marxists pay little or no heed to the importance Marx attaches to seeing the commodities produced including means of production. Most Marxists do not appreciate that Marx's criticism of Smith's explanation of the transfer of value from means of production to the value of the commodity produced with the means of production is premised on his (Smith's) neglect of means of production as part of what is produced, requiring him to have a layered income cost explanation of the value transferred. The neglect of Marx's criticism of Smith in this regard allows a number of Marxists to interpret Marx having a similar explanation of the value transferred from means of production to that of Smith (see below).

7.3.2 *Value of the Commodity*

Marxists agree that one of the basic building blocks of Marx's economic analysis is his theory of value. However there are considerable differences between them when it comes to the interpretation of his conception and explanation of the value of the commodity. Of particular relevance for the present study is the differences between, on the one hand, those adopting what I perceive to be a traditional interpretation, and, on the other hand, those adopting what I perceive to be a modern monetary interpretation. In what follows I will refer to the former grouping as Traditional Interpretation Marxists (TIMs) and the latter as Monetary Interpretation Marxists (MIMs). I take the former grouping to include those I have referred to in Nicholas (2011) as TI Marxists, viz., P. Sweezy, M. Dobb, and R. Meek, as well as their modern successors viz., A. Shaikh, B. Fine, M. Itoh, J. Weeks, C. Lapavitsas, and A. Saad-Filho, to name but a few. I take MIMs to include Marxists adopting approaches that have been labelled as New Interpretation (NI), Temporal Single System Interpretation (TSSI), and Monetary Circuit (MC), as well as individuals such as F. Moseley and R. Bellofiore.

TIMs

TIMs interpret Marx conceiving of the value of the commodity as the abstract (or, for some TIMs, the social) labour time expended in its production,[17] and its measure as a certain quantity of this labour time. This causes TIMs to implicitly, if not explicitly, interpret Marx seeing products acquiring values historically when they are produced in the context of a division of labour mediated by exchange,[18] and this value formed and reformed in the process of their production.[19] Lastly, TIMs interpret Marx explaining the magnitude of the value of the commodity by the quantity of the labour time used in its production.

The problems with the various TIM interpretations of Marx's explanation of the value of the commodity from the perspective of my interpretation of this explanation in Chapter 2 can be traced to their interpretation of his **conception** of the value of the commodity. To begin with, TIMs interpret Marx conceiving of the value of the commodity as the labour time actually expended in its production in the manner of Ricardo. They do not see that for Marx the value of the commodity is the labour time required to produce a standard commodity of a certain type, one produced by the bulk of producers of this commodity. Second, TIMs implicitly interpret Marx conceiving of the value of the commodity as its *relative* value and not in the first place its *absolute* value, where the

[17] See for example Sweezy (1968, p. 33), Meek (1973, p. 165), Fine and Saad-Filho (2004, pp. 20–21).

[18] See for example Meek (1973, 165–166), Itoh (1988, p. 115).

[19] See for example Shaikh (1977, p. 115), Fine (1980, p. 123).

relative value of the commodity is its absolute value relative to the absolute values of other commodities. Third, it causes some modern TIMs to at times collapse the value of the commodity into its exchange value, in much the same way Ricardo collapses the value of the commodity into its exchange value.[20]

Their mistaken interpretation of Marx's conception of the value of the commodity causes TIMs to interpret him conceiving of the **measure** of the commodity as a certain quantity of the labour time expended in the production of the commodity and not a certain quantity of the labour time that needs to be expended by the producers producing the bulk of the commodities of its type. They do not see that it is this labour time, and not that directly expended by the individual producer, that becomes the measure of the value of the commodity when producers use money to denote the general exchange values of their commodities.

Their interpretation of Marx's conception of the value of the commodity prevent many modern TIMs, viz., those seeing abstract labour time as the substance of the value of the commodity, from interpreting him seeing products **acquiring** values historically when they are produced in the context of a division of labour *per se*. They do not see that for Marx the products of labour acquire values historically before capitalism. Instead, their interpretation of Marx's conception of value requires them to interpret him seeing commodities acquiring values in capitalism, when they are produced in the context of a division of labour mediated by exchange where the labour time expended is either abstract labour time or becomes abstract labour time in the exchange of commodities for one another. TIMs do not see that for Marx products acquire values when they are produced with the expenditure of social labour time, as the labour time that needs to be expended to meet social demand. In pre-capitalist economic systems where production is based on a division of labour the expenditure of labour time is directly social. In capitalism the labour time expended in the production of the commodity is (simple) abstract and latently social labour time that only counts as part of the expenditure of necessary social labour time when the commodity is sold.

Their interpretation of Marx's conception of the value of the commodity prevents most TIMs, like most Marxists in general, from interpreting Marx seeing the values of commodities in capitalism **formed**

[20] See for example Rubin (1972 [1928], pp. 64–65), Meek (1977, p. 95), Shaikh (1977, pp. 113–114).

after their production and prior to them being put into the process of circulation. It prevents them from seeing the value of the commodity formed when producers denote the exchange values of their commodities as general exchange values prior to putting them into circulation.

Lastly, the problems with TIM interpretations of Marx's explanation of the **magnitude** of value of the commodity follow from the problems noted above with their interpretations of his conception of value and its formation. First, their conception of the value of the commodity precludes TIMs from interpreting Marx seeing the magnitude of the value of the commodity that needs explaining in the first instance as the magnitude of its *absolute*, and not *relative*, value. For Marx, the magnitude of the relative value of the commodity is the magnitude of its absolute value relative to the absolute value of another commodity. This has particularly important implications for understanding the impact of changes in the economy-wide productivity of labour on the magnitude of the value of money (see below). Second, TIMs do not see the importance Marx accords to the determination of the magnitude of the value of the commodity by the quantity of socially necessary labour time as the transformed form of the labour time actually expended in its production and, therefore, the importance he accords to the link between the value of the commodity and money. It was argued above that for Marx it is the use of money by producers to denote the general exchange values of their commodities that causes the quantity of labour time actually expended in its production to be transformed into that needed to produce the bulk of commodities. Third, their embodied labour time interpretation of Marx's explanation of magnitude of the value of the commodity prevents TIMs from interpreting him seeing the value transferred from the means of production to the commodity as the value of money that is required to repurchase them—the means of production. Instead, it requires TIMs to see the value transferred from the means of production to the value of the commodity as the labour time expended in the production of the means of production used to produce the commodity, and in the production of the means of production used to produce these means of production, and so on. That is, it requires them to interpret him seeing the value transferred from the means of production as the layered values of the means of production. Aside from this causing TIMs to see Marx having an indeterminate explanation of the value transferred from the means of production to the value of the commodity, it causes most TIMs to see Marx's transformation procedure as flawed because of his failure to transform the values of the means of production into their exchange values (money prices).

MIMs

MIMs interpret Marx conceiving of the value of the commodity as the money used to pay incomes (wages and profits) and buy means of production in the context of its production, where money is a token of a certain quantity of abstract labour time.[21] The abstract labour time represented by money is that used to produce all commodities whose circulation it facilitates. This interpretation of Marx's conception of the value of the commodity causes MIMs to implicitly, if not explicitly, interpret him conceiving of the measure of the value of the commodity as a certain quantity of money, and, for some, also the quantity of abstract labour time it represents.[22] Their interpretation of Marx's conception of the value of the commodity requires most MIMs to interpret him seeing commodities acquiring values historically, and the values of these commodities formed and reformed, when money is outlaid to undertake production. Lastly, it causes most MIMs to interpret Marx explaining the magnitude of value of the commodity by the quantity of money used to pay incomes and purchase means of production in the context of the production of the commodity.

Some MCs, those adopting an MC approach, implicitly, if not explicitly, interpret Marx conceiving of the value of the commodity as the quantity of money appropriated as incomes in the process of its production where money commands a certain quantity of wage labour.[23] This requires them to interpret Marx seeing the measure of the value of the commodity as a certain quantity of money or a certain quantity of wage labour. It also requires them to interpret Marx seeing commodities acquiring values when they are produced with wage labour and formed in the context of the wage bargain. Lastly, most MCs interpret Marx explaining the magnitude of value of the commodity, like other MIMs, by the money wage rate.

[21] See for example Kliman and McGlone (1999, p. 38), Moseley (2016, p. 288).

[22] Most adherents of the TSSI see the measure of value of the commodity as both money and abstract labour time.

[23] See for example Graziani (1997).

The problems with the various MIM interpretations of Marx's explanation of the value of a commodity from the perspective of the interpretation of his analysis presented in Chapter 2 begin with their interpretation of his **conception** of value. Although MIMs interpret Marx conceiving of the value of the commodity as the money outlaid on incomes appropriated in the immediate process of production of the commodity and means of production used in its production, since the means of production are themselves commodities they are in effect interpreting Marx conceiving of the value of the commodity as the money incomes appropriated directly and indirectly in the context of its production. That is to say, in attempting to defend Marx against his transformation procedure critics and reaffirm the relevance of his theory of value in the explanation of price, MIMs have ended up interpreting him conceiving of the value of the commodity in the manner of PKs; collapsing the value of the commodity into its exchange value or price of production and, consequently, interpreting him seeing the source of value as the money incomes appropriated in the process of the production of the commodity. Most importantly in this regard, MIMs interpret Marx conceiving of the value of the commodity in a way that abandons the link between and the labour time that needs to be expended in its production.

This interpretation of Marx collapsing the value of the commodity into its exchange value or price of production is most apparent in the TSSI interpretation of Marx's concept of value. For TSSI Marxists Marx's distinction between the value and exchange value of the commodity is that between the price of production and the market price of the commodity, i.e., between the trend money price of the commodity and the money price of the commodity that reflects supply–demand imbalances.[24] It is argued that Marx seeks to show with his transformation procedure that the formation of the general rate of profit results in the values of commodities being transformed into prices of production, and, correspondingly, values as distinct from prices of production disappearing from his analysis. As I have argued in Nicholas (2011), Marx's transformation procedure is his attempt to show the labour time that needs to be expended in the production of all commodities is redistributed between sectors in the context of the formation of the general rate of profit. Value does not disappear in this process. Instead, the magnitude of the exchange

[24] See for example Freeman and Carchedi (1996a, pp. xvi–xvii).

value of the commodity no longer directly corresponds to the magnitude of value. MIMs appear to ignore Marx's repeated contention that, even though the value of the commodity assumes the form of the price of production in the context of the formation of a general rate of profit, it remains distinct from the latter. Most Marxists, including MIMs, do not see that for Marx when producers use money to denote the exchange values of their commodities as general exchange values they transform the labour time actually expended in its production into the labour time expended by those firms producing the bulk of commodities in the sector (or socially necessary labour time) and, at the same time, transform the exchange value of the commodity into its price of production. They do not see that for Marx commodities still have values in spite of this transformation. However, for him the value of the commodity is no longer the labour time actually expended in its production, and its exchange value is no longer equal to this labour time, not even the labour time required to produce the bulk of commodities in the sector. It is their failure to recognise the distinction Marx makes between the value and exchange value of the commodity that prevents MIMs, and most Marxists, seeing the intrinsic connection for Marx between the value of the commodity and money, causing them to have a correspondingly mistaken interpretation of his explanation of both.

The mistaken MIM interpretation of Marx's conception of the value of the commodity leads, naturally enough, to an analogously mistaken interpretation of his conception of its **measure**. It causes them to interpret Marx conceiving of the measure of the value of the commodity as the measure of its exchange value or price of production, and *vice versa*. That is to say, Marx is interpreted by MIMs as conceiving of the measure of the value of the commodity as a certain quantity of money. Most MIMs interpret Marx seeing the quantity of money that serves as the measure of the value of the commodity commanding a determinate quantity of abstract labour time in the context of its use to facilitate the circulation of commodities produced with the expenditure of this labour time. A few MIMs, those adopting an MC approach, interpret Marx conceiving of the quantity of money serving as a measure commanding a certain quantity of the labour input. Interpreting Marx seeing money as the measure of the value of the commodity where money is a *token* of abstract labour time causes TSSI Marxists to interpret him seeing both money and abstract labour time as measures of the value of a commodity, where abstract labour time, like money, is observable.[25] MIMs, especially TSSI and MC Marxists, do not see that for Marx money is the *form* assumed by the measure of the value of the commodity when exchange comes to mediate the division of labour. Money is the measure of the exchange value of the commodity and not the measure of its value. Moreover, since money is the measure of the form assumed by the value of the commodity, there must be a connection between money and the measure of the value of the commodity. There must be a connection between the quantity of money as the measure of the exchange value of the commodity and the socially necessary labour time required for the production of all commodities as the measure of their values. MIMs do not see that for Marx money as the measure of the exchange value (price of production) of the commodity becomes the objectification of the measure of the value of the commodity; the objectification of a certain magnitude of socially necessary labour time. Most importantly, MIMs do not see that for Marx the labour time actually expended in the production of commodities becomes transformed into socially necessary labour time, and a certain quantity of this transformed labour time becomes the measure of the values of commodities and imminent measure of their exchange values when money is used as the measure of the exchange values of commodities. For Marx, the labour time that becomes the measure of the values of commodities is not, and cannot logically be, directly observable.

The MIM interpretation of Marx's concept of the value of the commodity, as its price of production, causes them to implicitly interpret him seeing commodities **acquiring** values historically when their production requires the payment of money incomes, and MC Marxists to interpret him seeing commodities acquiring values historically when they are produced with wage labour. MIMs do not see that for Marx products acquire values historically when they are produced in the context of cooperative efforts of individuals and the labour time expended by them counts as part of the total social labour required to sustain the economic system. As noted in Chapter 2, Marx argues that in rural patriarchal and communal systems goods are produced with the expenditure of labour time as directly social labour time. In other words, the goods produced are directly produced as values in both these system.[26] What changes with

[25] See for example Freeman and Carchedi (1996b, p. xvi), Kliman (2007, pp. 24–25).

[26] See Marx (1970, p. 33; 1976, p. 171).

capitalism is the way in which the expenditure of labour time counts as the expenditure of social labour time.

MIM interpretations of Marx's conception of value as its price of production cause them to have similarly mistaken implicit, if not explicit, interpretations of his explanation of the **formation** of the value of the commodity. MIMs do not see that for Marx the value of the commodity is formed in the context of the use of money to denote the general exchange value of the commodity, not the use of money to purchase the means of production and labour inputs *prior* to the production of the commodity.

The problems with MIM interpretations of Marx's explanation of the **magnitude** of the value of the commodity follow from the problems noted above with their interpretation of his conception of the value of the commodity, i.e., as the money incomes appropriated in the context of its production. Firstly, it requires them to interpret Marx denying any link between the magnitude of value of the commodity and the labour time actually expended, or that needs to be expended, in its production. MIMs can interpret Marx seeing the magnitude of the value of the commodity determined by the quantity of labour time *commanded* as incomes in the context of the production of the commodity, but not the quantity of labour time that needs to be *expended* in the production of the commodity. Most importantly, MIMs cannot interpret Marx explaining changes in unit money wage costs by changes in the unit labour time that needs to be expended in the production of the commodity, and, therefore, by changes in the productivity of labour. Needless to say, most MIMs would not accept that their interpretation of Marx's explanation of the magnitude of the value of the commodity requires them interpreting him ignoring the impact of changes in the productivity of labour on unit money wages, typically providing quotes from his various works to this effect.[27]

Second, and related to the preceding, it requires MIMs to interpret Marx seeing changes in the magnitude of value of the commodity as fundamentally attributable to changes in the money wage rate in the manner of PKs. The clearest among MIMs in this regard are MC Marxists. This interpretation of Marx's explanation of the magnitude of the value of the commodity in turn requires MIMs, like PKs, to interpret Marx seeing changes in the magnitude of the value of the individual commodity taking place in the context of changes in the magnitudes of values of all

[27] See, for example, Kliman (2007, p. 78), Moseley (2016, p. 289).

commodities. Hence, incidentally, the emphasis placed by many MIMs on their interpretation of Marx's theory of value being 'macro monetary' interpretations.[28]

Third, it requires MIMs to interpret Marx seeing changes in the money wage rate only having an impact on the *absolute* value of the commodity and not also its *relative* value. This is required to avoid having to interpret him seeing trend increases in the money wage rate accompanied by trend increases in the relative values of commodities produced with relatively more labour-intensive techniques of production. Since Marx's assumption of the formation of a general rate of profit precludes the interpretation of him explaining changes in relative values of commodities by changes in relative profit rates, this causes MIMs to be rather vague when it comes to interpreting his explanation of changes in the relative values of commodities.

Lastly, MIM interpretations of Marx's explanation of the magnitude of the value of the commodity prevents them from interpreting him seeing the values of the means of production transferred to the value of the commodity as the value of money required to *repurchase* the means of production. In fact, the logic of the MIM interpretation of Marx's explanation of the magnitude of value of the commodity is that he sees the value transferred from the means of production used in the production of the commodity to the value of the commodity as the layered money income costs of producing the means of production required to produce the commodity. TSSI Marxists are perhaps the clearest that this is the implication of their interpretation of Marx's explanation of the magnitude of value (price of production) of the commodity.[29] Indeed, they see themselves interpreting Marx having a "sequential" explanation of the magnitude of value of the commodity as opposed to the alternative more conventional "simultaneous" interpretation of his explanation in which the prices of production of both means of production and outputs are determined simultaneously in a general equilibrium system.[30]

[28] See, for example, Bellofiore (1989), Moseley (2016).

[29] See for example Freeman and Carchedi (1996b, p. xiv), Kliman and McGlone (1988, p. 70).

[30] Moseley (2016, pp. 296–301) criticises TSSI Marxists for their adoption of "iterative solutions" to Marx's transformation procedure, but fails to realise these solutions follow from their monetary explanations of the value of the commodity, an explanation he endorses.

7.4 Exchange and Exchange Value of the Commodity

7.4.1 *Exchange*

Marxists are divided in their interpretations of Marx's conception of the process of exchange, its purpose, historical emergence and nature. TIMs typically interpret Marx conceiving of the essence of the process of exchange as one commodity (C) for another (C'), i.e., C–C'.[31] When money (M) is brought into the analysis the process of exchange is conceived of as C-M-C'. TIMs tacitly interpret Marx seeing the purpose of exchange as the acquisition of other commodities, with the commodities acquired being commodity inputs when those exchanging the commodities are producers of commodities.[32] Their interpretation of Marx's conception of exchange requires TIMs to interpret him seeing exchange emerging prior to capitalism, initially as the exchange of commodities for one another and later as the exchange of commodities for one another mediated by money. Lastly, although TIMs interpret Marx conceiving of the process of exchange as in essence one commodity for another, they tacitly deny he sees this process as one of *barter* in the manner of Classical economics.

In contrast, MIMs interpret Marx conceiving of the essence of the process of exchange as the commodity for money, i.e., C-M, and money for a commodity, i.e., M-C.[33] A few MIMs, those adopting a NI approach, interpret him conceiving of the essence of the process of exchange in the manner of TIMs as C–C', albeit with money mediating the exchange of commodities.[34] MIMs interpret Marx seeing the purpose of exchange as facilitating the reproduction of the commodity by allowing producers to recover money outlays and obtain a profit in relation to these. This interpretation of Marx's conception of the process of exchange requires them to see it emerging historically with capitalism and the widespread exchange of commodities for money. Lastly, MIMs too tacitly deny Marx sees the process of exchange as one of barter.

[31] See for example Sweezy (1968, p. 23), Shaikh (1977, p. 114), Saad-Filho (2002, p. 98).

[32] See for example Shaikh (1977, p. 114).

[33] See for example Freeman (1996, p. 227).

[34] See for example Foley (1986, pp. 31–32), Mohun (1994, p. 395).

The problems with both TIM and MIM interpretations of Marx's explanation of exchange begin with their interpretation of his **conception** of the process of exchange. TIMs and MIMs do not see, or at least do not see clearly enough, that for Marx the process of exchange that characterises capitalism is the exchange of the commodity for something representing general exchange value. They do not see that what is commanded when the commodity is sold is something used by producers to denote the exchange values of their commodities as general exchange values. Nor do they see that for Marx the **purpose** of the process of exchange can only be seen as one of facilitating the reproduction of the commodity if what is commanded by the commodity in the process of exchange is something that permits the producer to repurchase all commodity inputs. They do not see that for Marx the exchange of commodities can only be seen as facilitating their reproduction if what is commanded in the process of exchange is something that represents general exchange value. Even though MIMs interpret Marx conceiving of the process of exchange as the exchange of the commodity for money, as I will argue below, they do not see money representing general exchange value.

Their interpretations of Marx's conception of the process of exchange prevents both TIMs and MIMs from seeing the process of exchange that is characteristic of capitalism **emerging** historically when producers use something representing general exchange value to denote the general exchange values of their commodities, allowing them to repurchase any and all commodities required to facilitate the reproduction of their commodities. For Marx, the process of exchange that is characteristic of capitalism does not emerge when producers directly exchange their commodities for the commodity inputs required to reproduce their commodities or for money outlaid on incomes.

Lastly, most Marxists do not see that Marx denies the process of exchange that characterises the process of exchange in capitalism can be interpreted as one of **barter** because he sees the commodities being exchanged having determinate money prices prior to them being put into the process of exchange (or circulation). It is not, as TIMs suggest, because he conceives of this process of exchange as one mediated by money or, as MIMs suggest, because he conceives of the process of exchange as the sale of the commodity for money.

7.4.2 *Exchange Value of the Commodity*

It follows from their different interpretations of Marx's explanation of the value of the commodity and process of exchange, that TIMs and MIMs have correspondingly different interpretations of his explanation of the exchange value of the commodity.

TIMs

TIMs interpret Marx conceiving of the exchange value of the commodity as the quantity of another commodity it is exchanged for, or more simply its relative price.[35] This requires them to interpret Marx conceiving of the measure of the exchange value of the commodity as any other commodity.[36] A few TIMs implicitly, if not explicitly, interpret Marx conceiving of one among the commodities a given commodity is exchanged for as the standard of all commodities as measures of the exchange values of one another, i.e., the numéraire commodity. This commodity is typically seen as gold.[37]

Although TIMs do not pay much attention to Marx's explanation the historical emergence and formation of the exchange values of commodities, these can be deduced from their interpretation of his conceptions of the process of exchange and the exchange value of the commodity. These require TIMs to interpret Marx seeing commodities acquiring exchange values historically when products begin to be exchanged for one another, and the exchange values of commodities formed in the context of the exchange of commodities for one another.

Lastly, TIMs interpret Marx explaining the magnitude of the exchange value of the commodity determined by the magnitude of its *relative* value.[38] Insofar as TIMs interpret Marx explaining the value of the commodity including the values of the means of production used in its production, they interpret him seeing the latter including the values of means of production required for the production of the means of production, and the values of the means of production required for their

[35] See for example Sweezy (1968, p. 27), Shaikh (1977, p. 113), Fine and Lapavitsas (2000, p. 364).

[36] See for example Sweezy (1968, p. 42), Shaikh (1977, p. 113).

[37] See Shaikh (1977, p. 114).

[38] See for example Sweezy (1968, pp. 45).

production, and so on.[39] Most (modern) TIMs see this explanation of the magnitude of the exchange value of the commodity by its value in Marx's work as problematic when the exchange value of the commodity is transformed into its price of production with the formation of the general rate of profit. Specifically, most TIMs accept that Marx failed to transform the values of means of production into their prices of production in his *transformation procedure*, and that if he had done so the two equalities, those between, on the one hand, aggregate values and aggregate prices of production, and, on the other hand, aggregate surplus value and aggregate profits, would not both hold.[40] The exception among TIMs is A. Shaikh, who argues that what is required is an extension of Marx's transformation procedure.[41]

Although the focus in all Marxist interpretations of Marx's explanation of the exchange value of the commodity has been his explanation of its magnitude, the problems with these interpretations begin with their interpretations of his **conception** of the exchange value of the commodity. In the case of TIMs, the major problem with their interpretation of Marx's conception of the exchange value of the commodity in a capitalist setting is they do not see that for him the exchange value of the commodity needs to indicate its general exchangeable worth if it is to facilitate the reproduction of the commodity. Instead, as argued above, TIMs interpret Marx conceiving of the exchange value of the commodity as representing its particular exchangeable worth; the quantity of another particular commodity it exchanges for. A second, and related, problem with the TIM interpretation of Marx's conception of the exchange value of the commodity is that they are not able to interpret him conceiving of the exchange value of the commodity as the *form* assumed by its value. This is because they do not see that for Marx the exchange values of commodities become the forms assumed by the values of the commodities when the representative of general exchange value, i.e., the general equivalent or money, is used to denote their exchange values as general exchange values and, in the process of doing so, transform the labour time embodied in them into magnitudes of socially necessary labour time while

[39] See Shaikh (1977, pp. 130–133; 2016, pp. 386–387).

[40] See Fine and Saad-Filho (2004) for a standard interpretation of Marx's transformation procedure and the flaws in it.

[41] See Shaikh (1977, p. 136).

at the same time causing the representative of general exchange value to embody a certain magnitude of this socially necessary labour time.

Their mistaken interpretation of Marx's conception of the exchange value of the commodity prevents TIMs from interpreting him conceiving of its **measure** as something representing general exchange value, i.e., money. Of note in this context is that the numéraire commodity cannot be conceived of as representing general exchange value since it is a standard of all commodities as measures of the exchange values of one another.

TIMs, especially modern TIMs, implicitly, if not explicitly, interpret Marx seeing commodities **acquiring** exchange values historically at the same time they acquire values, and not after. They do not see that for Marx the production of a good in the context of a division of labour is a precondition for it to acquire an exchange value. The source of the problem in this regard is that Marx is interpreted by TIMs, especially modern TIMs, seeing the substance of value as abstract labour time and the expenditure of labour time becoming the expenditure of abstract labour time in the process of exchange.

The logic of their interpretation of Marx's explanation of the exchange value of the commodity prevents them from seeing that for Marx the exchange values of commodities are only **formed** in the process of exchange in pre-capitalist economic systems. They do not, and cannot, see that for him the exchange values of commodities in capitalism, as general exchange values, are formed prior to the commodities being put into the process of circulation, when producers use the representative of general exchangeable worth to denote the general exchangeable worth of their commodities.

Lastly, the problems with TIM interpretations of Marx's explanation of the **magnitude** of the exchange value of the commodity follow from the above and their interpretation of his conception and explanation of the value of the commodity. To begin with, TIMs do not see that for Marx the magnitude of the exchange value that needs explaining in a capitalist setting in the first instance is the magnitude of its general exchange value; the quantity of something that represents general exchange value the commodity is seen as commanding in the process of circulation. TIMs do not see that it is this explanation that Marx uses as the basis for his explanation of the money exchange value or money price of the commodity, money being the representative of general exchange value *par excellence*. Although Marx begins his explanation of the magnitude of the general exchange value of the commodity by explaining the magnitude of its commodity exchange value, this is only to capture the essence of his explanation of the magnitude of its general exchange value. This essence being the magnitude of the value of the commodity. Marx does not see the explanation of the magnitude of the commodity exchange value of the commodity, or its relative price, as providing the basis for his explanation of the money price of the commodity.

Secondly, TIMs do not see that for Marx the magnitude of the exchange value of the commodity is determined by the quantity of socially necessary labour time required for its production, where this quantity is the transformed form of the quantity of (simple and abstract) labour time actually expended in the production of the commodity and corresponding to that embodied in the quantity of the universal equivalent (money) the exchange value of the commodity represents. TIMs do not see that for Marx this link between the magnitude of value of the commodity and its exchange value is manifest in the impact of changes in the productivity of labour on both the absolute and relative magnitudes of the exchange value of the commodity since neither the value of the commodity nor the value of money are visible. I will expand on this point below when assessing TIM interpretations of Marx's explanation of the magnitude of the money price of the commodity.

Lastly, their interpretation of Marx's explanation of the magnitude of the exchange value of the commodity in terms of the relative quantity of the labour time expended in the production of the commodity requires TIMs to deny Marx sees the magnitude of the exchange value of the commodity determined by the current exchange values of the means of production used to produce the commodity. Instead, as argued above, it requires them to interpret him explaining the magnitude of the exchange value of the commodity as its relative price by, in addition to the relative labour time expended in the immediate process of production, the relative labour times expended in the production of the means of production, and the relative labour times expended in the production of the means of production used in their production, and so on. Since there is no reason to suppose that the various layers of means of production are produced with the same techniques of production (viz., ratios of labour to means of production) there is no reason to suppose the quantity of value transferred from the means of production to the commodity is determinate in the context of the formation of the general rate of profit.[42] As should be apparent, it is this erroneous interpretation of Marx's explanation of the value transferred from the inputs used in the production of the commodity that is mostly responsible for his explanation of the magnitude of the exchange value of the commodity being seen as 'fatally flawed'.

MIMs

MIM interpretations of Marx's explanation of the exchange value of the commodity, like those of TIMs, follow from their interpretation of his explanation of the process of exchange and the value of the commodity. These cause MIMs to interpret Marx conceiving of the exchange value of the commodity as its money exchange value or money price, and its measure as a certain quantity of money where money is a token of a certain quantity of abstract labour time.[43] Particular emphasis is placed by MIMs on denying that Marx should be interpreted as conceiving of the exchange value of the commodity as its commodity exchange value or relative price.[44]

It follows from their interpretation of Marx's conception of the exchange value of the commodity that MIMs implicitly, if not explicitly, interpret him seeing commodities acquiring exchange values historically when money comes to be used to purchase the means of production and labour power needed to produce the commodities, and these exchange values formed prior to production in the context of the purchase of these inputs. A few MIMs, viz., MCs, implicitly interpret Marx seeing the exchange values of commodities emerging historically when money is used to pay wages, and formed in the context of the money wage bargain.[45]

Not surprisingly, most attention in MIM interpretations of Marx's explanation of the exchange value of the commodity is paid to his explanation of the determination of its magnitude, especially since it is this

[42] This is tacitly admitted to by Shaikh (2016, pp. 386–387).

[43] See for example Kliman (2007, pp. 24–25).

[44] Mohun (1994, p. 394) argues, confusingly, that the money exchange value of the commodity should be interpreted as its commodity exchange value expressed in terms of money.

[45] See Graziani (1997).

explanation, and in particular the alleged flaws in his transformation procedure, that has been subject to most of the criticisms levelled against Marx's theory of value. To repeat what was noted above, MIMs see the criticisms of Marx's transformation procedure stemming from a misunderstanding of what he is trying to do in his transformation procedure and, therefore, how he seeks to explain the magnitude of the exchange value or price of production of the commodity. They argue Marx is trying to explain this magnitude by the quantity of money outlaid on the wage and means of production, or, more fundamentally, by the quantity of money outlaid on the direct and indirect labour inputs used to produce the commodity, i.e., the labour inputs used in the immediate process of production of the commodity and in the production of the various layers of means of production used in its production.

From the perspective of the interpretation of Marx's explanation of the exchange value of the commodity presented in Chapter 2 the problems with the MIM interpretation of Marx's explanation of the exchange value of the commodity begin with their interpretation of his **conception** of this exchange value. One problem is MIMs are not able to explain why for Marx the exchange value or price of production of the commodity is the form assumed by its value where this value is the socially necessary labour time required for its production. This is because, as argued above, MIMs interpret Marx conceiving of the value of the commodity as the quantity of money appropriated as incomes in the context of its production and money as a token of abstract labour time. A second problem is that MIMs do not interpret Marx conceiving of the exchange value of the commodity as its general exchange value, i.e., the quantity of any and all commodities it can purchase. This is because MIMs do not see that for Marx the money exchange value of the commodity is formed when producers use money to denote the general exchange values of their commodities prior to putting them into the process of circulation.

It follows from this that MIMs are not able to explain why and how Marx sees the **measure** of the exchange value of the commodity as the form assumed by the measure of the value of the commodity, as the form assumed by the socially necessary labour time required for its production, or the latter being the imminent measure of its exchange value. This is because, as noted above, MIMs interpret Marx conceiving of the value and exchange value of the commodity as a certain quantity of money, where money is a token of abstract labour time or the labour input, requiring them to interpret him seeing the measures of the values and exchange values of commodities as certain quantities of money and abstract labour time. MIMs also do not see that for Marx money as the measure of the exchange value of the commodity is the embodiment of a certain quantity of labour time, not a token of it.

The conflation of Marx's conception of value with his conception of the exchange value or price of production of the commodity also prevents MIMs from interpreting Marx seeing commodities **acquiring** money prices of production historically *after* they acquire values. MIMs do not see that for Marx the historical acquisition of prices of production by commodities presupposes their acquisition of values. For Marx, products acquire values when they are produced with the expenditure of labour time in the context of a division of labour, as the expenditure of social labour time. They only acquire exchange values historically *after* this, when the division of labour is mediated by exchange and what functions as the representative of general exchange value or universal equivalent is used to denote the general exchange values of commodities.

The failure of MIMs to recognise the importance Marx attaches to producers using the universal equivalent to denote the general exchange values of their commodities also causes them to implicitly, if not explicitly, misinterpret his explanation of the **formation** of the exchange values of commodities. They do not see that for Marx the exchange values of commodities are formed after their production and prior to them being put into the process of circulation, not prior to the process of their production.

The problems with the MIM interpretation of Marx's explanation of the **magnitude** of the exchange value of the commodity follow from the above. First, their interpretation of Marx's conception of the value of the commodity, as the quantity of money appropriated as incomes, requires them to deny any link between the magnitude of the exchange value of the commodity and the quantity of labour time that needs to be expended in its production and, therefore, any link between changes in the magnitude of the exchange value of the commodity and changes in the productivity of labour. MC Marxists are the clearest in this regard, since they even deny what is commanded by money is labour time. As I argued above, MIMs can interpret Marx explaining the magnitude of the exchange value of the commodity determined by the labour time it commands, i.e., the labour time represented by the money appropriated as incomes in the production of the commodity, but not the labour time expended in the production of the commodity.

Second, and following from the preceding, their interpretation of Marx's explanation of the magnitude of value of the commodity requires MIMs to interpret him explaining the money exchange value or money price of production of the commodity by its money income components, especially the money wage rate, and denying that changes in the money prices of production of all commodities have a bearing on the money wage rate to avoid a circuitous explanation of the money prices of production of commodities. Needless to say, most MIMs do not acknowledge this to be the logical implication of their interpretation of Marx's conception of the value of the commodity and their corresponding explanation of the magnitude of its exchange value since it suggests they interpret him explaining the money price of production of the commodity in the manner of PKs. The exception in this regard is the MC approach.

A third, and related, problem with the MIM interpretation of Marx's explanation of the magnitude of the exchange value of the commodity is one alluded to above. It requires MIMs to interpret Marx ignoring the impact of changes in the money wage rate on the *relative* money exchange values or money prices of commodities, i.e., the money prices of commodities in relation to one another This is required to avoid interpreting Marx conceiving of money prices of commodities produced with more labour-intensive techniques of production rising continuously relative to those produced with less labour-intensive techniques in the context of continuous increases in the money wage rate over time. I argued in Chapter 6 that PKs also ignore the implications of continuous increases in the money wage rate on relative money prices of commodities for the same reason, and that this leaves them having to explain trend movements in relative money exchange value of commodities by trend sectoral rates of profit. Marx's assumption of the formation of a general rate of profits precludes a similar interpretation of his explanation of trend movements in relative money prices of commodities. Although it does not preclude him being interpreted seeing trend movements in the general rate of profit having an impact on trend movements in relative money exchange values of commodities, MIMs are no doubt aware that Marx sees this impact as relatively minor. This leaves MIMs having to tacitly accept Marx has no meaningful explanation of trend movements in the relative magnitudes of money prices of commodities. The obvious manifestation of this dilemma for MIMs is the dearth of their interpretations of Marx's explanation of the relative money exchange values of commodities, and the vagueness and *ad hoc* nature of those that are proffered.[46]

Lastly, the implicit MIM interpretations of Marx's explanation of the transfer of value from the means of production used in the production of commodities to these commodities requires them to interpret him denying the current money prices of the means of production have a bearing on the magnitudes of the money prices of the commodities produced with them.[47] This is because their interpretation of Marx's explanation of the magnitude of the money prices of the commodity requires them to interpret him seeing the prices of the means of production that matter for this explanation as their historic and not current prices, especially if one is to avoid interpreting Marx explaining the prices of outputs determined at the same time as the prices of means of production. MIMs do not see that for Marx the magnitudes of the money prices of commodities are set by producers with a view to reproducing these commodities. This requires producers to take into account the repurchase prices of the means of production when setting the prices of their own commodities.

7.5 Money and Its Functions

7.5.1 Money

Up to the early 1970s Marxist interpreters of Marx's work paid scant attention to his writings on money, with a few notable exceptions.[48] This changed largely as a result of the revival of interest in Marx's theory of price, as a theory of money price, by those I referred to above as MIMs.[49] In what follows I will focus particular attention on the works of those Marxists I have referred to above as TIMs and MIMs, with the former being for the most part modern TIMs.

[46] Moseley (2016, p. 289) suggests that Marx can be interpreted as explaining the relative magnitude of the exchange value of the commodity by the "real wage" and the productivity of labour.

[47] See Freeman and Carchedi (1996b, pp. x–xi), Kliman and McGlone (1999, p. 34), Kliman (2007, pp. 21–2).

[48] See for example Hilferding (1981).

[49] See for example Foley (1976, 1983).

Many sympathisers of Marx's work, along with its critics,[50] have interpreted him conceiving of money as a commodity possessing 'intrinsic worth'. This is certainly the interpretation found in the works of early Marxist interpreters of Marx's work,[51] and most of those I have referred to elsewhere as TI Marxists whenever they touch on Marx's understanding of money.[52] It is also an interpretation of Marx's conception of money found in several modern TIM interpretations of his work.[53] For all these Marxists the logic of Marx's analysis requires him to be interpreted seeing money as gold or tied to gold. Most modern Marxists, however, deny Marx's analysis requires him to be interpreted conceiving of money as something possessing, or linked to something possessing, intrinsic worth, even though they acknowledge he most certainly sees it doing so in the early phases of capitalist development.[54] They typically argue Marx explicitly sees money transitioning from something possessing intrinsic worth to an entity devoid of intrinsic worth with the development of capitalism, i.e., transitioning from gold to credit money resting on an inconvertible fiat currency base.[55] A few MIMs, those adopting an MC approach, interpret Marx seeing the latter form of money as the characteristic form of money in capitalism.[56] With the exception of MC Marxists, most modern Marxists interpret Marx conceiving of this form of money as a *token* of abstract labour time. MC Marxists interpret him conceiving of it as a token of the labour input.

Most Marxists implicitly, if not explicitly, interpret Marx seeing money emerging as a commodity along with the development of the exchange of commodities, when one particular commodity is used to facilitate the exchange of commodities for one another or circulate commodities with determinate money prices. Those Marxists adopting an MC approach

[50] Schumpeter (2006, p. 668) dismissively labels Marx, along with most Classical economists, as a "metallist".

[51] See for example Hilferding (1981, p. 35).

[52] See for example Sweezy (1968), Meek (1973), Mandel (1976).

[53] See for example Germer (2005), Weeks (2010), Shiakh (2016).

[54] See for example Lapavitsas (2000, 2005), Foley (2005), Nelson (2005).

[55] See for example Itoh and Lapavitsas (1999), Saad-Filho (2000, 2002), Lapavitsas (2000).

[56] See Graziani (1997, pp. 32–33, 36), Bellofiore and Realfonzo (2003, p. 215).

interpret Marx seeing money emerging with the development of credit, as credit money used primarily to denominate and settle debts.[57]

Lastly, little attention is paid to whether or not Marx sees money as a 'veil' in the manner of Classical economists, i.e., whether or not it is seen as having a bearing on output and employment. As one might expect, those few Marxists who pay attention to this issue deny Marx sees money as a veil.[58] However, little or no explicit rationale is provided for him doing so.

From the perspective of the interpretation of Marx's understanding of money presented in Chapter 2 the problems with Marxist interpretations of Marx's understanding of money begin with their implicit, if not explicit, interpretations of his **conception** of it. Most, if not all, Marxists do not see that for Marx money in capitalism is whatever is used by producers to denote the general exchange values of their commodities, with money becoming the embodiment of socially necessary time in the performance of this function. TIMs implicitly, if not explicitly, interpret Marx conceiving of money in capitalism as whatever is used to facilitate the exchange of commodities for one another, that becomes a valueless token of abstract labour time in the context of its use in this manner. A few TIMs interpret Marx conceiving of money as whatever is used to facilitate the exchange of commodities for the numéraire commodity, gold, with money being a valueless token of gold. MIMs implicitly, if not explicitly, interpret Marx conceiving of money as whatever is used to facilitate the circulation of commodities with determinate money prices and that becomes a valueless token of abstract labour time in the context of its use in this manner.

The mistaken Marxist interpretations of Marx's conception of money causes them, naturally enough, to have a mistaken interpretation of his explanation of its **emergence.** Even though most Marxists interpret Marx seeing money emerging prior to capitalism they do not see that for Marx the nature of money changes with the emergence of capitalism. They do not see that for Marx money emerges prior to capitalism as a representative of particular exchangeable worth while with the emergence of capitalism it becomes the representative of general exchangeable worth. This is because they do not see that for Marx money serves to facilitate

[57] See for example Graziani (1997, pp. 32–33).

[58] See Foley (1976, p. vii), Arthur (2004, p. 3).

the exchange of commodities as the standard of the commodities being exchanged for one another while in capitalism it facilitates the reproduction of commodities when producers use it as the representative of general exchange value to denote the general exchange values of their commodities.

Their interpretation of Marx's conception of money also causes Marxists to have a mistaken interpretation of the **form** he sees money assuming. They do not see that for Marx money assumes the form of whatever is used to facilitate the exchange of commodities for one another prior to capitalism and in capitalism it assumes the form of whatever is used by all producers to denote the general exchange values of their commodities. This means that for Marx money can assume the form of something with, as well as without, intrinsic value. That is to say, it can assume the form of a commodity, fiat currency, or even bit-coin in capitalism. All that is required is its use by the majority of producers to denote the general exchange values of their commodities. Of note in this regard is that, although for Marx there is every reason to suppose what is used to facilitate the circulation of commodities in capitalism (as a token of money) should be intrinsically valueless, or at least of a lesser value than money, there is no reason to suppose money is intrinsically valueless, much as there is no reason to suppose it has intrinsic value.

Lastly, Marxists do not see that the logic of Marx's analysis requires him to deny money is a **veil** in capitalism because of its fundamental link to the value of the commodity. For Marx, the value of the commodity in capitalism can only be understood with reference to money, much as money can only be understood with reference to the values of all commodities. This means that changes in the value and exchange value of money must logically have a bearing on the reproduction of the commodity and, therefore, the level of aggregate output and employment. TIMs implicitly, if not explicitly, interpret Marx denying money is a veil because of the alleged direct and indirect impact he sees changes in the quantity of it put into the process of exchange having on the quantity of commodities produced. They do not see that for Marx the quantity of money put into the process of circulation depends on the money prices of commodities, with the quantity of the commodities and their money prices determined before the commodities are put into circulation with determinate money prices and money with a determinate exchange value. MIMs implicitly, if not explicitly, interpret Marx denying money is a veil because they interpret him conceiving of the value of the commodity as the money incomes appropriated in the context of its production. They too do not see that for Marx money is not a veil because commodities are put into circulation with determinate money prices with the prices being those needed to facilitate the reproduction of the commodity.

7.5.2 *Functions of Money*

When interpreting Marx's explanation of the functions performed by money, most Marxists dutifully interpret him conceiving of these functions as those of the measure of value, means of circulation, means of payment, and hoard. They usually note that Marx sees the hoarding function of money assuming the form of a function of capital with the development of the financial system in capitalism.[59] The differences between the various Marxist interpretations of Marx's explanation of the functions performed by money pertain to the importance they see him according these functions. Most Marxists implicitly, if not explicitly, interpret Marx attaching primacy to money's medium of exchange or circulation functions. TIMs implicitly, if not explicitly, interpret Marx attaching primacy to money's function as medium of exchange[60] (although, confusingly, many refer to this as money's medium of circulation function[61]). A few TIMs explicitly interpret Marx attaching primacy to money function as 'money'—i.e., means of payment and hoard.[62] MIMs implicitly, if not explicitly, interpret Marx attaching primacy to money's medium of circulation function. A few MIMs, those adopting an MC approach, interpret Marx attaching primacy to money's function as denominator and settler of debts (means of payment).[63]

The basic problem with Marxist interpretations of Marx's explanation of the functions performed by money is they do not recognise the importance he attaches to the use of money by producers to denote the exchange values of their commodities as general exchange values, i.e.,

[59] See, for example, Bellofiore (2005).

[60] See for example Lapavitsas (2000, p. 635).

[61] See for example Hilferding (1981 [1928], p. 61), Lapavitsas (1991, p. 297).

[62] See for example (Fine and Lapavitsas 2000, p. 370).

[63] See for example Graziani (1997, p. 38).

to what Marx refers to as the **measure of value function** of money.[64] Many Marxists deny Marx can be interpreted as conceiving of money as a measure of the value of the commodity when it ceases to be a commodity possessing intrinsic worth.[65] Most Marxists are, however, relatively silent about his understanding of this function, apart from mechanically regurgitating what he writes in *Capital 1* and *Contribution.*[66] A few Marxists interpret this function as akin to that of a *numéraire* function; converting the commodity exchange values of commodities into numéraire exchange values.[67] As I argued above, this is a mistaken interpretation of Marx's understanding of money and its measure function. Money as measure serves to denote the exchange values of commodities in the form of something that represents general exchange value. Money as a numéraire reduces the exchange values of all commodities in terms of one another into their exchange values in terms of one particular commodity. There is no reason to suppose this particular commodity represents general exchange value, at least not unless it is used by all producers to denote the general exchange values of their commodities.

The neglect and misinterpretation by Marxists of Marx's conception of the measure function of money stems from their mistaken interpretations of his conception of the value of the commodity. These prevent Marxists from interpreting Marx's measure function as the use of money to denote the exchange values of commodities as general exchange values, causing the labour time expended in their production to be transformed into magnitudes of socially necessary labour time and money to become the form of the measure of the value of the commodity—the form of a certain quantity of the socially necessary labour time expended in the production of all commodities.

The TIM interpretation of Marx's conception of the value of the commodity prevents them from interpreting him conceiving of money as the measure of the exchange value of the commodity because it requires TIMs to interpret Marx conceiving of the exchange value of the commodity as its commodity exchange value and, therefore, its measure

[64] A notable exception is De Brunhoff (1976, p. 30).

[65] See Lapavitsas (2000, p. 634), Saad-Filho (2002, p. 99).

[66] The exceptions are Brunhoff (1976), Campbell (2005).

[67] See for example Graziani (2003, p. 5).

as another commodity. Conceiving of one of the commodities as a standard of all others as measures of the exchange values of one another, as the numéraire commodity, does not make it money or the numéraire exchange values of commodities money exchange values. For Marx, the numéraire is not used by producers to denote the exchange values of their commodities as general exchange values of their commodities and, therefore, does not become the representative of general exchange value. TIMs who interpret Marx as necessarily denying money serves as the measure of the exchange values of commodities when it is no longer a produced commodity are in fact interpreting him as denying it serves as a numéraire when it is no longer a produced commodity.[68] For Marx, as noted in Chapter 2, there is no need for money to have a physical presence when it is used as a measure of the exchange values of commodities.

MIM interpretations of Marx's conception of the value of the commodity as its exchange value or money price also prevents them from interpreting him conceiving of money as the measure of the exchange value of the commodity. This is because it prevents them from seeing the money price of the commodity as the form assumed by the value of the commodity and, correspondingly, money as the form assumed by the measure of the values of commodities when money is used to denote their exchange values as general exchange values.

The neglect, and/or mistaken interpretation, of Marx's measure function causes Marxists to have a mistaken interpretation of his understanding of the function money performs as a **medium of circulation**. It causes TIMs to interpret Marx's medium of circulation function as its *medium of exchange* function. In this case, commodities cannot be seen as put into the process of exchange with determinate money prices and circulated by money in accordance with these prices. Instead, Marx is tacitly interpreted as seeing commodities put into the process of exchange for one another with money facilitating this exchange and coming to represent certain quantities of the values of the commodities being exchanged in the performance of this function, i.e., representing a certain quantity of abstract labour time. The neglect, and/or mistaken interpretation, of Marx's measure of exchange value function causes, or rather requires, MIMs to interpret Marx conceiving of money as a medium of

68 See for example Saad-Filho (2002, p. 93).

circulation that facilitates the circulation of commodities with determinate money prices but where these prices are not linked to the labour time that is necessary for their production. It should be recalled here that MIMs interpret Marx seeing the value of the commodity determined by the quantity of money outlaid on wages (and means of production) where money is a token of the abstract labour time used in the production of all commodities. MC Marxists see Marx's medium of circulation function presupposing its *unit of account function*. The tacit assumption being that for Marx producers use money as token of the labour input to convert all labour costs into money costs, allowing them to set money prices of their commodities on the basis of these costs prior to putting them into the process of circulation.

Ignoring, and/or having a mistaken understanding of, Marx's measure of exchange value function, as well as seeing transactions increasingly credit-based, causes a few Marxists, viz., MC Marxists, to interpret Marx attributing primacy to money's function as the **denominator and settler of debts** in the manner of PK economists. These Marxists do not see that for Marx the use of money as a means of denominating and settling debts presupposes its measure of exchange value and medium of circulation functions.

Lastly, many Marxists also have a mistaken interpretation of Marx's understanding of money's function of **hoard** (i.e., its store of exchange value function). This stems from their conflation of the functions of money with those of financial capital in Marx's work. I will expand on the importance of this conflation in Nicholas (forthcoming), but note here it causes these Marxists to mistakenly interpret Marx seeing individuals as financial capitalists holding money in the form of deposits with banks and other financial institutions. As noted in Chapter 2, Marx argues that with the development of the capitalist mode of production hoards come to be used as capital by capitalists specialised in the use of these hoards to augment their wealth, making it appear that the function of money as hoard is a function of money capital, and those holding money as reserves of purchasing power are financial capitalists.

7.6 Value of Money

When interpreting Marx's explanation of the value of money, Marxists have historically focused on his explanation of the value of money as a commodity, gold, by the labour time required for its production, and its measure as a certain quantity of the labour time expended in its production. In contrast, most modern Marxists have focused on what they see as the logic of his analysis for the explanation of the value of credit money on a inconvertible fiat currency base.[69] They interpret him conceiving of the value of this money as the quantity of abstract labour time it comes to command or represent. For TIMs this quantity is what money indirectly commands when used as a medium of exchange, while for MIMs it is the quantity of abstract labour time money indirectly represents when it is used as a medium of circulation. This in turn suggests that TIMs see the measure of the value of money when it is credit money as a certain quantity of the abstract labour time it indirectly commands and for MIMs it is a certain quantity of abstract labour time it indirectly represents.

Since few, if any, Marxists pay attention to Marx's understanding of how money acquires value historically or how this value is formed, these need to be deduced from their interpretations of Marx's conception of the value of money and explanation of its magnitude. These suggest Marx is implicitly interpreted as seeing money acquiring value historically, and this value formed, when money is used to facilitate the exchange of commodities for one another (viz., TIMs) or to circulate commodities with determinate money prices (viz., MIMs).

Lastly, Marxists have traditionally interpreted Marx explaining the value of money as the value of gold by the quantity of labour time required for its production. While acknowledging Marx explains the magnitude of value of money as the magnitude of value of gold, most modern Marxists have focused on the implication of his analysis for the explanation of the magnitude of the value of credit money resting on an inconvertible fiat currency base. Modern TIMs implicitly, if not explicitly, interpret Marx explaining this magnitude by the quantity of it used to facilitate the exchange of commodities for one another relative to the quantity of these commodities, where the commodities are assumed to be produced with the expenditure of a certain mass of abstract labour time.[70] MIMs interpret Marx explaining this magnitude by the quantity of this money used to facilitate the circulation of commodities with determinate money prices where these commodities are also assumed to be

[69] See for example Foley (1983), Mohun (1994), Freeman and Kliman (1998), Lapavitsas (2000), Saad-Filho (2002).

[70] See for example Lapavitsas (2000), Saad-Filho (2002).

produced with the expenditure of a certain mass of abstract labour time and the quantity of money used to facilitate their circulation is endogenously determined in the sense of being determined by the quantity and prices of the commodities being circulated.

The problems with the preceding Marxist interpretations of Marx's explanation of the value of money begin with their implicit and explicit interpretations of its **conception**. To begin with, Marxist interpretations of Marx's conception of money as an intrinsically valueless token of the commodities whose exchange for one another or circulation with determinate money prices it facilitates precludes them from interpreting him conceiving of money as something possessing value as both a commodity and as money. This means they must interpret him conceiving of the value of gold as the value of a numéraire commodity and not also as money. Second, Marxist interpretations of Marx's conception of the value of money cause them to lose sight of the source of this value in much the same way their interpretations of his conception of the value of the commodity cause them to lose sight of its source. It causes them to interpret Marx seeing the source of the value of money as the abstract labour time actually expended in the production of all commodities and not the transformed form of this labour time that needs to be expended in the production of the bulk of commodities in each sector of the economy. Third, Marxist interpretations of Marx's conception of the value of money causes them to conflate this value with its exchange value. It is a conflation that results, naturally enough, from Marxist interpretations of Marx seeing money indirectly commanding or representing a certain magnitude of abstract labour time in the context of the performance of its medium of exchange or means of circulation functions.

The problem with Marxist interpretations of Marx's conception of the **measure** of the value of money follow from the problems noted above with their implicit interpretations of his conception of the value of money. First, their interpretations of Marx's conception of the value of money requires Marxists to interpret him conceiving of its measure as a certain quantity of the abstract labour time actually expended in the production of all commodities and not a certain quantity of the transformed form of labour time expended in the production of all commodities. Second, and related to the preceding, most Marxists cannot interpret Marx conceiving of labour time becoming the measure of the value of money at the same time it becomes the measure of the values of all commodities, i.e., when money is used by producers to denote the general exchange values of their commodities. This is because most Marxists neglect or misinterpret Marx's conception of the measure function of money. Lastly, since Marxists tend to conflate the value of money with its exchange value, they can be expected to conflate their respective measures.

Marxist interpretations of Marx's conceptions of money and its value prevent them from interpreting him seeing something **acquiring** value as money historically when it comes to be used to facilitate the reproduction of commodities that are produced for exchange. They do not see that for Marx money acquires value as money historically at the same time commodities that are produced for exchange acquire values as certain magnitudes of socially necessary labour time and general exchange values as money exchange values. Instead, their interpretations of Marx's conception of money and its value require them to interpret him seeing money acquiring value historically after it acquires exchange value, when it is used to facilitate the exchange of commodities for one another or their circulation with determinate money prices, and, for a few Marxists (MC Marxists), when it is used to purchase the labour input.

Most Marxists also do not see that for Marx the value of money is **formed** in the context of its use as measure of the exchange values of commodities *at the same time* as the formation of the exchange values of commodities as their general exchange values or money prices. Instead, their interpretations of Marx's conceptions of money and its value requires most Marxists to interpret Marx seeing the value of money formed in the context of it facilitating the exchange of commodities for one another or their circulation with determinate money prices, and, for a few Marxists (MC Marxists), in the context of the wage bargain.

The problems with the Marxist interpretations of Marx's explanation of the **magnitude** of value of money follow from the preceding. First, Marxists are not able to interpret Marx explaining the magnitude of value of money as a commodity. This is because it would require them to interpret him seeing money as something possessing value while functioning as a valueless token of the commodities, including itself, whose exchange for one another or circulation with determinate money prices it facilitates. It warrants recalling that for Marx money's function as the measure of the exchange value of the commodity does not require it to have a physical presence, and, therefore, allows for the possibility of the magnitude of value of money as a commodity to deviate from the magnitude of its value as money. In contrast, money's functions as medium of exchange or means of circulation require money to have a physical presence in the performance of these functions and, therefore, do not allow for such a deviation.

Second, Marxist interpretations of Marx's explanation of the magnitude of value of money require them to see this magnitude determined by the magnitude of its exchange value and not, as for Marx, *vice versa*. Specifically, for both TIMs and MIMs the magnitude of the value of money depends on the quantity of money relative to the quantity of commodities whose exchange or circulation money facilitates. I will return to this point below.

Third, Marxists do not see that for Marx the magnitude of value of money is determined by the quantity of the socially necessary labour time it comes to objectify when it is used as measure by producers and not the quantity of labour time it commands or represents when money is used to facilitate the exchange of commodities for one another or their circulation with determinate money prices. Of note in this context is that even though most modern TIMs deny Marx's labour theory of value is appropriate for the explanation of the relative price of the commodity they must implicitly accept its validity for such an explanation in the context of what they implicitly see to be his explanation of the magnitude of value of money if this value is to be seen as determined by the abstract labour time it commands in the process of facilitating the exchange of commodities for one another.

Lastly, Marxists are not able to interpret Marx seeing changes in the economy-wide productivity of labour having a bearing on the magnitude of value of money, notwithstanding their interpretation of his conception of the magnitude of value of money as the quantity of abstract labour time it represents or objectifies. In the case of TIMs, this follows from their implicit interpretation of Marx's conception of the value of the commodity as its *relative*, not *absolute*, value. It is a conception of the value of the commodity that precludes changes in the labour time expended in the production of individual commodities translating into changes in the aggregate labour time expended in the production of all commodities and, correspondingly, changes in the productivity of labour in the production of individual commodities translating into changes in the aggregate productivity of all commodities. In the case of MIMs, their inability to interpret Marx seeing changes in the economy-wide productivity of labour having a bearing on the magnitude of value of money stems from their interpretation of his conception of the value of the commodity. This conception, as noted above, requires them to interpret

Marx denying changes in the expenditure of labour time has any bearing on the magnitude of value of the commodity.

7.7 Exchange Value of Money

Marxists interpret Marx conceiving of the exchange value of money as the quantity of commodities commanded by the total quantity of money used to facilitate either their exchange for one another (TIMs) or their circulation with determinate money prices (MIMs). As noted earlier, Marxists interpret Marx conceiving of money assuming the form of whatever is used to facilitate the exchange of commodities for one another or the circulation of commodities with determinate money prices, or even what is used to denominate and settle debts (MC Marxists). Marxist interpretations of Marx's conception of the measure of the exchange value of money follow from this. That is to say, he is implicitly, if not explicitly, interpreted as conceiving of the measure of the exchange value of money, whatever form it assumes, as the cluster of all commodities whose exchange for one another, or circulation with determinate money prices, it facilitates.

TIM interpretations of Marx's explanation of the exchange value of money require them to interpret him seeing money acquiring exchange value historically when it is used to facilitate the exchange of commodities for one another, and the exchange value of money formed in the process of it facilitating the exchange of commodities for one another. MIM interpretations of Marx's explanation of the exchange value of money require them to interpret him seeing money acquiring exchange value historically when it is used to purchase commodities with determinate money prices, and the exchange value of money formed in the context of its use as a means of circulation. MC Marxist interpretations of Marx's explanation of the exchange value of money causes them to interpret him seeing money acquiring exchange value when it is used to denominate and settle debts, with this exchange value formed in the context of the outlay of money on wages.

When interpreting Marx's explanation of the exchange value of money, Marxists pay most attention to his explanation of the determination of its magnitude and his criticisms of the explanations of this magnitude by the Classical economists, i.e., his criticisms of the CQTM. In keeping with their interpretation of his conception of the exchange value of money, as the total quantity of money commanded by all commodities, Marxists interpret Marx explaining the magnitude of the exchange value of money as the general money price level. Divisions between Marxists pertain to whether they interpret Marx explaining this magnitude *prior* to money being put into the process of circulation to circulate commodities with determinate money prices or *in* the process of exchange when it is used to facilitate the exchange of commodities for one another. TIMs interpret Marx seeing the magnitude of the exchange value of money determined in the context of its use to facilitate the exchange of commodities for one another by the quantity of money used for this purpose relative to the quantity of commodities (and financial assets) whose exchange for one another it is used to facilitate. The resulting inflation is referred to by a number of modern TIMs as *extra money inflation*.[71] Given the similarity of their interpretation of Marx's explanation of inflation to that of the CQTM, TIMs, especially those subscribing to the extra money interpretation of Marx's explanation of the magnitude of the exchange value of money, are at pains to stress the differences between the two. They argue that, unlike the CQTM, Marx places emphasis on money's means of payment and hoard functions in addition to its "medium of circulation" (exchange) function, undermining the assumed proportionality between changes in the quantity of money put into circulation and the aggregate money prices of commodities, i.e., undermining the assumed stability in the velocity of circulation that is a cornerstone of the CQTM.[72] TIMs, especially those subscribing to the extra money inflation interpretation of Marx's explanation of the magnitude of the exchange value of money, also argue that the logic of Marx's explanation suggests that, unlike adherents of the CQMT, he sees the quantity of money used to facilitate the exchange of commodities for one another at least in part *endogenously* determined. Specifically, they interpret Marx seeing the (extra) money put into the process of circulation resulting from the activities of the monetary authorities in response to the demand for liquidity and/or the credit creation activities of private financial institutions.[73] In contrast, MIMs interpret Marx seeing the magnitude of the exchange value of money determined prior to it being put into the process of circulation, by the money wage rate.[74] This in turn requires them to interpret Marx

[71] See Saad-Filho (2002, p. 103).

[72] See Saad-Filho (2002, p. 96), Lapavitsas (2000, pp. 643–645).

[73] See Saad-Filho (2002, p. 104), Lapavitsas (2000, pp. 648–649).

[74] See Kliman (2007, pp. 129–130), Freeman (1998, p. 16).

seeing the quantity of money used to facilitate the circulation of these commodities as *endogenously* determined.

The problems with Marxist interpretations of Marx's explanation of the exchange value of money begin with their interpretations of his **conception** of it. They do not see that for Marx the exchange value of money in capitalism is the form assumed by its value when money is used to denote the general exchange values of commodities by all producers. This form is any and all commodities that are put into circulation with determinate money prices. Marxists do not interpret Marx conceiving of the exchange value of money in this way because they ignore the importance he attaches to the measure of exchange value function of money. This neglect, as I argued above, stems from their interpretations of his conception of the value of the commodity.

It follows from the preceding Marxists do not see that for Marx the **measure** of the exchange value of money is any and all commodities whose general exchange values money is used to denote. This is because they do not see that for Marx commodities become the measures of the exchange value of money at the same time, and in the same context, that money is used to measure the exchange values of commodities. In the same way Marxists do not see the money price of the commodity as the form assumed by the value of the commodity when money is used to measure the exchange value of the commodity, they do not see the commodity with a certain money price being the form assumed by the value of money when money is used to measure of the exchange values of all commodities.

From the preceding it follows Marxists do not see that for Marx a particular commodity **acquires** *general* exchange value as money historically when it is used to denominate the exchange values of all other commodities, and that the exchange value of money is formed in the context of its use for this purpose. Indeed, since most Marxists pay little heed to the importance Marx attaches to money's measure function, or his contention that money performs this function historically prior to it performing its other functions, it is not surprising they tacitly interpret him seeing something acquiring exchange value as money historically when it begins to perform one or another of its other functions; as a means of purchase or medium of exchange and, for a few, when it begins to be used to denominate and settle debts. It is also not surprising TIMs interpret Marx seeing the exchange value of money in capitalism **formed** in the process of money facilitating the exchange of commodities for one another, and MIMs interpret him seeing the exchange value of money formed prior to the production of commodities. Of note in this regard is that MIMs interpret Marx seeing the exchange value of money formed prior to the production and circulation of commodities while, as argued above, at the same time interpreting him seeing the value of money formed in the process of circulation, either in the current or a preceding period of time.

Lastly, the problems with Marxist interpretations of Marx's explanation of the **magnitude** of the exchange value of money follow from the preceding. To begin with, Marxists are unable to interpret Marx explaining the magnitude of the exchange value of money as commodity money for the same reason they are unable to interpret him explaining the magnitude of the value of money as a commodity because it would require them to conceive of a commodity possessing intrinsic value being used as a valueless token of commodities, including itself, whose exchange for one another, or circulation with determinate money prices, it facilitates.

Second, Marxist interpretations of Marx's explanation of the magnitude of value of money by the magnitude of its exchange value precludes them interpreting him explaining the latter by the former. This in turn precludes Marxists from interpreting Marx explaining the magnitude of the exchange value of money by the economy-wide productivity of labour. Even though adherents of the TSSI approach are particularly adamant they interpret Marx explaining the magnitude of the exchange value of money or aggregate money price level by economy-wide productivity of labour, they provide no indication how this is consistent with their interpretation of his explanation of the magnitude of the money price of production of the commodity which requires them to deny the productivity of labour has a bearing on it (see above).

Third, although the logic of Marxist interpretations of Marx's explanation of the magnitude of the exchange value of money allows them to interpret him seeing aggregate excess demand for commodities having a bearing on this magnitude, it is necessarily in a way that is inconsistent with his explanation of this magnitude. In the case of the TIMs, Marx can be interpreted as seeing increases in aggregate excess demand exerting upward pressure on the aggregate money price level only insofar as these increases correspond to an excess quantity of money put into the process of exchange. Moreover, it requires them interpreting Marx seeing commodities put into the process of exchange (for one another) without determinate money prices, or at least without money prices that are determined in the current period. In the case of MIMs, the implication is that aggregate excess demand has a bearing on the aggregate money price level only insofar as it has a bearing on the money wage rate and not also money profits since this would undermine their implicit interpretation of Marx's explanation of the magnitudes of the money prices of production of commodities by the money wage rate (see above).

Fourth, it also follows from Marxist interpretations of Marx's explanation of the magnitude of the exchange value of money that they must ignore the importance he accords to the impact of changes in raw material prices on this magnitude. For TIMs, this follows from their interpretation of Marx having an essentially CQTM explanation of the magnitude of the exchange value of money. For MIMs, this follows from their interpretation of Marx's explanation of the magnitudes of money exchange values of commodities as determined by the money wages outlaid in their production. I will expand on this point in Nicholas (forthcoming).

Lastly, their interpretation of Marx's explanation of the magnitude of the exchange value of the commodity requires Marxists to interpret him seeing the quantity of money used to facilitate the exchange of commodities for one another, or to facilitate their circulation with determinate money prices, as *exogenously* determined. This is readily apparent in the case of TIM interpretations of Marx's explanation of the magnitude of exchange value of money which suggests he sees money used to facilitate the exchange of commodities for one another in accordance with their commodity exchange values without reference to the quantities of these commodities and their money prices. What is less apparent is that it also applies to MIM interpretations of Marx's explanation of the magnitude of the exchange value of money. Their neglect of Marx's measure function of money suggests they too must interpret him as seeing commodities put into the process of circulation without determinate magnitudes of money prices, or at least without money prices determined in the current period. The TSSI interpretation of Marx as seeing money circulating commodities with money prices determined in a preceding period is perhaps the clearest testimony to this neglect.[75]

[75] See, for example, Freeman (1996, p. 235).

7.8 Money Price of the Commodity

When considering Marxist interpretations of Marx's explanation of the money price of the commodity, it is pertinent to again consider the interpretations of TIMs and MIMs separately. This allows for the two interpretations of Marx's explanation of the money price of the commodity to be more readily linked to their respective interpretations of his explanation of the value and exchange value of the commodity.

7.8.1 TIMs

TIMs implicitly, if not explicitly, interpret Marx conceiving of the money price of the commodity as its commodity exchange value for a given value of money. As argued above, some TIMs interpret Marx conceiving of gold as the numéraire commodity and money as a token of it. Their interpretation of Marx's conception of the money price of the commodity requires TIMs to interpret Marx conceiving of money as a token of commodities as measures of the exchange values of one another, and for some a token of gold as the standard of commodities as measures of the exchange values of one another.

Their implicit interpretations of Marx's conception of the money price of the commodity requires TIMs to interpret him seeing money acquiring money prices historically when money begins to be widely used to facilitate the exchange of commodities for one another, and these prices formed in the context of the use of money to facilitate the exchange of commodities for one another. That is to say, TIMs interpret Marx seeing commodities acquiring money prices when money begins to be used as a medium of exchange and formed in the context of the performance of this function.

Lastly, TIMs interpret Marx seeing the magnitude of the money price of the commodity determined by the relative price of the commodity (and this in turn by the relative labour time required for its production) for a given value of money. As noted above, most TIMs see Marx's explanation of the magnitude of money price of the commodity as flawed because of the flaw in his transformation procedure and corresponding explanation of the relative price (commodity exchange value) of the commodity.

The problems with the TIM explanation of the money price of the commodity begin with its **conception**. First, TIMs are unable to interpret Marx conceiving of the money price of the commodity as its money exchange value. This follows from their interpretation of his conception of the value of the commodity as having no link to money. As argued in chapter 2, for Marx the value of the commodity is the transformed form of the labour time actually expended in its production where this transformation takes place when money is used to denote the general exchange value of the commodity. Second, their interpretation of Marx's conception of money prevents TIMs from interpreting Marx conceiving of the money price of the commodity as its commodity money price. This is because their interpretation of Marx's conception of money is as an intrinsically valueless token of the commodities whose exchange for one another it facilitates. This means that when TIMs interpret Marx conceiving of commodities having gold prices it must mean they are interpreting him seeing commodities having certain numéraire prices in the manner of Ricardo. Third, their interpretation of Marx's conception of the money price of the commodity prevents TIMs interpreting him conceiving of these prices as the forms assumed by their values. This is because they do not see commodities acquiring values in the context of money being used by producers to denote the general exchange values of their commodities, and causing both commodities and money to become the embodiments of a certain magnitude of socially necessary labour time. Lastly, TIM interpretations of Marx's conception of the money price of the commodity preclude them from interpreting him conceiving of the relative price of the commodity as its money price relative to that of another commodity and the aggregate money price level as the aggregate money prices of all commodities. Instead, it causes TIMs to interpret Marx conceiving of the relative money price of the commodity as its commodity exchange value, where money is a token of the abstract labour time that governs the exchange of commodities for one another, and the aggregate money price level as the aggregate quantity of money used to facilitate the exchange of a certain aggregate quantity of commodities for one another relative to this quantity of commodities.

The consequence of their mistaken interpretation of Marx's conception of the money price of the commodity is that TIMs are unable to interpret Marx conceiving of money as its **measure** and the form of the measure of the value of the commodity. Rather, it requires them to interpret him conceiving of money as a token of commodities as the measures of the exchange values of one another. For TIMs to be able to interpret Marx conceiving of money as the measure of the money price of the commodity, they would need to interpret him conceiving of the money price of the commodity as its money exchange value. Moreover, for TIMs to be able to interpret Marx conceiving of money as the form of the measure of the value of the commodity, they would need to interpret Marx conceiving of the value of the commodity having an intrinsic link to money. As I have argued above, this is precluded by their interpretation of Marx's conception of the value of the commodity.

Their implicit interpretation of Marx's conception of the money price of the commodity prevents TIMs from interpreting Marx seeing the historical **acquisition** of money prices of commodities that facilitate their reproduction taking place with the emergence of capitalism and the use of one particular commodity as the measure of the general exchange values of all others. It also prevents them from interpreting Marx seeing the money prices of commodities **formed** prior to them being put into the process of circulation (exchange). Indeed, as argued above, their interpretations of Marx's conception of the money price of the commodity suggest that for TIMs Marx should be interpreted as seeing commodities acquiring money prices prior to capitalism and these prices formed in the process of the exchange of commodities for one another.

The problems with TIM interpretations of Marx's explanation of the **magnitude** of the money price of the commodity follow from the preceding. To begin their interpretation of Marx's explanation of the money price of the commodity prevents TIMs from interpreting him explaining this magnitude as the magnitude of its money exchange value. Instead, as argued above, their interpretations of Marx's conception of the money price of the commodity require him to be interpreted as explaining its magnitude as the magnitude of its commodity exchange value for a given value of money. Second, it prevents TIMs from interpreting Marx explaining the magnitude of the money price of the commodity as the magnitude of its commodity money price unless he is interpreted as explaining this magnitude as the magnitude of its numéraire price and money as a numéraire commodity. Third, the TIM interpretation of Marx's explanation of the magnitude of the money price of the commodity requires them to interpret him seeing changes in the relative money prices of commodities taking place independently of changes in the aggregate money price level. This is because it prevents them from interpreting Marx explaining the magnitude of relative money price of the commodity as the magnitude of its money price relative to the magnitude of the money price of another commodity, and the aggregate money price level as the aggregate of the money prices of all commodities. Lastly, since TIMs see Marx's explanation of the magnitude of the commodity exchange value of the commodity as flawed due to the alleged problem with his transformation procedure, they must also interpret him having a correspondingly flawed explanation of the magnitude of the money price of the (individual) commodity. I noted above, this is certainly the conclusion of many modern TIMs. To repeat what I have argued above, not only do TIMs misunderstand Marx's transformation procedure, they misunderstand the sense in which he sees the magnitude of the value of the commodity determining the magnitude of its money exchange value or money price. Once it is recognised that for Marx the value of the means of production transferred to the money exchange value or money price of the production of the commodity is the value of money needed to repurchase the means of production, his alleged transformation problem disappears. More fundamentally, since for Marx value cannot be seen, its impact on the magnitude of the money price of the commodity only becomes manifest in the link between changes in the relative productivity of labour and changes in the relative money prices of commodities.[76]

7.8.2 MIMs

Since MIMs interpret Marx conceiving of the exchange value of the commodity as its money exchange value, much of what follows is necessarily informed by what was argued above in relation to their interpretation of Marx's explanation of the exchange value of the commodity as its money exchange value.

For MIMs, Marx conceives of the money price of production of the commodity as the quantity of money commanded by it in the process of its circulation by money, with money being whatever is used to facilitate the circulation of commodities or, for a few MIMs, to denominate and settle debts. It follows from this that MIMs implicitly, if not explicitly, interpret Marx conceiving of the measure of the money price of the commodity as a certain quantity of money, where money is a token of abstract labour time or (for a few MIMs) the labour input. It also follows they interpret Marx seeing commodities acquiring money prices historically when money comes to be used to purchase the inputs used in

[76] It warrants noting that Marx does not allude to this relationship being also manifest in the link between changes in the economy-wide productivity of labour and the aggregate money price level even though there should logically be a link between these two as well.

production, viz., the means of production and labour power, and these money prices formed in the context of the purchase of these inputs. Lastly, most MIMs interpret him explaining the magnitude of the money price of the commodity by the quantity of money outlaid on wages and used to purchase means of production, with the emphasis being on the money outlaid on wages given that means of production are also produced commodities. As I noted above, MC Marxists are the clearest that this interpretation of Marx's explanation of the magnitude of the money price of the commodity is the logical consequence of the MIM interpretation of the value of the commodity.

The problems with MIM interpretations of Marx's explanation of the money price of the commodity begin with its **conception**. As I argued above in the context of MIM interpretations of Marx's conception of the exchange value of the commodity, they do not see that for Marx the money price of the commodity is the *form* assumed by its value. This is because their interpretation of Marx's conception of value prevents them from seeing that for him the value of the commodity assumes the form of its money price when money is used to denote the general exchange value of the commodity. As I have also argued above, Marx stresses the value of the commodity cannot be seen. Instead, its existence is evidenced by the impact changes in the productivity of labour have on the magnitude of its money price. Second, MIMs do not see that for Marx the money price of the commodity represents its *general exchange value*, i.e., the quantity of any and all commodities it is able to command, and not the quantity of abstract labour time or the labour input it is able to command.

The consequence of the MIM interpretation of Marx's conception of the money price of the commodity is, as one might expect, a confused interpretation of his conception of its **measure**. Specifically, as argued above, it causes MIMs to implicitly, if not explicitly, interpret Marx conceiving of both money and labour time as the measures of the money price of the commodity, and not money alone as this measure. What MIMs are necessarily ignoring is the importance Marx attaches to socially necessary labour time as the *intrinsic* measure of the money price of the commodity, and money the *extrinsic* form assumed by this intrinsic measure. Even more fundamentally still, MIMs do not see that for Marx when money is used by producers to denote the general exchange values of their commodities it converts the labour time actually expended in the production of commodities into magnitudes of socially necessary labour time—the average labour time expended in the production of the bulk of commodities in all sectors.

Their interpretation of Marx's conception of the money price of the commodity and its measure prevents MIMs from interpreting Marx seeing the historical **acquisition** of money prices by commodities that facilitate their reproduction taking place with the emergence of capitalism and the use of money by producers to denote the general exchange value of their commodities. It also causes MIMs to ignore the emphasis he places on the **formation** of the money prices of commodities after their production and prior to them being put into the process of circulation. MIMs do not see that for Marx when producers set the prices of their commodities before putting them into the process of circulation they take into account the prices set by the producers producing the bulk of the commodities of this type in the context of relative changes in the unit costs of production in their own production processes as well as the general condition of the market—e.g., the extent of excess demand for the products of the type produced by the particular producer.

The problems with the MIM interpretation of Marx's explanation of the **magnitude** of the money price of the commodity follow from the above and correspond in part to those noted above in the context of MIM interpretations of Marx's explanation of the magnitude of the exchange value of the commodity. First, like TIMs, MIMs are not able to interpret Marx explaining the magnitude of the money price of the commodity as the magnitude of its commodity money price. This is because, as for TIMs, their interpretation of Marx's conception of money precludes such an interpretation. To the extent that MIMs interpret Marx explaining the magnitudes of the money prices of commodities as magnitudes of their gold prices,[77] they must be interpreting him explaining these as the magnitudes of the numéraire prices of commodities, with the exchange value of the numéraire (gold) being unity.

Second, as argued in the context of MIM interpretations of Marx's explanation of the magnitude of the exchange value of the commodity, their interpretation of Marx's conception of value prevents them from interpreting him explaining the magnitude of the money price of the commodity by the (socially necessary) labour time expended in its production. Instead, it requires MIMs to interpret Marx explaining the

[77] See for example Moseley (2011).

magnitude of the money price of the commodity by the money wage rate in the manner of PKs. As I have argued above, this interpretation of Marx's explanation of the magnitude of the money price of the commodity is clearest in the MC approach.

Third, one consequence of their interpretation of Marx's explanation of the money price of the commodity by the money wage rate is it requires MIMs to deny Marx has a meaningful explanation of trend changes in the *relative money prices* of commodities. As I argued above, this is because, on the one hand, MIMs need to deny Marx sees changes in money wages having a bearing on relative money prices to avoid interpreting him seeing the prices of labour-intensive products rising continuously alongside increases in the money wage rate, and, on the other hand, MIMs are unable to interpret Marx explaining changes in these prices by changes in sectoral profit rates in the manner of PKs due to their acceptance of Marx's assumption of the formation of a general rate of profit. As I also argued above, this causes MIMs to either ignore Marx's explanation of trends in the relative magnitudes of money prices or interpret him explaining these trends by all manner of *ad hoc* factors.

Fourth, a consequence of the preceding is that it requires MIMs, like TIMs, to interpret Marx seeing changes in the relative money prices of commodities taking place independently of changes in the aggregate money price level, and not also in the context of the latter. Crucially, like TIMs, MIMs are not able to interpret Marx seeing changes in the productivity of labour having a bearing on changes in both the relative money prices of commodities and the aggregate money price level.

Lastly, and also in accordance with MIM interpretations of Marx's explanation of the magnitude of the exchange value of the commodity noted above, their interpretation of his explanation of the magnitude of the value of the commodity precludes them from interpreting Marx seeing the money prices of means of production, including raw materials, having a bearing on this magnitude and, therefore, the magnitude of the money price of the commodity. It was argued above that the MIM interpretation of Marx's explanation of the magnitude of the value of the commodity requires them to interpret him seeing the value of the means of production transferred to the value of the commodity produced with them as the values of the means of production used directly and indirectly in their production, and not the value of money required to repurchase the means of production.

7.8.3 *The Source of the Problem*

The source of the problem with the Marxist interpretations of Marx's explanation of money price discussed in this chapter is their interpretation of Marx's conception of the value of the commodity and its link to money. TIMs interpret Marx seeing the value of the commodity having no intrinsic link to money while MIMs interpret him collapsing value into money. This causes both approaches to have a mistaken interpretation of Marx's conception of money as an intrinsically valueless token of abstract labour time (or, for MC Marxists the labour input) and a correspondingly mistaken interpretation of Marx's explanation of the money price of the commodity, with the most obvious manifestation of the latter being that it requires both approaches to interpret Marx seeing changes in the relative money prices of commodities taking place independent of changes in the aggregate money prices of all commodities, at least insofar as they are able to interpret Marx having an explanation of changes in the former. It will be recalled that most TIMs accept Marx cannot be interpreted as having a logical explanation of the relative (money) price of the individual commodity because of alleged flaws in his transformation procedure, and the MIM interpretation of Marx's explanation of the money price of the commodity requires them to deny he has any meaningful explanation of the relative money price of the commodity.

References

Arthur, C. J. (2004). *The new dialectic and Marx's 'Capital.'* Brill.

Baran, P. A., & Sweezy, P. M. (1966). *Monopoly capital: An essay on the American economic and social order*. Monthly Review Press.

Bellofiore, R. (1989). A monetary labor theory of value. *Review of Radical Political Economics, 21*(1+2), 1–25.

Bellofiore, R. (2005). The monetary aspects of the capitalist process in the Marxian system: An investigation from the point of view of the theory of the monetary circuit. In F. Moseley (Ed.) (pp. 124–139).

Bellofiore, R., & Realfonzo, R. (2003). Money as finance and money as universal equivalent: Re-reading Marxian monetary theory. In L.-P. Rochon & S. Ross (Eds.), *Modern theories of money: The nature and role of money in capitalist economies*. Edward Elgar.

Brenner, R. (1976). Agrarian class structure and economic development in pre-Industrial Europe. *Past & Present, 70*, 30–75.

Campbell, M. (2005). Marx's explanation of money's functions: Overturning the quantity theory. In P. Moseley (Ed.) (pp. 143–159).
De Brunhoff, S. (1976). *Marx on money* (M. J. Goldbloom, Trans.). Urizen Books.
Duménil, G. (1983–1984). Beyond the transformation riddle: A labor theory of value. *Science and Society, 47*(4), 427–450.
Fine, B. (1980). *Economic theory and ideology*. Edward Arnold.
Fine, B., & Lapavitsas, C. (2000). Markets and money in social theory: What role for economics? *Economy and Society, 29*(3), 357–382.
Fine, B., & Saad-Filho, A. (2004). *Marx's 'Capital'*. Pluto Press.
Foley, D. K. (1976). Preface. In S. de Brunhoff (pp. v–ix).
Foley, D. K. (1983). On Marx's theory of money. *Social Concept, 1*(1), 5–19.
Foley, D. K. (1986). *Understanding 'Capital': Marx's economic theory*. Harvard University Press.
Foley, D. K. (2005). Marx's theory of money in historical perspective. In F. Moseley (Ed.) (pp. 36–49).
Foster, J. B. (2000). *Marx's ecology: Materialism and nature*. Monthly Review Press.
Freeman, A. (1996). Price, value and profit—A continuous, general, treatment. In A. Freeman & G. Carchedi (Eds.), (pp. 225–279).
Freeman, A. (1998). *Time, the value of money and the quantification of value* (MPRA Paper, No. 2217). University Library of Munich, Germany.
Freeman, A., & Carchedi, G. (Eds.). (1996a). *Marx and non-equilibrium economics*. Edward Elgar.
Freeman, A., & Carchedi, G. (Eds.). (1996b). Foreword. In A. Freeman & G. Carchedi (Eds.) (pp. vii–xx).
Freeman, A., & Kliman, A. (1998). *Simultaneous and temporal valuation contrasted* (MPRA Paper, No. 52805, revised 23 Sep 1998). University Library of Munich, Germany.
Germer, C. (2005). The commodity nature of money in Marx's theory. In P. Moseley (Ed.) (pp. 21–35).
Graziani, A. (1997). The Marxist theory of money. *International Journal of Political Economy, 27*(2), 26–50.
Graziani, A. (2003). *The monetary theory of production*. Cambridge University Press.
Hardt, M., & Negri, A. (2000). *Empire*. Harvard University Press.
Hilferding, H. (1981). *Finance capital: A study of the latest phase of capitalist development* (M. Watnick & S. Gordon, Trans.). Routledge and Kegan Paul (Originally published in 1910).
Hilton, R. (Ed.). (1978). *The transition from feudalism to capitalism*. Verso.
Itoh, M. (1988). *The basic theory of capitalism: The forms and substance of the capitalist economy*. Macmillan Press.

Itoh, M., & Lapavitsas, C. (1999). *Political economy of money and finance*. Palgrave Macmillan.
Kliman, A. J. (2007). *Reclaiming Marx's 'Capital': A refutation of the myth of inconsistency*. Lexington Books.
Kliman, A. J., & McGlone, T. (1988). The transformation non-problem and the non-transformation problem. *Capital & Class, 35*, 56–83.
Kliman, A. J., & McGlone, T. (1999). A temporal single-system interpretation of Marx's value theory. *Review of Political Economy, 11*(1), 33–59.
Lapavitsas, C. (1991). The theory of credit and money: A structural analysis. *Science & Society, 55*(3), 291–322.
Lapavitsas, C. (2000). Money and the analysis of capitalism: The significance of commodity money. *Review of Radical Political Economics, 32*(4), 631–656.
Lapavitsas, C. (2009). Financialised capitalism: Crisis and financial expropriation. *Historical Materialism, 17*(2), 114–148.
Mandel, E. (1976). *'Introduction' in Marx's Capital: Volume I* (B. Fowkes, Trans.). Penguin Books.
Marx, K. (1970). *A contribution to the critique of political economy* (Trans. from German by S. W. Ryazanskaya). Progress.
Marx, K. (1976). *Capital: Volume I* (B. Fowkes, Trans.). Penguin Books.
Meek, R. L. (1973). *Studies in the labor theory of value* (2nd ed.). Lawrence & Wishart.
Meek, R. L. (1977). *Smith, Marx, & after: Ten essays in the development of economic thought*. Chapman & Hall.
Mohun, S. (1994). A re(in)statement of the labour theory of value. *Cambridge Journal of Economics, 18*(4), 391–412.
Moseley, F. (Ed.). (2005). *Marx's theory of money: Modern appraisals*. Palgrave Macmillan.
Moseley, F. (2011). The determination of the "Monetary Expression of Labor Time" ("MELT") in the case of non-commodity money. *Review of Radical Political Economics, 43*(1), 95–105.
Moseley, F. (2016). *Money and totality: A macro-monetary interpretation of Marx's logic in capital and the end of the 'Transformation Problem.'* Brill.
Moulier-Boutang, Y. (2012). *Cognitive capitalism* (E. Emery, Trans.). Wiley.
Nelson, A. (2005). Max's objections to credit theories of money. In F. Moseley (Ed.) (pp. 65–77).
Nicholas, H. (2011). *Marx's theory of price and its modern rivals*. Palgrave Macmillan.
Nicholas, H. (forthcoming). *Explorations in Marx's theory of price, Volume 2: Profits and business cycles*. Palgrave Macmillan.
Rubin, I. I. (1972). *Essays on Marx's theory of value*. Black & Red (Originally published in 1928).

Saad-Filho, A. (2000). Inflation theory: A critical literature review and a new research agenda. In P. Zarembka (Ed.), *Value, capitalist dynamics and money* (Vol. 18, pp. 335–362). Bingley.

Saad-Filho, A. (2002). *The value of Marx: Political economy for contemporary capitalism*. Routledge.

Schumpeter, J. A. (2006). *History of economic analysis*. Taylor and Francis (Originally published in 1954).

Shaikh, A. (1977). Marx's theory of value and the "transformation problem." In J. Schwartz (Ed.), *The subtle anatomy of capitalism* (pp. 106–139). Goodyear.

Shaikh, A. (2016). *Capitalism: Competition, conflict, crises*. Oxford University Press.

Sweezy, P. M. (1968). *The theory of capitalist development: Principles of Marxian political economy*. Monthly Review Press.

Weeks, J. (2010). *Capital, exploitation and economic crisis*. Routledge.

CHAPTER 8

Neoclassical Explanations of Money Price

8.1 Introduction

What has come to be referred to as the Neoclassical school of thought is generally acknowledged as having its origins in the writings of Jevons, Walras, and Menger around the latter part of the nineteenth century.[1] Its emergence was the culmination of a reaction against the Classical school that began with what Marx describes as the disintegration of the Ricardian school.[2] Today the Neoclassical school is by far the dominant school of thought in most universities and policy circles around the world, in spite of the inroads made by the PK school in more recent times. I have argued elsewhere the Neoclassical school comprises a number of sub-schools, the most important of which are the Austrian, Walrasian, and New Keynesian.[3] Notwithstanding the divergent explanations of various economic phenomena proffered by adherents of these and other sub-schools making up the Neoclassical school, they all share one unifying principle; the explanation of economic phenomena in terms of the decisions made by individuals in the processes of consumption, exchange, and production.

[1] See Dobb (1973).

[2] See Marx (1972).

[3] See Nicholas (2011, 2012) for an elaboration of the Neoclassical school.

H. Nicholas, *Explorations in Marx's Theory of Price—Why Marx Is Still Relevant for Understanding the Modern Economy*,
https://doi.org/10.1057/978-1-137-56564-8_8

8.2 Object and Approach

Most Neoclassicals see the purpose of their economic analyses to show how the behaviour of individuals explains observed economic phenomena, and, more specifically, how this process fosters an increasing division of labour and optimal allocation of resources resulting in a maximisation of welfare. When explaining economic phenomena, Neoclassicals too use the method of abstraction. Most Neoclassicals also typically abstract in the first instance from capital, money, and supply–demand imbalances. A few modern Neoclassicals have, to one extent or another, deviated from this, particularly with respect to the need to abstract from capital and money, denying the need to abstract from either.

From the perspective of Marx's analysis the problem with the Neoclassical focus on the process of exchange and the behaviour of the individual in this process is that it shifts the focus of economic analysis away from the production of commodities towards their exchange. This shift of focus is most clearly in evidence in the works of the founders of the subjective approach to the explanation of price. Two of these, Carl Menger and Leon Walras, begin their analyses of the economic system with what is referred to as a 'pure exchange' economy comprising individuals *endowed* with commodities seeking to exchange these for other commodities with a view to enhancing their consumption satisfaction or utility. They bring in production after the analysis of the pure exchange economy to explain the endowments of individuals, but in a way that does not alter the results of the analysis of this pure exchange economy. Moreover, even when Neoclassicals bring production into the analysis from the outset, the emphasis remains on individuals taking decisions with a view to enhancing their consumption satisfaction. Neoclassicals conceive of producers as surrogate consumers producing commodities with a view to directly or indirectly maximising their consumption satisfaction. Consequently, the distinction made by Smith between different systems of production involving the appropriation of the net product by owners of different factor inputs is no longer seen as an important foundation of the analysis. This foundation shifts to that of the behaviour of individuals as consumers engaged in exchange with one another as owners of commodity outputs and 'factor inputs' (see below).

The problem with the Neoclassical method of abstraction is that, like most other approaches, its purpose is not to capture the essence of the phenomena being studied. It is to make the study of the economic system more manageable by dealing with one aspect of it at a time, albeit beginning with what is perceived to be the most important aspects of it.[4] Consequently, it leads to a distorted understanding of the economic system. For example, whether or not Neoclassicals abstract from capital used in the process of production in the first instance, they conceive of it as a collection of (long-lasting) commodity inputs whose owners are in effect surrogate consumers. What Neoclassicals do not see in this regard is that capital used in the process of production is a certain quantity of value that expands over time and assumes the forms of commodities and money in the process of its expansion.

The abstraction from money in the first instance causes Neoclassicals to have a similarly distorted understanding of it when it is brought into the analysis. It causes money to be seen as a token of the commodities being exchanged, with the system of the exchange of commodities being essentially one of barter, i.e., the exchange of one commodity (C) for another (C'). When money is brought into the analysis such that C-C' becomes C-M-C', individuals are deemed to still have in mind the relative satisfaction they expect to derive from the purchase of C' with the money they obtain from selling C.[5] This results in money being seen as a veil, and 'monetary phenomena', such as inflation and external payments balances, seen as distinct from 'real phenomena' such as economic growth and employment. The former are explained by monetary decisions of individuals and the latter by their quantity decisions. Some Neoclassicals (e.g., Modern Austrians, Monetarists, and New Keynesians) tacitly deny there is need to abstract from money in the first instance when explaining economic phenomena. Many of them see monetary decisions of individuals impacting on real economic phenomena and quantity decisions impacting on monetary phenomena, with Austrians referring to money as

[4] In a debate with critics of the Neoclassical approach, Katzner (2008, p. 329) describes the Neoclassical process of abstraction as one focusing on certain aspects of economic phenomena that are thought to be of primary significance for its subsequent explanation.

[5] In fact, even when exchange is seen as mediated by credit, the exchange process is conceived of as one of barter in the sense what when the commodities are sold on credit the individuals selling the commodities are assumed to have in mind the subjective value they expect to derive from the commodities they intend to purchase in the future when the debt is repaid. Mises (1971, p. 35) argues "Credit transactions are in fact nothing but the exchange of present goods against future goods".

something of a 'fluttering veil' in this context.[6] However, these Neoclassicals see this impact taking place over the 'short run' or 'short period', accepting that money is in essence a veil and monetary phenomena are in the final instance separate from real phenomena. What these, and all other Neoclassicals, do not see is that the economy is fundamentally a monetary economy in which the exchange of the commodity is for money *per se*. There is no separation between the real and monetary economy. Commodities are not sold for other commodities in accordance with the subjective value attached to them, nor are inputs purchased with commodities or clusters of commodities.

Lastly, Neoclassicals also abstract from demand–supply imbalances in the first instance in a way that reinforces their understanding of the system as essentially one in, or tending to, balance or 'equilibrium' in commodity, 'factor', and money markets. When demand and supply imbalances are admitted to, they are seen as explaining, to one degree or another, deviations from equilibrium. There are considerable differences among Neoclassicals, even within the different sub-schools, regarding the equilibrium tendencies of markets. At one extreme are the so-called 'rational expectations' Neoclassicals who deny any significant divergences of markets from equilibrium, and, at the other extreme, there are the Austrians who see markets as nearly always in disequilibrium. What all Neoclassicals agree on, however, is the tendency of the movement of the variables being analysed towards equilibrium, and that this movement is the outcome of the behaviour of individuals. This view of the essential nature of the system denies that it is characterised by recurrent periods of expansion and contraction in economic activity. That is, Neoclassicals deny 'business cycles' are inherent to, let alone necessary, for the functioning of the capitalist system of production. In fact, for Neoclassicals business cycles are more appropriately described as 'fluctuations' in aggregate economic activity resulting from random real or monetary 'shocks', with the extent of the fluctuations depending on the severity of the shocks.[7] There are most certainly differences between Neoclassicals regarding the sources and nature of the fluctuations. However,

[6] Horwitz (2000, p. 67).

[7] See Ikeda (2019) for an elaboration of this point.

there is broad agreement that the capitalist system is for the most part in equilibrium or tending towards equilibrium.[8]

8.3 Neoclassical Economics as Ideology

Although the first major Neoclassical works, i.e., those of Menger, Jevons, and Walras, only make their appearance towards the end of Marx's life, he is most certainly aware of the emergence of this line of economic thought, referring to it as 'vulgar' and its exponents as 'apologists' for the capitalist class in general, even identifying elements of this approach in the works of Smith and Ricardo. Marx sees the Neoclassical approach as vulgar in that their explanations of economic phenomena are superficial.[9] He sees them as apologetic in that their explanations of economic phenomena have the sole purpose of mystifying and sanitising the workings of the economic system, justifying the role played by the capitalist class in these workings.[10] For Marx, the most obvious consequences of the ideological nature of this approach are the conception of capital and distorted explanation of the sources of incomes, especially profit.[11] One can add to this the confused and confusing conception of money, the justification of the role of financial capitalists, and the distorted explanation of cycle phenomena.

Mention should also be made of the tendency of Neoclassicals towards the increasing mathematical presentations of arguments and their econometric validation. Whether intentionally or otherwise, there can be no doubting that the mathematical presentation of economic arguments conveys the impression of their *logical rigour*, deflecting attention from the unrealistic assumptions underlying them and ambiguity of the concepts being used. A case in point is the mathematical presentations of neo-Walrasian general equilibrium explanations of money prices of commodities (see below). Also, whether intentionally or otherwise, there can similarly be no doubting that the use of econometric techniques is intended to convey the impression of *scientific rigour*, often masking

[8] One of the clearest expressions of the need to conceive of the system as tending towards equilibrium even when it is seen as characterised by overproduction, unemployment, and the like is provided by Schumpeter (1964, pp. 42–45).

[9] Marx (1969, pp. 266–267, 485).

[10] Marx (1972, 453).

[11] Marx (1972, pp. 462, 454).

the real purpose of such studies as providing support for certain desired policy stances and shifts. Take for instance the vast number of supposedly scientific econometric studies of the 1970s, 80s, and 90s purporting to provide incontrovertible evidence of a determinate link between printing of money (viz., changes in the central banks asset base) and inflation. These studies appear to have been conveniently forgotten in the aftermath of the great 2007–2009 global economic crisis when most of the central banks of the advanced countries embarked on unprecedented expansions of the monetary bases of their financial systems which should have resulted in nothing short of hyperinflation if those studies were to be believed. Not only did the predicted hyperinflation not materialise, its absence elicited barely any acknowledgement from either the authors of those studies or the policy makers who made use of them.

8.4 Production and Value of the Commodity

8.4.1 Production

Like Smith, Neoclassicals conceive of the production of commodities as undertaken by firms with the aid of 'factors of production', where factors of production are conceived of as labour, capital, and land, whose owners receive an income for their supply in the forms of wages, interest, and rent, respectively. The incomes are seen as commodity incomes determined in markets for the factor inputs, with changes in them providing signals for decision-making by individuals as sellers and buyers of the factor inputs. Neoclassicals see the process of production as a producer using the productive services of factor inputs to produce outputs. They see the commodities produced in capitalism as those required to meet the consumption needs of owners of factor inputs, and argue, in the manner of Smith, that the increasing productivity of labour and other factor inputs accompanying the increasing division of labour is the result of a broadening and deepening of the process of exchange.[12]

From the perspective of Marx's analysis the problems with the Neoclassical explanation of production begin with the general **conception** of production. Like most other approaches considered above, Neoclassicals do not see production as social production. They do not see it involving the cooperation of human beings in the production of the goods needed

[12] See for example Menger (2007),Walras (1954), Marshall (2009).

to reproduce the material base of the system. Instead, they conceive of production as a technical process involving the use of material inputs and labour to produce outputs. The material inputs and labour are seen as provided by individuals seeking to enhance their consumption satisfaction. There is no discussion of the social setting in which the inputs, particularly the labour input, are provided, or recognition that in capitalism labour is compelled to work for a wage. It is not recognised that wage labour is characteristic of capitalism as opposed to previous historical epochs.

Related to this, Neoclassicals also do not see that the **purpose** of production changes in different social settings. They do not see that in capitalism this purpose is the accumulation of wealth in the form of capital (i.e., a form of wealth that begets more wealth) and not the satisfaction of the consumption needs of the producers. The distorted Neoclassical view of the purpose of production in capitalism stems from its point of departure for the analysis of the capitalist system; the exchange of commodities by individuals with a view to enhancing their consumption satisfaction. It is a starting point that assumes individuals exchanging commodities with one another are naturally endowed with these commodities. Even when this assumption is relaxed to allow for endowments of commodities held by individuals to be seen as produced, Neoclassicals continue to assume the purpose of the exchange of the commodities is the satisfaction of the consumption needs of those exchanging them and not the reproduction of the commodities.

The mistaken conception of the nature and purpose of production in capitalism causes Neoclassicals to have a distorted understanding of the capitalist **producer**. The capitalist producer, or entrepreneur, is seen as providing the superintendence services of a manager and appropriating a wage in the form of a profit. There is no indication where profits come from and how the rate of profit is formed. The only possible conclusion available to Neoclassicals for where profits come from is that they are deductions from incomes accruing to owners of factors of production in a disequilibrium setting. In fact, Neoclassicals try to avoid conceiving of the entrepreneur as the owner of capital that appropriates a profit in relation to the magnitude of the capital advanced to undertake production. This is because it undermines their conception of capital as a factor input that is borrowed by the entrepreneur from the owner of capital. The most obvious manifestation of the erroneous Neoclassical understanding of the entrepreneur and profits is the *ad hoc* cameo appearances the entrepreneur makes in most Neoclassical economics textbooks, usually in the context of discussions of supply responses to increases in the relative demand for a commodity, or their analyses of perfect and monopoly competition.

The Neoclassical conception of the nature and purpose of production also causes them to have a mistaken conception of the **inputs** used in the production of the commodity as factor inputs, i.e., borrowed inputs whose owners appropriate incomes for lending them to entrepreneurs. A distinction is drawn between factor and commodity inputs, with the latter being those non-long-lasting commodities that are directly purchased by entrepreneurs. Neoclassicals conceive of *capital* as a composite of long-lasting produced commodities that, as noted above, are borrowed by the entrepreneur paying an income to the lender of capital (the 'capitalist') in the form of (commodity) interest. They do not explain why and how capital can be conceived of as a composite of long-lasting commodity inputs, or how the commodities commanded as interest by the owners of the composite of long-lasting inputs can be conceived of as having a determinate relation to this composite. The Neoclassical conception of production also causes them to have a mistaken conception of the *labour* input. It causes them to conceive of what is purchased with the wage as certain skills of the worker. They do not see that what is purchased is the *ability* of the worker to expend energy over a certain period of time in the production of commodities that can be sold for greater sums of money than they cost to produce. Neoclassicals also do not see that the wage rate is not determined in the market for labour but in the processes of the production of commodities. Newly employed workers are paid standard rates for standard jobs prevailing in the firms and not a rate determined by the supply of and demand for workers in the labour market.

Neoclassicals conceive of the process of production as a technical combination of the factor inputs not the productive consumption of the means of production in the context of the expenditure of labour time. In fact, given that Neoclassicals see the factor inputs as essentially marketable inputs that can be purchased with the commodities produced with their assistance, they implicitly see the process of production in the final instance as the production of commodities by means of commodities. That is, they implicitly see the process of production as the productive consumption of commodity outputs. This allows them to bypass the problem of having to explain the link between the labour input and the commodities produced.

Like Smith, Neoclassicals see the commodity **outputs** produced excluding (long-lasting) means of production. This is because Neoclassicals, like Smith, see the expenditure on goods and services stemming from incomes and not from the revenues of companies, part of which assumes the form of incomes and part of which is necessarily spent on replacing used-up means of production. Neoclassicals avoid conceiving of incomes spent on commodities including what is spent on long-lasting capital goods because doing so would imply capital is simply another produced commodity. In this case, capital cannot be differentiated from the produced commodities appropriated with incomes accruing to owners of factor inputs. They would have to admit that capital is a produced commodity that can simply be bought like any other commodity.

Lastly, as noted in the context of Smith's argument with respect to the link between the division of labour and exchange, there is no historical evidence to support this link. Nor is there any reason to suppose that the main driver of the increasing productivity of labour is the increasing division of labour and, therefore, the process of exchange. Rather, this driver is the tendency in capitalist systems to develop technologies that result in the ever-increasing displacement of labour in the production of any commodity, a tendency that is inherent in these systems.

8.4.2 *Value of the Commodity*

When it comes to the explanation of the value of the commodity, Neoclassicals are divided. On the one hand there are those who conceive of it as the subjective value attached to the commodity by the individual whether or not they are in possession of it. On the other hand, there are those who *implicitly* conceive of the commodity having objective value, even if they deny doing so. Specifically, even though adherents of the latter group admit to explaining the prices of commodities in the final instance by the commodity costs of producing them (where these costs are the commodities used to pay wages and interest), they try to give the explanation a subjective character in the manner of Marshall. In what follows I will refer to the former group as Subjective Value Neoclassicals (SVNs) and the latter as the Objective Value Neoclassicals (OVNs). The SVNs comprise the Austrian and Walrasian approaches. The OVNs comprise the New Keynesians and their predecessors the Neoclassical Synthesis approach. It warrants remarking that most popular economics textbooks are written from an OVN perspective.

SVNs

Although all SVNs conceive of the value of a commodity as the subjective value attached to it by the individual, there are differences between them in terms of how they conceive of this subjective value. Some SVNs conceive of the subjective value attached as the relative utility or satisfaction. Others conceive of it as the ranking of preferences of individuals for different commodities.[13] For all SVNs there can be no measure of the value of the commodity as such, only a ranking of subjective value. Commodity A yielding more or less subjective value than commodity B, or commodity A being preferred to commodity B. Given their conception(s) of the value of a commodity, SVNs must also logically see commodities acquiring values prior to their production and exchange,[14] and these values formed and reformed independently of the latter, independently of the production and exchange of the commodities. Lastly, also following from the SVN conception of the value of the commodity, they do not explain the magnitude of the value of the commodity, since, by definition, subjective value cannot have magnitude.

From the perspective of Marx's analysis the problems with the Neoclassical explanations of the value of the commodity begin with how they conceive it. The problem with the SVN **conception** of value is that it is premised on a conception of the economy comprising individuals naturally endowed with commodities who exchange them to enhance their consumption satisfaction. In such an economy it makes sense to conceive of the value of a commodity as the subjective value attached to it by those exchanging it. However, once it is accepted that the economy being explained is one where the process of exchange facilitates the reproduction of commodities, this conception of value no longer makes sense. Indeed, the problem with the subjective conception of value becomes particularly manifest when production is brought into the analysis since it requires SVNs (and also OVNs) to explain the means of production purchased by firms having subjective value attached to them even though they do not directly satisfy the consumption needs of individuals. Consequently, most Neoclassicals avoid conceiving of firms as buyers of products. Those that do attempt to explain the subjective value attached to the inputs bought

[13] See Hicks (1946, pp. 11–25) for a comprehensive discussion of the distinction between utility and subjective preference.

[14] See Mises (1971, pp. 38–39).

by the firm argue it corresponds to the satisfaction expected to be derived by the producer either from the commodities produced with the inputs or those exchanged for the produced commodities.[15]

It follows from the preceding that their conception of the value of the commodity prevents SVNs from seeing commodities **acquiring** value historically when they are produced in the context of a division of labour. In fact, it presumes they see products acquiring values independently of their production. The SVN conception of the value of the commodity not only prevents them seeing the **formation** and reformation of this value in capitalism taking place in the context of the production of the commodity but also in the context of the formation and reformation of its exchange value. Consequently, not only are they unable to see the link between the formation of the value of the commodity and its production, i.e., between what is commanded in the process of exchange by the individual commodity and its value. What SVNs do not see in this regard is the intrinsic link between money and the value of the commodity.

Lastly, the SVN conception of the value of the commodity, as the subjective value attached to it, means this value cannot be seen as having a quantitative dimension, a certain **magnitude**. As noted above, this requires Neoclassicals to deny it is meaningful to explain the magnitude of the value of the commodity. Some SVN, especially a number of those adopting a Walrasian approach, give the impression they conceive of the value of the commodity as the commodities appropriated as incomes by owners of factor inputs. However, for Walrasians, as for Austrians, the commodity incomes appropriated by owners of factor inputs used to produce the commodity are determined by the subjective value attached to the commodity (see below).

OVNs

OVNs conceive of the value of the commodity as the commodities commanded as incomes by owners of factor inputs used in its production. The commodities commanded as incomes are seen as wages, interest, and rent by owners of labour, capital, and land, respectively. Their conception of the value of the commodity causes OVNs to implicitly see the measure of this value as a certain quantity of the commodities commanded as incomes. OVNs implicitly see commodities acquiring values when they

[15] See for example Horwitz (2000, p. 44).

are produced using factor inputs whose owners appropriate incomes in the form of commodities. It also causes them to see these values formed in the process of production for given real factor incomes. Lastly, OVNs explain the magnitude of the value of the commodity by the relative quantity of commodities commanded by owners of factor inputs required to produce the commodity, drawing a distinction between short and long periods of time based in the relative fixity of the capital input in the manner of Marshall. OVNs see the short period as a period of time when the quantity of the capital input is fixed and the long period when all factor inputs are variable.[16] They see changes in the magnitude of value of the commodity brought about by changes in the relative demand for the commodity,[17] with changes over the short period explained by changes in unit labour costs resulting from changes in the marginal productivity of labour and over the long period by changes in unit factor costs resulting from 'economies of scale'—unit costs falling and rising due to efficiencies and inefficiencies brought about by changes in the scale of production.[18] By implication, OVNs see movements in the magnitude of the value of the commodity over the short period as fluctuations in these magnitudes around their long period averages due to demand and supply imbalances.

The problem with the OVN explanation of the value of the commodity from the perspective of Marx's analysis also begins with its **conception**. First, OVNs tacitly conceive of the value of a commodity as a certain *cluster* of all commodities, and in particular an aliquot part of the net product, commanded as incomes by owners of the factors of production used in the production of a commodity. Since OVNs are unclear that this is how they conceive of the value of a commodity, they are, naturally

[16] Marshall actually distinguishes between four periods of time; the market, short, long, and secular periods. The market period is the shortest time period and is a period of time when it can be assumed output is fixed, while the secular period is the longest and is a period of time when all factor inputs are completely flexible and there are changes in technology and skills (2009, pp. 312–315).

[17] An increase in the relative demand for a product is seen as resulting in an increase in the magnitude of the exchange value of the commodity in the context of an increase in the magnitude of the profit appropriated by the entrepreneur. The increase in the magnitude of profit causes her/him to increase the output of the commodity using more labour and intermediate commodity inputs. This in turn result in a diminishing marginal productivity of labour and an increase in unit commodity wage costs, causing unit profits to fall back to their original equilibrium levels.

[18] See for example Mankiw (2017, pp. 259–262).

enough, unclear about how they conceive of the commodities comprising the net product as an aggregate cluster in a way that allows for aliquot parts of it to be seen as appropriated as incomes in the context of the production of the commodities. Second, like all other approaches, OVNs do not see the costs incurred in the production of the commodity as the transformed form of the costs actually incurred in the production of the commodity, with these costs being what need to be incurred in its production as a standard commodity of a certain type.

The problems with the implicit OVN conception of the **measure** of the value of the commodity follow from their implicit conception of its value. First, the OVN conception of the value of the commodity requires them to see its measure as a certain aliquot part of the net product. Problematically, this requires OVNs to conceive of the net product as a homogeneous and divisible entity. Needless to say, OVNs ignore the problem, tacitly assuming it is possible to conceive of the net product as a homogeneous entity that is divisible into aliquot parts. Second, the implicit OVN conception of the measure of the value of the commodity prevents them from conceiving of a unit of this measure.

The OVN conception of the value of a commodity requires them to see commodities **acquiring** values historically *after*, not prior to, them acquiring exchange values. This view of the historical emergence of the values of commodities is consistent with their view of production based on the use of marketable factor inputs facilitated by the emergence of exchange. Like Smith, OVNs appear to conveniently ignore the fact that products are produced historically long before they are exchanged for one another.

The OVN conception of the value of the commodity prevents them from seeing it **formed** after the process of production of the commodity at the same time as the formation of its exchange value. This is because, like all other approaches, OVNs do not see the value of the commodity is the costs that need to be incurred in the production of a standard type of the commodity in question, with the costs actually incurred in the production of the particular commodity becoming transformed into those that need to be incurred when producers set the prices of their commodities prior to putting them into circulation.

The problems with the OVN explanation of the **magnitude** of value of the commodity follow from the above. First, the OVN explanation of the magnitude of value over the short period presumes it is possible to conceive of the labour input as quantifiable in a way that permits the explanation of changes in unit labour costs pertaining to changes in the (marginal) productivity of labour. Since OVNs conceive of the labour input in the manner of Smith, there is no reason to suppose it lends itself to the sort of quantification required for this purpose. Specifically, the conception of unit labour costs that are related to the productivity of labour requires the labour expended in the production of the commodity to be conceived of as labour time. Second, their explanation of the magnitude of value over the long period requires OVNs to tacitly assumes it is meaningful to conceive of factor inputs being perfectly substitutable for one another in accordance with their relative marginal productivities and 'prices' (i.e., the commodity incomes appropriated in relation to the quantity of the factor input) such that changes in the magnitude of the value of the commodity can be explained by changes in the quantities of these factors and corresponding productivities for given trend factor prices. I will take up and expand on these and other problems with the OVN explanation of the magnitude of value of the commodity over both the short and long periods in Nicholas (forthcoming), but note in passing that these explanations require the entrepreneur to be conceived of as a manager and profits as their wages, and capital to be conceived of as a composite of 'long lasting' commodity means of production. Lastly, like most other approaches OVNs pay little attention to the value of the means of production transferred to the value of the commodity produced with them. They certainly do not see that the implication of their conception of the value of a commodity requires them to explain the value transferred from the means of production as the income costs incurred in the production of the various layers of means of production required to produce a commodity, and that there is no reason to suppose this constitutes a determinate magnitude.

8.5 Exchange and Exchange Value of the Commodity

8.5.1 Exchange

Most Neoclassicals conceive of the process of exchange in capitalism as essentially one commodity (C) for another (C'), or C-C', with this process mediated by money (M), and depicted as C-M-C'. The money acquired from the sale of the commodity is seen by Neoclassicals as held only fleetingly, although it is accepted individuals may hold part of their wealth in the form of money. Walrasian Neoclassicals deny that money serves the purpose of facilitating the exchange of commodities since exchange is presumed as having taken place at the exchange values computed by an auctioneer.[19] Neoclassicals typically see the purpose of the exchange of commodities as one of meeting the consumption desires of individuals, with those Neoclassicals adopting an income cost explanation of the magnitude of value seeing the purpose of the exchange of commodities as, additionally, to enable the producer to acquire the necessary commodities to pay (commodity) incomes to owners of factor inputs. Like Smith, Neoclassicals see the process of exchange as historically preceding that of the production of commodities in the context of a division of labour. Also like Smith, Neoclassicals conceive of the process of exchange as essentially one of barter, in the sense that there is no separation between the sellers and buyers of the products being exchanged. Those selling products are seen as attaching a certain subjective value to these products that they then compare with the subjective value of the products they seek to purchase.

From the perspective of Marx's analysis, the problems with the Neoclassical explanation of the process of exchange begin with its **conception**. The problem in this regard is that Neoclassicals do not conceive of the process of exchange in capitalism as the exchange of the individual commodity for something representing general exchange value, albeit with a view to purchasing other commodities. In fact, even when the process of exchange in capitalism is conceived of as C-M-C', money is conceived of as representing particular exchange value as a token of the commodities being exchanged for one another and not something representing general exchange value and allowing those selling their commodities to purchase any and all other commodities.[20] Neoclassicals do not see the purpose of exchange in capitalism is the reproduction of the commodity. Instead, they see its purpose as the satisfaction of the wants of those exchanging the products for one another, whether or not production is brought into the analysis. This view of the purpose of exchange is readily apparent in the case of SVN analyses, but less so in the case of OVN analyses. SVNs see the process of exchange in capitalism,

[19] See Debreu (1959).

[20] See below for an expansion of this point.

as in all modes of production, as independent of the material reproduction of the economic system. Although, in contrast, OVNs see exchange facilitating the process of the reproduction of the commodity, they see it doing so by enabling producers to acquire the commodities needed to pay incomes thereby satisfying the consumption needs of the owners of factor inputs. They do not see that it facilitates the reproduction of the commodity by enabling the producer to repurchase all the commodity inputs used up in the process of production, including labour power.

Neoclassicals do not see the **emergence** of widespread exchange presupposing the production of commodities in the context of a division of labour, because they see the process of exchange as either independent of production or driving the division of labour. SVN typically begin their analyses of exchange by assuming the commodities being exchanged are those which individuals are naturally endowed with, only bringing production into their analyses to explain the endowments. Even though OVNs do not begin their analyses of the process of exchange in similar fashion, they typically follow Smith in arguing the increasing division of labour that has taken place in respect of the production of commodities has been historically driven by exchange.[21]

Lastly, even when Neoclassicals bring money into their analyses of the process of exchange, they conceive of the latter as one of **barter**. This is because they conceive of the process of exchange as in the final instance one commodity for another, or for a cluster of commodities, with all commodities being put into the process of exchange without determinate exchange values. The characteristic feature of a barter system is that products acquire exchange values in the process of their exchange for one another and not prior to this.

8.5.2 Exchange Value of the Commodity

The Neoclassical explanations of the exchange value of the commodity are related to their explanations of its value. Since a distinction is required between subjective and objective explanations of the value of the commodity, a corresponding distinction is required when considering Neoclassical explanations of the exchange value of the commodity.

[21] See, for example, Krugman and Wells, (2006, p. 12).

SVNs

SVNs conceive of the exchange value of the commodity as the quantity of another commodity a unit of it commands in the process of exchange, viz., Q_y/Unit *x* where Q_y is the quantity of another commodity, *y*, commanded by a unit of commodity *x*. That is to say, SVNs see the exchange value of a commodity as its *commodity exchange value* or *relative price*. This conception of the exchange value of the commodity does not change when SVNs bring production into their analyses and owners of factor inputs are conceived of as appropriating commodity incomes in the context of the production of the commodity.

Most Austrian SVNs argue the purpose of the exchange value of a commodity is the *signals* it provides for individuals to base their decisions on with respect to the quantities of commodities (and services) they seek to buy or sell.[22] When the individuals exchanging commodities include producers of commodities, the exchange values of commodities are seen as providing signals for producers to base their decisions regarding the quantities of the commodities to be produced. The exchange values that provide the signals are seen as 'disequilibrium' exchange values. Walrasian SVNs who see an auctioneer setting equilibrium exchange values deny these have any signalling role since the decisions of individuals are taken as given in the formation of the exchange values.[23]

All SVNs see the measure of the exchange value of the commodity as any and every commodity commanded by in the process of exchange. A few SVNs follow Walras in conceiving of one of the commodities as a standard of all commodities as measures of the exchange values of one another; as a numéraire commodity. The rationale offered for the adoption of a numéraire commodity is that it aids multiple exchanges.[24] This is not, however, a view shared by all SVNs, particularly not Austrian SVNs.[25]

Although SVNs, like most other approaches, pay little or no attention to how commodities acquire exchange values historically, the logic of their analyses suggests they see this accompanying the emergence of the process

[22] See for example Menger (2007), Mises (1971).

[23] See Hahn (1987, p. 55).

[24] See for example Hicks (1946, p. 58), Malinvaud (1985, pp. 9–10).

[25] Hayek (1941, pp. 31–32) argues the numéraire contributes nothing to "triangular and multi-angular exchanges".

of exchange *per se*, after individuals have assigned subjective value to the commodities to be exchanged. SVNs typically pay more explicit attention to the formation of the exchange values of commodities. Austrian SVNs see this formation taking place in the context of bargaining between individual buyers and sellers of commodities. Walrasians see exchange values of commodities formed outside of the process of exchange, by the auctioneer. The auctioneer is seen as weighing up the various quantities of commodities that are demanded and supplied and calling out corresponding equilibrium exchange values ensuring balance between them—the quantities of commodities demanded and supplied.[26] By implication, buyers and sellers are assumed to be 'price takers'.[27]

For all SVNs the magnitude of the exchange value of the commodity is explained by the demand for, and supply of, it relative to another commodity, and this in turn by the values of the commodities, i.e., the subjective worth attached to the commodities by the individuals exchanging them. The supply of the commodity is seen as the inverse of the demand for it, even if the commodity being exchanged is produced. An increase in the demand for a given commodity implies a decrease in its supply, and *vice versa*. For SVNs, changes in the quantities of commodities held by individuals as a result of changes in their production are always the result of prior changes in the relative demand for them, given an initial balance between demand and supply. To the extent that SVNs bring commodity income costs into their analyses, it is to argue that they are explained by the exchange value of the commodity and not the other way around. For example, Walras (2005, pp. 71–72) argues,

> Where there is equilibrium of exchange and production the price of [factor] services is determined by the price of the products (and not the price of the products by the price of the services), and that the price of the products is determined by the condition of maximum satisfaction of the needs, which is therefore the basic condition of economic equilibrium.

In a similar vein the Austrian economist Holcombe (2014, p. 32) argues,

[26] Walker (2006, p. 150) argues that Walras "did not mention or imply a central price quoter or decentralised price quoters in any connection".

[27] See for example Arrow and Hahn (1971).

The value of inputs into the production process is determined by the value consumers place on what those inputs produce. So, the cost of production is ultimately determined by the value of what is being produced.

Moreover, for SVNs the production costs incurred in the production of the commodity are determined by the subjective value attached to the inputs in terms of the satisfaction foregone as a result of their supply. Thus, the real wage appropriated by labour is the reward for the leisure foregone by the worker and the real interest appropriated by owners of capital is the reward for the present consumption foregone by them.

From the perspective of Marx's analysis the problems with the SVN explanation of the exchange value of the commodity begin with its **conception**. SVNs do not see that in capitalism what is commanded in the process of exchange by a particular commodity is something representing general exchange value. This is because SVNs conceive of the process of exchange as one commodity for another and its purpose as the enhancement of the consumption satisfaction of those exchanging their commodities with one another. They do not see that this conception of the exchange value of the commodity corresponds to a mode of production in which the commodities being exchanged are not produced for exchange i.e., pre-capitalist economic systems. In capitalism, when commodities are produced for exchange, the commodity is exchanged by the producer of the commodity for something representing general exchange value causing the exchange value of the commodity to assume the form of general exchange value, or money exchange value, allowing the producer to repurchase all the commodity inputs (including labour power) used up in the production of the commodity. To the extent SVNs see the exchange value of the commodity assuming the form of money, they conceive of this as a token of its particular exchange value, a token of the particular commodity to be commanded in the process of exchange, and not the form of its general exchange value.

The problem with the SVN conception of the **measure** of the exchange value of the commodity follows from the problems with its conception. Since SVNs do not see the exchange value of the commodity in capitalism as its general exchange value, they do not see its measure as necessarily something representing general exchange value that is readily divisible into homogeneous parts. In fact, since SVNs see the exchange value of the commodity as the particular commodity it commands in each transaction they see this measure continuously changing with no reason to suppose it lends itself to divisibility into homogeneous parts. For those SVNs recognising the problem, the proposed solution is the adoption of a homogeneous standard or numéraire commodity. Apart from the necessary arbitrariness of the choice of the numéraire, these SVNs do not make clear why the numéraire is not money. Walras, who is generally credited with developing the concept of the numéraire, recognises the problem and corresponding importance of distinguishing the numéraire from money. However, his attempt to distinguish between the two is confused and confusing, as the following passage demonstrates:

> The role of the numéraire and money are different. We may suppose that one commodity is chosen as numéraire and another as money...For the time being, and in order to study the effect of choosing a commodity as money on its value, we shall suppose the commodity both numéraire and money at the same time. (Walras, 2005, p. 77)

Hicks reiterates and expands on the need for a numéraire commodity as well as the problem of distinguishing between it and money. The confusion this gives rise to is evident in the following:

> We shall find it convenient, when dealing with multiple exchange, always to take some particular commodity as a standard of value. So far, this commodity is invested with some of the qualities of money. But it is not necessary to assume that our traders actually use the standard commodity as money; they may do or they may not. If, for some purposes, we do decide to identify the standard commodity with money, then it must be clearly understood that it has not yet been given any more of the qualities of money than these – that it is an object of desire, and that it is used as a standard of value. Later on we shall be able to endow our standard commodity with other qualities, so that we can actually employ it as a means for analysing genuinely monetary problems; for the present it is very much a shadow. But we shall find that it is much more useful to have even a shadow in the early stages of our analysis than to have no money at all...
>
> Thus we shall assume for the present that our standard commodity is a real commodity like any other, with an ordinary place on the scale of preferences of an ordinary individual... (Hicks, 1946, pp. 58–59)

The SVN conception of the exchange value of the commodity along with the conception of exchange on which it is based causes adherents to see products **acquiring** exchange values historically when they are less scarce in the sense of being less naturally abundant. Although it is evident freely available goods do not have exchange values, it does not follow products acquire exchange values historically when they begin to be less scarce, less naturally abundant. In all social systems, except possibly so-called hunter-gatherer systems, the availability of products to satisfy consumption needs depends on their production. SVNs, like most other economists, do not see that products acquire exchange values historically after they come to be produced in the context of a division of labour, when the division of labour comes to be mediated by exchange. They do not see that the form of the exchange value that the commodity acquires prior to the emergence of capitalism is not the form of exchange value it acquires in capitalism. The form of the exchange value it acquires prior to the emergence of capitalism is the form of particular exchangeable worth, i.e., the form of commodity exchange value, even when it assumes a money form. The form of exchange value it acquires in capitalism is the form of general exchangeable worth, even when the exchange value assumes a commodity form i.e., the form of commodity money.

Their conception of the exchange value of the commodity and underlying process of exchange prevents SVNs from seeing it **formed** *prior* to commodities being put into the process of exchange. SVNs do not see the exchange values of commodities formed by producers denoting the exchange values of their commodities as certain magnitudes of general exchange values prior to putting them into the process of circulation. Instead, they see the exchange values of commodities formed either in the process of the exchange of commodities for one another and the bargaining of individuals exchanging the commodities (viz., Austrians) or outside of the economic system by the actions of an auctioneer (viz., Walrasians).

The problems with the SVN explanation of the **magnitude** of the exchange value of the commodity from the perspective of Marx's approach follow from the above. First, SVNs do not see that the magnitude of the exchange value to be explained in a capitalist economic system is the magnitude of its general exchange value and not its particular exchange value, i.e., its money price or money exchange value and not its relative price or commodity exchange value. Again, this is because SVNs conceive of the magnitude of the exchange value of the commodity to be explained as, in effect, that pertaining to the exchange of commodities in pre-capitalist economic systems. Second, SVNs cannot explain the magnitude of the exchange value of the commodity by the magnitude of its value since for them value does not have a magnitude. Instead, they explain the magnitude of the exchange value of the commodity by the relative value of the commodity, i.e., the relative subjective worth attached to it. This causes SVNs to implicitly see the magnitude of exchange value of the commodity changing with each and every transaction involving different individuals, denying that there is any tendency for different buyers of commodities to pay the same amount of another commodity to purchase it. That is to say, it requires SVNs to see each buyer of a commodity exchanging a different amount of another commodity for the commodity in question since the relative subjective worth attached to the commodities must differ between buyers. Lastly, their explanation of the magnitude of the exchange value of the commodity requires SVNs to ignore costs in this explanation, even when the production of the commodity is brought into the analysis. In fact, as noted above, when SVNs bring producers into their analysis they conceive of them as surrogate consumers, whose demand for inputs stems from the satisfaction they expect the commodities they intend to produce with these inputs to directly or indirectly yield.

OVNs

The point of departure for a consideration of the OVN explanation of the exchange value of the commodity is also its conception. Most OVNs conceive of the exchange value of the commodity in the manner of the SVNs, i.e., as the quantity of another commodity commanded by a unit of it. A few OVNs conceive of it as the quantity of 'all commodities' or a part of the net product commanded by a unit of a given commodity.[28] This conception follows logically from the implicit OVN conception of the value of the commodity as the commodities appropriated as incomes by owners of factors of production in the context of the production of a commodity. A few OVNs conceive of the exchange value of the commodity as 'all other commodities' commanded by a unit of it where all commodities are denominated in terms of money.[29] This conception is a legacy of the attempt by M. Friedman to reformulate Marshall's assumption of a constant value of money (as the constant marginal utility of money) when explaining the magnitude of the exchange value of

[28] See for example Lipsey and Chrystal (2007, p. 50).

[29] See for example Mankiw (2017, p. 43), Varian (1992, p. 150).

a commodity.[30] Whichever of these conceptions OVNs adopt, they all tacitly see the exchange value of the commodity providing signals on which individuals base their consumption and production decisions.[31]

Their conception of the exchange value of the commodity requires most OVNs to conceive of its measure as the commodity or cluster of commodities for which it is exchanged. For those OVNs conceiving of the exchange value of the commodity as a certain aliquot part of the net product it commands in the process of exchange the measure of the commodity is implicitly seen as an aliquot part of the net product, and for those conceiving of the exchange value of the commodity as a certain cluster of all other commodities it commands in the process of exchange the measure is implicitly seen as a certain quantity of this cluster.

The logic of the OVN explanation of the exchange value of the commodity suggests that, like SVNs, OVNs see commodities acquiring exchange values historically with the development of exchange *per se*, but unlike SVNs they see this taking place at the same time as, or even before, commodities acquire values. This follows from the OVN conception of the value of the commodity as the commodity incomes appropriated by factor owners where the commodities appropriated have exchange values. The logic of the OVN explanation of the exchange value of the commodity also suggests OVNs see it formed in the process of exchange, albeit the exchange of commodities by producers seeking to recover the quantity of commodities outlaid on incomes required to pay owners of factor inputs for the supply of these inputs.

Lastly, like SVNs, OVNs explain the magnitude of the exchange value of the commodity by the demand for, and supply of, the commodity. Where OVNs diverge from SVNs is in seeing the magnitude of the exchange value of the commodity reflecting its relative real income costs, and these in turn reflecting relative quantities of factor inputs. Following Marshall, these real income costs are linked to the 'efforts' and 'sacrifices' of individuals.[32] Distinguishing between the short and long periods, OVNs argue that over the former period, when the labour input alone is variable, the income costs that matter are real wage costs, while over the long period, when all factor inputs are variable, the income costs that

[30] See Friedman (1949), Hahn (1984).

[31] See for example Mankiw (2017, p. 7).

[32] See Marshall (2009, pp. 282–283, 289).

matter are the real incomes pertaining to all the factor inputs. It has to be said, however, that most OVN explanations of the magnitude of the exchange value of the commodity are rather vague on the connection between factor incomes and factor inputs.

From the perspective of Marx's analysis, the problems with the OVN explanation of the exchange value of the commodity also begin with its **conception**. The basic problem with this conception from the perspective of Marx's approach is the same as that with the SVN conception; the exchange value of the commodity is seen as its commodity exchange value or particular exchange value and not its general exchange value, and where what represents general exchange value is homogeneous and divisible. Conceiving of the exchange value of the commodity as the quantity of a certain cluster of commodities commanded by it is not the same as conceiving of it as the general exchange value of the commodity, even when the cluster of commodities is conceived of as an aliquot part of the net product. This is because the exchange value of the commodity is still being conceived of as the quantity of a particular commodity commanded by it, except in this case the particular commodity is an artificial construct. Moreover, there is no reason to suppose this construct is any more homogeneous and divisible than an individual commodity, or that it is used by the producer to pay incomes. The problem with conceiving of the exchange value of the commodity as an artificial construct has caused most OVNs to formally conceive of it in the manner of SVNs, as the quantity of another commodity commanded by a given commodity in the process of exchange, with many OVNs fluctuating between the two in their explanations of the exchange value of the commodity. Whatever conception of the exchange value of the commodity OVNs adopt, like SVNs, they do not see the exchange value of the commodity as its general exchange value because they do not see its purpose one of enabling the producer of the commodity to repurchase all the commodity inputs used up in its production.

The problem with the implicit OVN conception of the **measure** of the exchange value of the commodity follows from its conception. The basic problem in this regard is that, as for SVNs, OVNs see the measure of the exchange value of the commodity as a particular commodity, i.e., the particular commodity the commodity in question exchanges with, and not something that represents general exchange value. This means that for OVNs, as for SVNs, the measure of the exchange value of the commodity changes with each and every transaction, without any reason to suppose the measure is either homogeneous or divisible—two necessary qualities of a measure of the exchange value of a commodity. There is also no reason to suppose that a certain quantity of the net product as a composite commodity can be conceived of as the representative of general exchange value, let alone that it is homogeneous and divisible, since it is tacitly assumed to be a particular commodity.

Like SVNs, OVNs do not see commodities **acquiring** exchange values historically after they come to be produced in a division of labour, or acquiring *general* exchange value with the emergence of capitalism—and the use by producers of something representing general exchange value to denote the general exchange values of their commodities with a view to facilitating their reproduction. Instead, and like SVNs, OVNs see commodities acquiring exchange values historically prior to their production in the context of a division of labour, and the form of this exchange value remaining the same in capitalism.

Also like SVNs, OVNs do not see the exchange value of the commodity in capitalism **formed** prior to the commodity being put into the process of exchange (circulation). Even though, unlike the SVNs, OVNs see the purpose of the exchange value of the commodity as the reproduction of the commodity, like SVNs, they do not see its formation taking place in the context of producers denoting the general exchange values of their commodities prior to putting them into the process of exchange (circulation). This is because they see the reproduction of the commodity requiring producers to exchange their commodities for those commodities required to pay incomes and not to exchange them for a certain quantity of money that enables the producers to repurchase the commodity inputs (including labour power) used up in the process of production.

The problems with the OVN explanation of the **magnitude** of the exchange value of the commodity follow from the above. First, like SVNs, OVNs do not see the magnitude of the exchange value that needs explaining as the magnitude of its general exchange value, even when the commodity commanded is seen as a part of the net product. This follows from their failure to see the purpose of the exchange value of the commodity as one of facilitating its reproduction by enabling the producer to repurchase all the commodities used up in their production. Second, although OVNs explain the magnitude of the exchange value of the commodity by the magnitude of its value, as I argued above they are not able to conceive of factor inputs in a way that allows them to explain the values of commodities having determinate magnitudes over either the short or long periods. Of particular note in this regard is their conceptions of the labour and capital factor inputs as well as the assumed substitutability between all factors. Third, changes in the magnitude of the exchange values of commodities are seen as resulting from changes in the quantities of them put into the process of exchange as a result of changes in their relative values. OVNs do not see that the magnitudes of exchange values of commodities change before they are put into the process of exchange since, as argued above, they do not see exchange values of commodities formed prior to them being put into the process of exchange (circulation). Lastly, OVNs must logically deny the exchange values of commodity inputs having a direct bearing on the exchange values of commodity outputs. This follows from their explanation of the magnitude of the exchange value of the commodity by the embodied income costs of producing the commodity. To the extent that the inputs used in the production of the commodity are seen by OVNs as including commodity inputs in addition to factor inputs, the magnitudes of the former need to also be explained by the commodity incomes appropriated in the context of their production, and the commodity inputs used in their production by commodity incomes appropriated in the context of their production, and so on.

8.6 Money and Its Functions

8.6.1 Money

Most Neoclassicals (viz., Austrians and OVNs) conceive of money as whatever is used by individuals to facilitate the exchange of commodities or assets for one another. Differences between Neoclassicals pertain to their conceptions of what is commanded by money in the process of exchange and their values (see below). Austrian SVNs conceive of what is commanded by money in the process of exchange as a particular commodity or asset,[33] the value of which is the subjective value attached to it.[34] OVNs conceive of what is commanded by money in the process of exchange as the commodities appropriated in the form of incomes, the

[33] I take an asset for Neoclassicals to mean something which entitles the owners to a certain stream of income.

[34] See for example Mises (1971, pp. 119–120).

values of which are the quantities of commodities commanded as factor incomes in the context of their production. Walrasian SVNs are divided between those who deny money has an existence because they deny there is need for something to facilitate the exchange of commodities given that this role is ascribed to the auctioneer, and those that accept it has an existence but not something that facilitates the exchange of commodities for one another. The latter grouping, referred to in the literature as neo-Walrasians,[35] conceive of money as 'a temporary abode of purchasing power' that individuals hold as a form of wealth, the value of which is the subjective worth they attach to it.[36]

Most Neoclassicals follow Smith in seeing money emerging historically with the process of exchange. Like Smith, they see money facilitating an economy-wide extension of this process, making possible an increasingly complex division of labour.[37] Neoclassicals accept that money emerges in the first instance as a commodity, although it is denied it needs to be a commodity.[38] Indeed, whether money's primary purpose is seen as facilitating the exchange of commodities (assets) for one another or serving as a temporary abode of purchasing power, for Neoclassicals it logically shouldn't be a commodity. Instead, it should be either a valueless token of commodities or an asset.

Lastly, Neoclassicals see money as a 'veil' in the sense that changes in its quantity and exchange value have no bearing on the production and reproduction of commodities, at least over the long run or long period. Most Neoclassicals see money having an impact on the production of commodities over the short run or short period due to 'expectation errors', with some modern Austrians referring to money being akin to a 'fluttering veil'.[39] Neo-Walrasians are the exception among Neoclassicals in that they tacitly deny money is a veil over either the short or the long period.

From the perspective of Marx's analysis the problems with the Neoclassical understanding of money begin with its **conception**. First, Neoclassicals conceive of money in capitalism as what is used to facilitate the

[35] See Clower (1999).

[36] See for example Patinkin (1949),Fischer (1974),Lucas (1980).

[37] Horwitz (2000, p. 138), Krugman and Wells (2006, p. 12).

[38] Mises (1971).

[39] Horwitz (2000, p. 67).

exchange of commodities for one another presuming that the process of exchange in capitalism can be characterised as the exchange of commodities for one another, albeit mediated by money. Second, their conception of money requires Neoclassicals to see money as an intrinsically valueless token of the commodities whose exchange for one another it facilitates and, therefore, a token of the values of these commodities. This means it requires Austrians to conceive of money as a token of subjective worth which must, by implication, change with each and every transaction, and OVNs to conceive of money as a token of a certain aliquot part of the net product where all those using money to facilitate the exchange of commodities for one another are aware of the quantity of the net product it represents. Third, it follows from the preceding that it requires Neoclassicals, like all other approaches to deny money is, or has ever been, a commodity in capitalism. Lastly, it requires Neoclassicals to see money representing particular exchange value and not general exchange value. It requires them to see it representing the quantity of the particular commodity that is to be acquired in the process of exchange and not any and all other commodities. It requires them to deny what is observably one of the most important characteristics of money; its use to purchase any and all commodities.

Neo-Walrasians give the impression they see money as what is commanded in the process of exchange, having intrinsic value and representing general exchange value. However, this impression is illusory. First, since they see money as an arbitrarily chosen asset that is in principle the same as any other asset, they are conceiving of the process of exchange in which it is what is commanded as the exchange of one asset for another. Second, it is not money that neo-Walrasians see having value but rather an ordinary asset, like any other asset, with no reason to suppose any one asset held as wealth is more useful than another as a hedge against uncertainty. Lastly, there is no reason to suppose what is held as wealth can be used to purchase any and all other assets, i.e., that it represents general exchange value.

Neoclassicals see money **emerging** historically with the development of exchange, but not prior to capitalism. In fact, Neoclassical must deny money emerges as a numéraire commodity prior to capitalism to avoid having to conceive of commodities being put into the process of circulation with determinate money prices. This means that, as with Smith, they must deny money emerges as a commodity like gold or silver, whether in pre-capitalist systems or even in capitalism. Neoclassicals who conceive of money as an asset held as part of an individual's wealth, i.e., neo-Walrasians, can conceive of money emerging prior to capitalism, but as an *arbitrarily* chosen 'asset' which is much the same as any other asset.

Neoclassicals who conceive of money as a token of commodities (viz., Austrians and OVNs) must deny it assumes the **form** of a commodity or, indeed, the form of whatever facilitates the exchange of commodities. This is to avoid conceiving of money as something possessing value that is simultaneously a valueless token of the commodities whose exchange for one another it facilitates. Neoclassicals who conceive of money as an asset to which individuals attach subjective value (i.e., neo-Walrasians) are unable to explain why it assumes any particular form. This is because there is no reason to suppose money assumes the form of what is required to facilitate the exchange of commodities for one another since it is assumed the process of exchange is facilitated by the auctioneer. In the final instance, neo-Walrasians have to assume money acquires the form of whatever asset is arbitrarily selected as the numéraire store of wealth.

Lastly, Neoclassicals see money as a **veil**, albeit a fluttering veil for some, because they do not acknowledge the fundamental role it plays in the reproduction of the commodity. They do not see producers using money to denote the general exchange values of their commodities with a view to facilitating their reproduction in the context of appropriating a profit. Indeed, since Neoclassicals see money's purpose as facilitating the exchange of commodities with a view to enhancing the satisfaction of those exchanging commodities, or even providing the individual with a hedge against uncertainty, there is no reason to suppose they see changes in the quantity of money and corresponding changes in its exchange value having any bearing on the reproduction of commodities.

8.6.2 *Functions*

Neoclassicals accept money has in principle several functions, but most Neoclassicals (viz., Austrians and OVNs) attach primacy to its medium of exchange function, seeing the other functions as derivative of this function. As medium of exchange, money facilitates the exchange of commodities for one another according to their values. The other functions of money Neoclassicals usually refered to are those of unit of account and store of purchasing power.[40] Neoclassicals see money's function as a unit of account as its use to denominate the exchange value of the commodity in terms of money. They see money's store of purchasing power function as that of holding wealth in its most liquid and least risky form.[41] A few Neoclassicals, those neo-Walrasians who see money as an asset, assign primacy to money's store of purchasing power function, formally denying it is used as a medium of exchange. Lastly, even though Neoclassicals acknowledge money is used to denominate and settle debts, they typically pay scant attention to this function of money.

From the perspective of Marx's analysis, the major problem with the Neoclassical explanations of money's functions is their neglect of its function as the **measure** of the general exchange values of commodities and the corresponding primacy they attach to one or another of its other functions, most notably its medium of exchange function. The neglect of money's measure function follows for most Neoclassicals (viz., Austrians and OVNs) from their conception of the process of exchange as the exchange of commodities for one another by individuals with the purpose of maximising their satisfaction. They see the exchange values of commodities that are formed in this process measured by one another and not by something representing general exchange value. This is also true for those Neoclassicals who see money used to facilitate the exchange of commodities for a numéraire commodity. The neglect of money's measure function in the case of neo-Walrasians follows from their tacit assumption that prices are set by an auctioneer.

Money's **unit of account** function that Neoclassicals admit to should not be confused with Marx's measure of exchange value function. The unit of account function of money for Neoclassicals is the use of a unit of whatever serves to facilitate the exchange of commodities for one another to denominate the exchange values of the commodities being exchanged. It is not the use by producers of something that represents general exchange value to denote the general exchange values of their commodities with a view to facilitating their reproduction, nor the use of various names (e.g., a pound sterling) to denote units of whatever is used as the measure of the exchange value of the commodity.

[40] See Mankiw (2017, p. 605).

[41] Friedman (1989, pp. 20–21) argues that this function of money is similar to Keynes' liquidity preference function except that for Neoclassicals money as a store of wealth is compared to all other stores of wealth and not only financial assets.

The neglect of money's function as measure of the exchange value of the commodity by Neoclassicals requires them to ignore its function as **medium of circulation**. It should be recalled that the use of money as the measure of the exchange values of their commodities by producers results in them putting their commodities into the process of circulation with determinate money prices, requiring money to facilitate their circulation in accordance with these prices. Since Neoclassicals see the process of exchange as the exchange of commodities for one another, they see money facilitating this process as a **medium of exchange**, attaching primacy to this function of money in the absence of an auctioneer. Money as a medium of exchange is necessarily a valueless token of the commodities whose exchange for one another it facilitates. In contrast, money as a medium of circulation is either what serves as the measure of the exchange value of the commodity or a token of it that facilitates the circulation of commodities with determinate money prices. As a medium of circulation money enters the process of circulation with a determinate magnitude of value and exchange value.

Although Neoclassicals who attach primacy to money's medium of exchange function accept it also performs the functions of **denominator and settler of debts** and **store of purchasing power**, they pay less heed to these functions. They tacitly assume the quantity of money used for these purposes is a stable function of the quantity of money used as a medium of exchange, albeit allowing for variations in the rate of interest. What Neoclassicals do not see is that money's primary function as medium of exchange logically precludes it from being seen as held outside of the process of facilitating the exchange of commodities for one another, since money cannot be seen as possessing value and representing a certain quantity of exchange value outside of this process.

The problem with the neo-Walrasian understanding of money's store of purchasing power function of money is, on the one hand, their conflation of this function with the function of money as capital, and, on the other hand, their need to formally deny money's function as medium of exchange while tacitly admitting to it. The confusion of money with capital follows from seeing money held as a store of purchasing power assuming the form of an asset or capital. Neo-Walrasians do not see that money held as capital is for the purpose of expanding its magnitude, while money held as a reserve of purchasing power does not imply this motive for holding it, notwithstanding it is held in banks and other financial institutions that use money in this way. The need for neo-Walrasians to formally deny money's medium of exchange function follows, as noted above, from their contention that the exchange values of commodities and/or assets are set by an auctioneer, while their implicit admission of this function of money is apparent in their conception of money as a repository of purchasing power. This is the contradiction inherent in the neo-Walrasian conception of money alluded to above, and noted by Clower (1999, p. 407) in the following;

> The point to note is that, when dealing with the apparently simple task of incorporating money into economic theory, some of the greatest minds in the discipline (Baumol, Tobin, Samuelson, Friedman, Patinkin, Fama, Black and Hall, among others) have been led into outright contradiction.

8.7 Value of Money

Neoclassicals who explain the value of money fall into one of two groups; those who deny money has value in itself, and those who argue it has value in itself.[42] The former conceive of the value of money as the value of the commodities (assets) commanded by money in the process of exchange. Some of these (viz., Austrians) conceive of this value as the subjective value attached to the commodities (assets) whose exchange for one another money facilitates.[43] Others (viz., OVNs) implicitly conceive of it as a cluster of commodities whose exchange for one another money facilitates. Neoclassicals who see money having value in itself (viz., those referred to above as neo-Walrasians), conceive of this value as the subjective value attached by individuals to the services provided by money.[44]

Neoclassicals who conceive of money having subjective value directly or indirectly attached to it, i.e., the Austrians and neo-Walrasians, deny this value can be measured. It can only be ranked in relation to the subjective value attached to something else. Neoclassicals who conceive of money having objective value in the form of the commodities commanded as incomes whose exchange for one another money facilitates, i.e., the OVNs, tacitly see money having a measure. This measure is logically the

[42] Graziani (2003, pp. 108–109) refers to the two groupings as the "direct" and "indirect" approaches to the explanation of the value of money.

[43] See for example Mises (1971).

[44] See for example Brunner and Meltzer (1989).

cluster of commodities appropriated as incomes by owners of factor inputs used to produce all the commodities exchanged for one another.

The preceding suggests that for most Neoclassicals (viz., Austrians and OVNs) what functions as money is implicitly, if not explicitly, seen as acquiring value historically when it comes to be used to facilitate the exchange of commodities, where this value is either the subjective value attached to the services provided by money or the value of the commodities whose exchange for one another it facilitates. It also suggests that for most Neoclassicals (viz., Austrians and OVNs) the value of money is formed in the process of exchange. A few Neoclassicals (viz., neo-Walrasians) tacitly see the value of money formed independently of the process of exchange, in the manner of the formation of the value of any commodity (asset), when individuals attach subjective value to the services performed by it other than that of medium of exchange.

Neoclassical explanations of the magnitude of value of money follow from the above. Most SVNs, whether they conceive of money having direct or indirect subjective value, deny this value has a certain magnitude. This is because they see the value of money as the subjective value attached to either the services provided or the commodities commanded by it. In contrast, the OVN conception of the value of money allows for an explanation of its magnitude. It requires this magnitude to be explained by the quantity of the commodities appropriated as incomes in the context of the production of the commodities whose exchange for one another money facilitates.

From the perspective of Marx's analysis, the problems with the Neoclassical explanation of the value of money begin with its **conception**. First, like all other approaches, the Neoclassical conception of money and the functions it performs requires them to conceive of the value of money as the value of the aggregate quantity of money used to facilitate the exchange of commodities for one another, and this value as the values of all the commodities whose exchange for one another it facilitates. Like all other approaches, Neoclassicals are unable to conceive of the value of money as the value of any commodity with a determinate money price whose circulation a unit of it facilitates. The exception in this regard is the neo-Walrasians, who are able to conceive of the value of money as the value of a unit of it because they conceive of money as an asset, like any other asset, to which individuals attach subjective worth. Second, their conception of the value of the commodity requires

Austrians to deny money has value and OVNs to collapse the value of money into its exchange value. It requires Austrians to deny money has value because they conceive of the value of the commodity as the subjective worth attached to it. This concept precludes the aggregation of the values of commodities required by the Neoclassical conception of the value of money, i.e., as the values of commodities whose exchange for one another money is used to facilitate. Their conception of the value of the commodity causes OVNs to collapse the value of money into its exchange value because the aggregate quantity of commodities commanded as incomes in the context of the production of all commodities commanded by money must logically equal the aggregate quantity of commodities commanded by money when it is used to facilitate their exchange for one another. This is analogous to, and stems from, the OVN collapse of the value of the commodity into its exchange value. Of note in this context is that the neo-Walrasian conception of the value of money, as the value of an arbitrarily chosen asset, requires them to deny the existence of money as distinct from any other asset.

The problems with the Neoclassical conception of the **measure** of the value of money follow the problems noted above with its conception. Since SVNs cannot conceive of money having value, they obviously cannot conceive of it having a measure. Although neo-Walrasians can conceive of money having value, i.e., the value of the numéraire asset, they also cannot conceive of this value having a measure since, as noted above, subjective worth has no quantitative dimension. Since OVNs conflate the value of money with its exchange value, it follows they must also conflate their respective measures. Indeed, insofar as OVNs conceive of the value of money having a measure, it must logically be a certain quantity of all commodities commanded as incomes in the context of their production, which must logically be the same as the measure of the exchange value of money (see below).

Since Austrians are unable to conceive of the value of money, they are logically unable to explain its historic emergence and formation. Neo-Walrasians are in principle able to explain these, but as pertaining to the value of an arbitrarily chosen asset that is not in any way distinct from any other asset. Although OVNs can in principle explain the historic emergence of the value of money and its formation, their conflation of the value of money with its exchange value suggests that this explanation is premised on a similar conflation. What requires adding here is that the Neoclassical conception of money prevents them from seeing money **acquiring** value historically as a numéraire commodity, when one commodity comes to be adopted as a standard of all commodities as measures of the exchange values of one another. Seeing money acquiring value historically as a numéraire commodity in this manner is precluded in Neoclassical analyses because it requires them seeing money as a numeraire commodity and not a token of the commodities whose exchange for one another it facilitates or even a token of the numeraire commodity. In fact, neo-Walrasians are only able to conceive of money acquiring value historically as a numéraire asset because they conceive of the latter as akin to any asset, and not money as such, acquiring value like any other asset when individuals assign subjective worth to it in respect of the services it performs as a hedge against uncertainty.

The Neoclassical neglect of money's function as measure of the exchange values of commodities prevents them from seeing its value **formed** prior to it being put into the process of the circulation of commodities and at the same time as the formation of its exchange value and the money prices of commodities. Instead, it causes them to see the value of money formed in the process of exchange and its use as a medium of exchange, after the formation of its exchange value and the formation of the money prices of commodities. As I will argue below, it is this implicit view of the formation of the value of money that precludes Neoclassicals from explaining the magnitude of the exchange value of money by the magnitude of its value. Although neo-Walrasians do not see the value of money formed in the process of the exchange of these assets for one another, they see its value formed like the values of all other assets, outside of the economic system by an imaginary auctioneer.

The problems with the Neoclassical explanation of the **magnitude** of the value of money follow from the above. To begin with, the SVN conception of the value of money does not allow adherents of this approach to explain its magnitude, whether the value of money is conceived of as the subjective value attached to the services provided by money as a form of wealth or the subjective value attached to the commodities whose exchange it facilitates. This is because, as noted above, subjective worth has no quantitative dimension.

Even though their conception of the value of money allows OVNs to explain its magnitude, it should be apparent from the above that this explanation is problematic. To begin with, the OVN conception of money precludes them from explaining the magnitude of value of money as the magnitude of value of money as a commodity. This is because, as for other approaches, money must be something that is intrinsically valueless to facilitate the exchange of commodities for one another. Money cannot be a particular commodity. Second, the logic of the OVN conception of the value of money suggests its magnitude is explained by the magnitude of its exchange value. That is to say, the quantity of commodities comprising the incomes appropriated in the context of the production of the commodities commanded by money in the process of facilitating their exchange depends on the exchange value of money. It depends on the quantity of the commodities commanded by money in the performance of its medium of exchange function. Third, the OVN conception of the value of the commodity as its relative value, prevents them from conceiving of changes in the magnitudes of values of commodities having a bearing on the magnitude of the value of money. Lastly, and most importantly from the perspective of Marx's analysis, their conception of the value of the commodity precludes them from seeing the economy-wide productivity of labour and value of raw materials having a bearing on its magnitude and, therefore, the magnitude of the value of money.

8.8 Exchange Value of Money

Austrians and OVNs conceive of the exchange value of money as the quantity of all commodities (and assets) commanded by money in the context of it facilitating the exchange of commodities for one another. By implication the measure of the exchange value of money is the cluster of all commodities (and assets) whose exchange for one another money is seen as facilitating, and this cluster becoming the measure of the exchange value of money in the context of it being used as a medium of exchange. Neo-Walrasians implicitly conceive of the exchange value of money as the exchange value of a numéraire asset held by an individual in the form of wealth, and its measure as any other asset held by an individual as wealth alongside money.

The preceding implies Austrians and OVNs see money acquiring exchange value historically when it is chosen to facilitate the exchange of commodities for one another. As noted above, this implies that for these Neoclassicals money is seen as acquiring exchange value historically prior to it acquiring value, and after commodities acquire exchange values. It also implies these Neoclassicals see the exchange value of money formed in the process of it facilitating the exchange of commodities (and assets) for one another when money is used as a medium of exchange. The neo-Walrasian conception of the exchange value of money implies adherents of this approach see money acquiring exchange value historically when it is held by individuals as a form of wealth, and this exchange value, like the exchange values of all other assets, is formed outside of the process of exchange by an auctioneer.

Lastly, all Neoclassicals explain the magnitude of the exchange value of money by the demand for, and supply of, money, where the demand for, and supply of, money are seen as independent of one another with changes in the supply of money exogenously given and resulting in changes in the stock of money held by individuals. The demand for money by individuals is seen as a function of the quantity and prices of commodities and/or assets held by them, allowing for the impact of changes in the rate of interest on this demand. The stock of money is conceived of as comprising the cash and liabilities of the commercial banking system held by individuals. This is seen as linked to the cash base of the financial system—notes and coins that circulate in the financial system. Consequently, changes in the magnitude of the exchange value of money are explained by changes in the stock of money, and this in turn by changes in the cash base of the system. Differences between Neoclassical explanations of the magnitude of the exchange value of money pertain to the conception of the money stock, the transmission of changes in the money stock to changes in the prices of commodities and/or assets, and the nature and extent of the impact of increases in the money stock on the quantity of commodities produced over the short run. Differences between Neoclassicals with regard to the money stock revolve around the commercial bank liabilities included in it, with considerable attention paid to the alleged liquidity of the liabilities included in different definitions.[45] Differences between Neoclassicals regarding the transmission of money stock impulses to prices revolve around the assumed behaviour of individuals in response to changes in their holdings of real money balances, i.e., money balances in relation to the prices of all the commodities and/or assets that a representative individual holds in the form of wealth.[46]

[45] See Friedman (1989, p. 2),Mises (1971, pp. 132–133).

[46] See Friedman (1989, p. 2).

Austrians and OVNs assume that individuals hold a certain amount of real money balances to meet their various transactions and other needs, and respond to increases/decreases in these balances by increasing/decreasing their expenditure of the nominal money balances they hold in an attempt to restore their holdings of real money balances to their equilibrium levels. The increase/decrease in expenditure can take the form of the purchase/sale of commodities, securities, and services, the repayment/acquisition of debt, the purchase/sale of property, etc. Equilibrium levels of real money balances are assumed to be restored by a decrease/increase in nominal money balances held by the individual, an increase/fall in the aggregate money price level (or at least its rate of increase), and, for some of these Neoclassicals, also an increase/decrease in the quantity of commodities and/or assets put into the process of circulation. Fundamental to the whole process of transmission is the use of money as a medium of exchange to facilitate the exchange of commodities for one another. The increase in the stocks of money held by individuals result in more money being used to facilitate the exchange of commodities for one another resulting in the money prices of commodities rising.

Neo-Walrasians also assume individuals hold a certain amount of real money balances, but for non-transactions purposes. Increases in the stocks of their money holdings are supposed to elicit changes by the auctioneer in aggregate money prices of all assets that restore equilibrium holdings of real money balances. Logically, there cannot be any disequilibrium changes in aggregate output over the short run for neo-Walrasians.

The problems with the Neoclassical explanation of the exchange value of money begin with its **conception**. First, in the same way the Austrian and OVN conceptions of money precludes them from conceiving of it possessing value as a commodity, it also precludes them from conceiving of the exchange value of money as the exchange value of money as a commodity. Second, their conceptions of money also precludes Austrians and OVNs, like Smith and Ricardo, conceiving of the exchange value of money as the quantity of any and every commodity a unit of it commands. This is because, like Smith and Ricardo, Austrians and OVNs do not conceive of the commodities put into the process of circulation having determinate money prices. Consequently, like Smith and Ricardo, Austrians and OVNs too conceive of the exchange value of money as the exchange value of the aggregate quantity of money used to facilitate the exchange of commodities (assets) for one another relative to the quantity of these commodities (assets). That is, they conceive of the exchange value of money as in effect the reciprocal of the aggregate money price level. What these Neoclassicals do not explain in this regard is how the commodities whose exchange for one another money facilitates can be conceived of as a homogeneous mass in the absence of their reduction to equivalence in terms of a numéraire commodity or money.

In contrast with Austrians and OVNs, the neo-Walrasian conception of money does not preclude them from conceiving of money possessing exchange value when it assumes the form of a commodity, or conceiving of the exchange value of money as the quantity of any commodity it commands in the process of exchange. This is because, as argued above, neo-Walrasians conceive of money as simply one among all assets held by individuals, i.e., as an arbitrarily chosen numéraire asset, that is not required to perform the function of medium of exchange. Consequently, for neo-Walrasians the exchange value of money is not the exchange value of something representing general exchange value, even though it is conceived of as a repository of purchasing power. Rather, it is the exchange value of any asset to which individuals attach subjective value, and represents particular exchange value.

The problems with the Neoclassical conceptions of the **measure** of the exchange value of money follows from their conceptions of it. It follows from their conception of the exchange value of money that Austrians and OVNs see what is measured as the exchange value of the aggregate quantity of money used to facilitate the exchange of commodities for one another and not a unit of money. It also follows from this conception that the measure of the exchange value of money is the aggregate quantity of commodities whose exchange for one another it facilitates and not any commodity with a determinate money price. As should be evident, Neoclassicals are not able to conceive of the measure of the exchange value of money as the quantity of any commodity with a determinate money price commanded by a unit of it because of their neglect of the measure of exchange value function of money. It will be recalled Austrians see commodities as the measures of the exchange values of one another in the process of their exchange for one another, and OVNs see clusters of commodities or assets as these measures. Although neo-Walrasians implicitly see any asset as the measure of the exchange value of money, they see these assets as the measure of the exchange value of money as a particular asset like the measure of the exchange value of any other asset, and not uniquely the measure of the exchange value money—as the general asset.

The Neoclassical conception of money prevents them, and in particular Austrians and OVNs, from seeing money **acquiring** exchange value historically as a numéraire commodity that is used to facilitate the exchange of commodities for one another. This is because it would require them to see money acquiring exchange value prior to the emergence of capitalism. Instead, their conception of money requires Austrians and OVNs to see money as credit money acquiring exchange value in capitalism when it comes to be used to facilitate the exchange of commodities for one another. In contrast with Austrians and OVNs, neo-Walrasians see money as a numéraire asset acquiring exchange value prior to the emergence of capitalism. However, this is because they see it acquiring exchange value, like any other asset, outside of the economic system, as a result of the actions of the omniscient auctioneer.

The primacy attached to money's medium of exchange function by Austrians and OVNs precludes them from seeing its exchange value **formed** in the context of its use by producers to set the money prices of their commodities prior to money being put into the process of circulation to circulate commodities with determinate money prices. For Austrians and OVNs to admit that the exchange value of money is formed prior to its entry into the process of circulation, and, therefore, that commodities are put into the process of circulation with determinate money prices, would undermine the entire theoretical edifice of their explanations of price; one premised on prices being formed in the market on the basis of the demand for, and supply of, commodities. The neo-Walrasian explanation of the formation of the exchange value of money allows them, in contrast, to conceive of it being formed outside of the process of exchange, but only because it allows them to see it formed outside of the economic system—by the omniscient auctioneer. Moreover, it requires them to see the formation of the exchange value of money like the formation of the exchange value of any other asset held as a hedge against uncertainty, with no reason to suppose that one asset more than any other has this attenuated role.

The problems with the Neoclassical explanation of the **magnitude** of the exchange value of money follow from the preceding. First, the Austrian and OVN conception of money precludes them from explaining the exchange value of money as the magnitude of the exchange value of a unit of money by the quantity of any commodity with a determinate money price commanded by it in the process of its circulation. Instead, the logic of the Austrian and OVN explanations requires them to explain the magnitude of the exchange value of money as the exchange value of the aggregate quantity of money used to facilitate the exchange of all commodities relative to the quantity of these commodities.

Second, Austrians and OVNs cannot explain the magnitude of the exchange value of money by the magnitude of its value. This follows from their explanation of the magnitude of value of money by the magnitude of its exchange value (see above).

Third, Austrians and OVNs are unable to conceive of changes in aggregate excess demand for commodities having a bearing on the magnitude of the exchange value of money (aggregate money price level) unless these changes are seen as constituting changes in the excessive quantity of money used to facilitate the exchange of commodities for one another, the excess quantity of money being in relation to the quantity of commodities whose exchange for one another it is used to facilitate. This requires Austrians and OVNs to, for example, deny credit expansions by commercial banks have a bearing on the magnitude of the exchange value of money, and that these expansions have consequences for the cash base and banking liabilities of the system.

Fourth and related to the preceding point, the Austrian and OVN explanations of the magnitude of the exchange value of money are premised on the assumption that the quantity of what is used to purchase commodities (or assets) in the process of circulation is exogenously determined in the sense of being independent of the quantities of commodities (or assets) put into the process of circulation and their prices. This has led to a considerable amount of time and energy being spent by these Neoclassicals and their critics alike debating the validity of this or that definition of money stock and the time the lag between changes in the stock of money and the money prices of commodities (or assets). The source of the problem is that Austrians and OVNs do not see money prices of commodities set by producers before they put their commodities into the market. Once it is accepted commodities enter the process of circulation with determinate money prices there is no need to see what facilitates their circulation as any specific media of circulation. These media can include both bank liabilities and credit. Changes in the quantity of cash and bank liabilities must follow, not precede, changes in the quantities and money prices of commodities (and financial assets, property, etc.) put into the process of circulation.

Fifth, Austrian and OVN explanations of the magnitude of the exchange value of money also require them to conceive of what is purchased with the aggregate quantity of money put into the process of circulation including 'assets' or even constituting assets. This conception stems from the recognition that money is also spent on other things apart from commodities, including financial assets. This in turn implies that for these Neoclassicals money is used to facilitate the exchange of assets for one another in accordance with their relative values. The need to bring into the analysis the array of things that money is spent on arises from the denial that commodities, like financial assets, property, and other forms of wealth, enter the process of circulation with determinate money prices and are circulated by money and various substitutes for money in accordance with their money prices.

Lastly, the debates among Austrians and OVNs, as well as between these Neoclassicals and their critics, regarding whether or not the expenditure of money by individuals results in a 'temporary' increase in aggregate output, also stem from their denial that commodities are put into the process of circulation with determinate money prices. Whether or not changes in money prices are accompanied by corresponding changes in aggregate output, and whether or not these changes are protracted depends, like the money prices of the commodities, on the conditions governing the production of the commodities. It depends in particular on the conditions governing the profitability of production.[47]

The problems with the neo-Walrasian explanation of the magnitude of the exchange value of money, like the problems with the Austrian and OVN explanations of the same, follow from their conception of money and its exchange value. To begin with, neo-Walrasians are able to explain the magnitude of the exchange value of money by the magnitude of its value because they conceive of money as something to which individuals attach subjective value much like any other asset. An increase in the quantity of any asset relative to all other assets held by individuals implies the subjective value attached to it falls relative to that attached to all other assets, causing the auctioneer to ascribe a lower exchange value to it in order to restore balance between the relative demand for and supply of the asset. Since money is seen as a numéraire asset, an increase in the relative quantity of it held by all individuals and a corresponding fall in its

[47] See Nicholas (forthcoming) for a more extensive discussion of this point.

exchange value with respect to all other assets implies an increase in their money (numéraire) exchange values. As noted above, one of the important implications of the neo-Walrasian explanation of the magnitude of the exchange values of assets is their necessary denial that the productivity of labour (or any factor input for that matter) has a bearing on it.

Even though, as argued above, the neo-Walrasian explanation of the magnitude of the exchange value of money is in many ways different from those of the Austrian and OVN explanations, a fundamental premise of their explanation is also that changes in the stock of money (the numéraire asset) held by individuals are exogenously determined. This implies that neo-Walrasians, like the Austrians and OVNs, need to deny that changes in the stock of money are related to changes in credit. Unlike the Austrians and OVNs, this does not require neo-Walrasians to deny that individuals use credit to facilitate the exchange of assets since they deny what is held as money is used to facilitate the exchange of assets. Rather, as for Austrians and OVNs, what is required is the denial by neo-Walrasians that changes in the quantity of credit induce changes in the quantity of the numéraire asset put into the system. Since neo-Walrasians pay no attention to the process of exchange of commodities and what facilitates this, they can ignore the impact of changes in the quantity of credit on the stock of the numéraire asset in the system. It warrants remarking in this context that their neglect of credit requires neo-Walrasians to deny that increases in the stock of money allow individuals to reduce their holdings of debt. However, this consequence is often neglected in neo-Walrasian accounts of the impact of changes in the stock of money or numéraire asset held by individuals, with many adherents of the approach explicitly arguing that one of the consequences of individuals holding increased money (numéraire asset) balances is the reduction of their holdings of debt.[48]

8.9 Money Price of the Commodity

When considering the Neoclassical explanations of the money price of an individual commodity, a distinction needs to be again drawn between SVN and OVN approaches which allows these explanations to be linked

[48] See Friedman (1974).

to their respective explanations of the value and exchange value of the commodity.

8.9.1 SVNs

The SVNs considered in this section comprise the Austrians and neo-Walrasians. It will be recalled that in principle Walrasians cannot admit to the existence of money because of the role accorded to the auctioneer in setting prices, but neo-Walrasians get around this by assuming that the primary function of money is other than that of a medium of exchange.

Austrians conceive of the money price of the commodity as its commodity exchange value for a given value of money, where the commodity exchange value of the commodity is the quantity of another commodity commanded by a unit of it in the process of exchange, and the value of money is tacitly seen as the quantity of subjective worth commanded by money when performing the function of medium of exchange. Neo-Walrasians conceive of the money price of a commodity as the money price of an asset held as wealth by individuals where money is one among these assets, the numéraire asset, and the money price of an asset is its numéraire exchange value. These conceptions of the money price of the commodity suggest that Austrians conceive of money as a token of commodities as measures of the exchange values of one another, and neo-Walrasians conceive of it as the standard of all assets as measures of the exchange values of one another.

The Austrian conception of money requires them to see commodities acquiring money prices historically when money is used to facilitate the exchange of commodities for one another, and these prices formed in the process of exchange in the context of the formation of the exchange values of commodities. The neo-Walrasian conception of money requires them to see commodities acquiring money prices historically when money is held by individuals as a form of wealth, with money prices formed by the auctioneer.

Lastly, Austrians explain the magnitude of the money price of the commodity as the magnitude of the exchange value of the commodity for a given magnitude of value of money, framing this explanation in the context of the demand for, and supply of, commodities for one another. As argued above, Austrians explain the magnitude of the exchange value of the commodity by the subjective value attached to the commodities being exchanged for one another with the aid of money as a medium of exchange, and the value of money by the values of the commodities whose exchange for one another money facilitates. Neo-Walrasians explain the magnitude of the money price of an asset as the magnitude of its numeraire exchange value. They too frame this explanation in the context of demand and supply, except as the demand for, and supply of, assets as forms of the wealth held by individuals where money is assumed to be the numéraire asset.

The problems with the SVN explanations of the money price of the commodity/asset begin with its **conception**. First, Austrians are unable to conceive of the money price of the commodity as the quantity of money commanded by a unit of a given commodity, i.e., as the money exchange value of the commodity. This is because they do not conceive of what is commanded in the process of exchange as something representing general exchange value. Second, and related to the preceding, Austrians are unable to conceive of the relative money price of the commodity as its money price relative to the money price of another commodity and, correspondingly, the aggregate money price level as the aggregate of the money prices of all commodities. Instead, they conceive of the relative money price of the commodity as its relative price, and the aggregate money price level as the quantity of all commodities commanded by the aggregate quantity of money used to facilitate their exchange for one another. Although, in contrast, neo-Walrasians appear to conceive of the money price of the commodity or asset as the quantity of money it commands in the process of exchange, this conception of money price is in effect the asset exchange value of an asset where money is any arbitrarily chosen numéraire asset that represents a certain magnitude of particular exchange value like all other assets. That is, the money price of an asset is in effect its numeraire asset exchange value, or relative price. Moreover, although neo-Walrasians give the impression that they conceive of the relative money price of the commodity as the money price of one asset relative to the money price of another and the aggregate money price level as the aggregate of the money prices of all assets, they are only able to conceive of the money price of the asset and aggregate money prices of all assets in this way by assuming money to be an arbitrarily chosen asset that is like all other assets.

The problems with the SVN conceptions of the **measure** of the money price of the commodity/asset follow from this. For Austrians the measure of the money price of the commodity is the measure of its commodity exchange value, with money a token of this measure and not its measure as such. That is to say, for Austrians the measure of the money price of the commodity is another particular commodity, with money a token of this commodity and in the final instance a token of the subjective worth attached to the commodity. This means, as noted above, the measure of the money price changes with each and every transaction, with no reason to suppose what serves as measure in each case is homogeneous and divisible. For neo-Walrasians the measure of the money price of the commodity is an asset held as wealth that is chosen as the standard of all assets held as wealth. There is no reason to suppose any one asset is more suited to functioning as this standard than another because it is not clear what purpose the numeraire asset is supposed to be serving.

The Austrian conception of money prevents them from seeing commodities **acquiring** money prices historically before the emergence of capitalism and money assuming the form of credit money. That is to say, it requires them to deny commodities acquire prices denominated in terms of a numéraire commodity, such as gold, prior to the emergence of capitalism. In fact, it also requires them to deny commodities acquire gold prices even after the emergence of capitalism, prior to them acquiring credit money prices. Although, in contrast, neo-Walrasians are able to conceive of commodities acquiring money prices prior to capitalism, they see these commodities as assets that are held as a 'hedge against uncertainty' with the numéraire used to denominate the prices as an arbitrarily chosen asset. That is to say, neo-Walrasians see commodities as assets acquiring money prices historically when one of the assets held by individuals as a hedge against uncertainty is arbitrarily chosen as a numéraire asset, and used to denominate the exchange values of all other assets with respect to one another in terms of one and the same asset.

Their denial of money's function as measure of the exchange value of the commodity and the corresponding denial of money's medium of circulation function, prevents Austrians from seeing money prices**formed** prior to commodities with determinate money prices being put into the process of circulation. Instead, the primacy they accord to money's medium of exchange function requires them to see the money price of the commodity formed in the context of the use of money to facilitate the exchange of commodities with one another in accordance with the values and corresponding commodity exchange values of the commodities being exchanged for one another. The neo-Walrasian conception of the money price of an asset as its relative price, coupled with their view of the role of the auctioneer in the formation of the relative prices of assets, suggests they see the money prices of assets formed in the manner of the formation of the asset exchange value of any asset, outside of the process of the exchange of assets for one another but also outside of the economic system.

The problems with the SVN explanations of the **magnitude** of the money price of the commodity follow from their conception of the money price of the commodity. First, the Austrian conception of the money price of the commodity prevents them from explaining its magnitude as the quantity of money directly commanded by the commodity. Second, this in turn prevents Austrians from explaining the relative price of the commodity as its money price relative to the money price of another commodity, and the aggregate money price level as the (weighted) average of the money prices of all commodities. Instead, it causes them to explain the magnitude of the money price of the commodity as its commodity exchange value where money is seen as token of the commodities being exchanged for one another, and the aggregate money price level as the quantity of all money required to facilitate the exchange of all commodities relative to the quantity of these commodities. Third, and following from the preceding, it causes Austrians to see changes in the relative prices of commodities taking place *independently* of changes in the aggregate money price level. Logically, changes in the money price of an individual commodity should take place in the context of changes in the aggregate money prices of all commodities, even if changes in the former also take place independently of the latter. Lastly, and most importantly from the perspective of Marx's analysis, their explanation of the magnitude of the money price of the commodity requires Austrians to deny changes in the productivity of labour have any bearing on changes in the relative price of the commodity and the aggregate money price level.

Although neo-Walrasians can be interpreted as explaining the magnitude of the money price of an asset as the magnitude of its money exchange value, what they are explaining in this regard is in effect the numéraire asset exchange value of the asset, or, more simply, its relative price. Moreover, although the neo-Walrasian concept of the money price of the asset allows them to be interpreted as seeing changes in the relative money prices of commodities taking place in the context of changes in the aggregate money price level as well as independently of the latter, this is only because they explain changes in the latter as in effect changes in the former; changes in the relative price of the asset. Thus, when one asset is arbitrarily chosen as a numéraire asset and the quantity of it is deemed to increase relative to the quantities of all other assets held by individuals, the relative numéraire asset prices of all other assets must logically be seen as increasing in the context of an increase in the aggregate numéraire price level. Needless to say, there is no reason to suppose changes in the productivity of labour are seen by neo-Walrasians as having a bearing on changes in the money prices of assets.

8.9.2 OVNs

The OVN conception of the money price of a commodity is, like the Austrian conception, the exchange value of the commodity for a given value of money. It warrants recalling that the exchange value of the commodity is for OVNs the quantity of an aliquot proportion of the net product commanded by a unit of it, and the value of money is the quantity of the net product commanded by it. By implication OVNs see money as a token of the measure of the exchange value of the commodity, i.e., a token of an aliquot part of the net product.

Like Austrians, OVNs implicitly see commodities acquiring money prices historically when money comes to be used to facilitate the exchange of commodities for one another. And, also like Austrians, OVNs see money prices formed in the process of the exchange of commodities for one another, when money is used to facilitate this exchange.

Lastly, OVNs explain the magnitude of the money price of the commodity by the magnitude of its exchange value for a given value of money in the context of the relative demand for, and supply of, the commodity. It will be recalled that this suggests changes in the magnitude of the money price of the commodity result from changes in the relative demand for, and supply of, the commodity and are accompanied by changes in the factor inputs used to produce the commodity. OVNs see a change in the value of money resulting from changes in the exchange value of money.

From the perspective of Marx's analysis the problems with the OVN explanation of the money price of the commodity begin with its **conception**. Like Austrians, OVNs are unable to conceive of the money price of a commodity as the quantity of money directly commanded by a unit of the individual commodity and, correspondingly, the aggregate money price level as the aggregate of the money prices of individual commodities. This is because, like Austrians, OVNs do not conceive of the process of the exchange of commodities as particular commodities for something representing general exchange value, something that can be used to purchase any and all commodities, notwithstanding their conception of what is commanded in the process of exchange as implicitly an aggregate cluster of commodities. As argued above, there is no reason to suppose that an artificially constructed composite of commodities can be used to purchase any and all commodities and, accordingly, come to represent general exchange value.

The problem with the OVN conception of the **measure** of the money price of the commodity follows from the problems noted above with its conception of the money price of the commodity. Like Austrians, OVNs tacitly see the measure of the money price of the commodity as the measure of its commodity exchange value, with money a token of this measure. That is to say, they implicitly see the measure of the money price of the commodity as a certain quantity of an artificially constructed cluster of commodities, and money a token of this cluster. Needless to say, OVNs provide no indication how money is to be seen as a token of an artificially constructed cluster, typically seeing it as a token of particular commodities exchanged for one another in the manner of Austrians.

Like Austrians, the OVN conception of money prevents them from seeing commodities **acquiring** money prices historically prior to the emergence of capitalism and the assumption by money of the form of credit money. Specifically, it prevents them from seeing commodities acquiring gold prices prior to capitalism in the context of the use of gold as a numeraire commodity. Their conception of money also prevents OVNs, like Austrians, seeing commodities acquiring gold prices in capitalism, prior to them acquiring credit money prices.

Their neglect of money's function as measure prevents OVNs, like Austrians, seeing money prices of commodities **formed** prior to the commodities being put into the process of exchange (circulation). Specifically, it prevents them seeing commodities put into the process of circulation with determinate money prices and circulated by money or various substitutes of money including credit. Instead, the primacy they accord to money's medium function as a result of their neglect of its measure function causes them to see commodities put into the process of exchange for one another acquiring money prices in this process, and in the context of them acquiring certain magnitudes of exchange values.

The problems with the OVN explanation of the **magnitude** of the money price of the commodity follow from the problems with its conception. To begin with the OVN conception of the money price of the commodity prevents them from explaining the magnitude of the money price of the commodity as the magnitude of its money exchange value, i.e., as the quantity of money the commodity directly commands. Consequently, like Austrians, OVNs do not see changes in the magnitude of the value of the commodity having a direct bearing on the magnitude of its money price. Second, the OVN conception of the money price of the commodity and corresponding conception of the aggregate money price level prevents them, like all other approaches from seeing changes in the relative prices of commodities taking place in the context of changes in the aggregate money price level as well as independently of the latter. Specifically, the OVN conception of the money price of the commodity prevents them from explaining the relative price of the commodity as its money price relative to that of another commodity and the aggregate money price level as the aggregate of the money prices of all commodities such that factors having a bearing on the latter must be seen as having a bearing on the former. Lastly, and most importantly from the perspective of Marx's analysis, OVNs do not see trend movements in the relative and economy-wide productivity of labour having a fundamental bearing on trend movements in relative and aggregate money prices of commodities.

8.9.3 OVN Textbooks

Although for the most part textbooks written from an OVN perspective follow the OVN explanation of the money price of the commodity outlined above, there are some important deviations from it that warrant attention. These deviations begin with, and indeed centre on, their conception of the price being explained. Many authors of popular economics textbooks give the impression that the prices they are explaining from the very outset are money prices and not in the first instance relative prices. For example, Mankiw (2017, pp. 76–7) explains how markets work by explaining the money price of ice-cream cones as determined by the demand for, and supply of, these cones, with the implication being that the demand for, and supply of, the commodity is with respect to money and not another commodity or cluster of commodities. As should be apparent from what has been argued above, conceiving of the price of the individual commodity to be explained as the quantity of money commanded by it from a Neoclassical perspective requires the adoption of a neo-Walrasian approach. It requires conceiving of money as a numéraire commodity (asset) and the exchange values of all commodities (as assets) denominated in terms of it according to the relative subjective worth attached to them. This allows the relative price of the commodity to conceived of as its 'money' price, where money is the numéraire commodity, and its magnitude explained by the demand for, and supply of, the commodity with respect to money as a commodity, the numéraire commodity.

As is readily apparent, however, this is not how most OVN textbook authors explain the money prices of commodities. They implicitly, if not explicitly, explain these by the relative price of the commodities where money is a token of the commodities being exchanged for one another and not one of the commodities being exchanged. They explain the relative price of the commodity by the relative demand for, and supply of the commodity with respect to another commodity and not money, where the relative demand is explained by the subjective worth attached to the commodity relative to another, and the relative supply by the commodity income costs of producing it relative to another. In other words, the demand-supply diagrams depicting the determination of the price of the commodity as its money price found at the beginning of most popular economics textbooks are fundamentally misleading. It would appear that what the authors of these textbooks are trying to avoid by conceiving of the price of the commodity as its money price and not relative price in the first instance is having to explain how relative prices translate into money prices, and the sense in which money can be seen as a token of the commodities being exchanged for one another, let alone a token of an aliquot part of the net product.

8.9.4 The Source of the Problem

The source of the problem with all of the above Neoclassical approaches to explaining the magnitude of the money price of the commodity from the perspective of Marx's analysis, like the source of the problem with all other approaches, is their conception of the value of the commodity and its link to money. Their conception of value prevents Austrians and OVNs from explaining relative money prices as the money price of one commodity relative to another, and the aggregate money price level as the weighted average of the individual money prices of all commodities. This in turn prevents Austrians and OVNs from conceiving of changes in relative money prices of commodities taking place in the context of changes in the aggregate money price level as well as independently of the latter. Indeed, their concept of value causes Austrians and OVNs to conceive of the relative prices of commodities and the aggregate money price level in a way that requires them to see changes in the former taking place independently of changes in the latter. As argued above, the Austrian and OVN conceptions of the value of the commodity causes, or rather requires, them to conceive of the relative money price of the commodity as its commodity exchange value where money is a token of the commodity or cluster of commodities commanded in the process of exchange, and the aggregate money price level as the quantity of money used to facilitate the exchange of all commodities for one another relative to the quantity of these commodities.

In contrast, the neo-Walrasian conception of value of the commodity and its link to money allows them to conceive of changes in relative prices of commodities (assets) taking place in the context of changes in the aggregate money price level as well as independently of the latter. However, this is because neo-Walrasians conceive of money possessing value in itself and not as a reflection of the commodity (asset) it commands in the process of exchange. It is a conception of money that allows neo-Walrasians to conceive of the relative price of the commodity (asset) as its money price relative to that of another, and the aggregate money price level as the aggregate of the money prices of the individual commodities (assets). It is these conceptions of the money price of the individual commodity (asset) and aggregate money price level that allows neo-Walrasians to conceive of changes in the former taking place in the context of changes in the latter, as well as independently of the latter. As I argued above, neo-Walrasians are only able to conceive of changes in relative and aggregate money prices in this way because they assume money to be an arbitrarily chosen numeraire commodity (asset) that is in principle no different from any other commodity (asset) in the economic system. Unlike all other approaches, neo-Walrasians do not postulate a certain link between the value of the commodity (asset) and money, but rather collapse money into a commodity (asset).

References

Arrow, K. J., & Hahn, F. H. (1971). *General competitive analysis*. Oliver and Boyd.

Brunner, K., & Meltzer, A. H. (1989). *Monetary economics*. Basil Blackwell.

Clower, R. (1967). A reconsideration of the microfoundations of monetary theory. *Economic Inquiry, 6*(1), 1–8.

Clower, R. (1999). Post-Keynes monetary and financial theory. *Journal of Post Keynesian Economics, 21*(3), 399–414.

Debreu, G. (1959). *Theory of value: An axiomatic analysis of economic equilibrium*. Yale University Press.

Dobb, M. (1973). *Theories of value and distribution since Adam Smith: Ideology and economic theory*. Cambridge University Press.

Fischer, S. (1974). Money and the production function. *Economic Inquiry, 12*(4), 517–533.

Friedman, M. (1949). The Marshallian demand curve. *Journal of Political Economy, 57*(6), 463–495.

Friedman, M. (1974). A theoretical framework for monetary analysis. In R. J. Gordon (Ed.), *Milton Friedman's monetary framework: A debate with his critics* (pp. 1–62). University of Chicago Press.

Friedman, M. (1989). Quantity theory of money. In J. Eatwell, M. Milgate, & P. Newman (Eds.), *The new Palgrave: Money* (pp. 1–40). Macmillan Press.

Graziani, A. (2003). *The monetary theory of production*. Cambridge University Press.

Hahn, F. H. (1984). *Equilibrium and macroeconomics*. Basil Blackwell.

Hahn, F. H. (1987). The foundations of monetary theory. In M. de Cecco & J.-P. Fitoussi (Eds.), *Monetary theory and economic institutions: Proceedings of a conference held by the international economic association at Fiesole, Florence, Italy* (pp. 21–43). Palgrave Macmillan.

Hayek, F. A. (1941). *The pure theory of capital*. University of Chicago Press.

Hicks, J. R. (1946). *Value and capital: An inquiry into some fundamental principles of economic theory* (2nd ed.). Clarendon Press.

Holcombe, R. G. (2014). *Advanced introduction to The Austrian School of Economics*. Edward Elgar.

Horwitz, S. (2000). *Microfoundations and macroeconomics: An Austrian perspective*. Routledge.

Ikeda, E. (2019). *Global business cycles and developing countries*. Routledge.

Jevons, W. S. (1970). *The theory of political economy*. Pelican. Originally published 1871.

Katzner, D. W. (2008). On the analytical and methodological significance of microeconomic theory. *Review of Radical Political Economics, 40*(3), 324–330.

Krugman, P., & Wells, R. (2006). *Economics*. Worth.

Lipsey, R. G., & Chrystal, K. A. (2007). *Economics* (11th ed.). Oxford University Press.

Lucas, R. E., Jr. (1980). Equilibrium in a pure currency economy. *Economic Inquiry, 18*(2), 203–220.

Malinvaud, E. (1985). *Lectures on microeconomic theory* (2nd ed.). North-Holland.

Mankiw, N. G. (2017). *Economics* (8th ed.). Cengage Learning.

Marshall, A. (2009). *Principles of economics: Unabridged* (8th ed.). Cosimo. Originally published in 1890.

Marx, K. (1969). *Theories of surplus value: Part II* (translated from German by R. Simpson). Lawrence & Wishart.

Marx, K. (1972). *Theories of surplus value: Part III* (translated from German by J. Cohen, J. & S.W. Ryazanskaya). Lawrence & Wishart.

Menger, C. (2007) *Principles of Economics*. Ludwig von Mises Institute. Originally published in 1871.

Mises, L. von. (1971). *The theory of money & credit*. Foundation for Economic Education. Originally published in 1912.

Nicholas, H. (2011). *Marx's theory of price and its modern rivals*. Palgrave Macmillan.

Nicholas, H. (2012). What is the problem with neoclassical price theory. *World Review of Political Economy, 3*(4), 457–477.

Parkin, M., Powell, M., & Matthews, K. (2005). *Economics*. Pearson Education.

Patinkin, D. (1949). The indeterminacy of absolute prices in classical economic theory. *Econometrica, 17*(1), 1–27.

Schumpeter, J. A. (1964). Business *cycles: A theoretical, historical, and statistical analysis of the capitalist process*. McGraw-Hill. Originally published in 1936.

Walker, D. A. (2006). *Walrasian Economics*. Cambridge University Press.

Walras, L. (1954). *Elements of pure Economics* (translated by W. Jaffé). Allen & Unwin. Originally published in 1874.

Walras, L. (2005). *Studies in applied economics: Theory of the production of social wealth* (translated by J. van Daal, 2 Volumes). Routledge.

Varian, H. R. (1992). *Microeconomic analysis* (3rd ed.). W.W. Norton.

CHAPTER 9

Conclusions

The purpose of this volume, which is part of a three-volume work seeking to expand on Marx's explanation of the price of the commodity, is to clarify and expand on his explanation of the money price of the commodity. I see this requiring, on the one hand, a reinterpretation of his concept of the value of the commodity in the context of an elaboration and extension of his explanation of money, and, on the other hand, critical evaluations of the explanations of the money price of the commodity found in the approaches of Smith, Ricardo, Sraffa, PKs, and Neoclassicals, as well as other Marxist interpretations of Marx's explanation of the money price of the commodity. My purpose in focusing on these other approaches is to showcase Marx's approach and highlight the fundamental problems with these approaches. I see the reinterpretation of Marx's conception of the value of the commodity requiring recognition of the link he sees between the value of the commodity and money in the context of the primacy he attaches to money's function as the measure of the general exchange value of the commodity. I see the problems with all other approaches to the explanation of the money price of the commodity stemming from their conceptions of the value of the commodity and its link to money. In this regard, I distinguish between, on the one hand, the works of Smith, Ricardo, Sraffa and the Neoclassicals, and, on the other hand, the works of the PKs. The explicit and implicit conceptions

H. Nicholas, *Explorations in Marx's Theory of Price—Why Marx Is Still Relevant for Understanding the Modern Economy*, https://doi.org/10.1057/978-1-137-56564-8_9

of the value of the commodity in the former cause them to deny any direct link between the value of the commodity and money, while the implicit conception of the value of the commodity in the works of the latter, the PKs, causes them to collapse the value of the commodity into money. The consequence of their conceptions of the value of the commodity and its link to money in both cases is a confused and confusing explanation of the money price of the individual commodity and corresponding explanations of the relative price of the commodity and aggregate money price level.

My reinterpretation of Marx's explanation of the money price of the commodity begins with his concept of the value of the commodity in capitalism. I see this for Marx as linked to money in the sense that he sees the value of the commodity formed in the context of the use of money by capitalist producers to denote the general exchange values of their commodities, causing the labour time expended in the production of the commodity to be transformed into socially necessary labour time, i.e., into units of economy-wide standard labour time, that is required to produce the bulk of commodities of a certain type. Marx conceives of the money price of the commodity as the quantity of money that is commanded by a unit of it and formed in the context of the formation of its value, prior to it being put into the process of circulation. He sees the trend magnitude of the money price of the commodity determined by the trend magnitude of its value with the link between the two being manifest in the link between changes in the relative productivity of labour and relative money price of the commodity. Marx uses his explanation of the trend magnitude of the money price of the commodity to not only explain movements in the money prices of commodities relative to one another but also movements in the aggregate money price level. Crucially, Marx sees changes in relative money prices taking place in the context of changes in the aggregate money price level as well as independently of the latter.

From the perspective of Marx's analysis the problems with the analyses of Smith, Ricardo, Sraffa and the Neoclassicals stem from their conceptions of the value of the commodity and its link to money. All these analyses conceive of the value of the commodity being formed independently of money, and money becoming a token of a certain quantity of the value of the commodity in the context of it being used to facilitate the exchange of commodities for one another according to their relative values. This in turn requires them to conceive of the money price of the commodity as its relative price for a given value of money, and the aggregate money price level as the aggregate quantity of money required to facilitate the exchange of commodities comprising the net product for one another relative to the quantity of these commodities. That is to say, it requires them to deny that the relative money price of the commodity is the money price of one commodity relative to another and the aggregate money price level is an aggregate of the money prices of commodities. I see the most obvious manifestation of the problem with the explanation of the money price of the commodity by Smith, Ricardo, Sraffa, and Neoclassicals is that it causes them to see changes in the relative price of the commodity taking place independently of changes in the aggregate money price level and not in the context of the latter.

In contrast with Smith, et. al., PKs collapse the value of the commodity into money and conceive of money as a token of a certain quantity of the labour input. This causes PKs to conceive of the money price of the commodity as the quantity of money it directly commands, and explain it by the money wage rate. The explanation of the money price of the commodity by the money wage rate is necessarily an explanation of the aggregate money price level since the money wage rate pertains to the labour used in the production of all commodities. PKs deny that changes in the money wage rate have a bearing on the relative money prices of commodities to avoid having to conceive of the money prices of commodities produced with more labour-intensive techniques of production continuously rising relative to those produced with less labour-intensive techniques in the context of a continuous increase in the money wage rate. Consequently, like all other approaches, the most obvious manifestation of their mistaken explanation of the money prices of commodities is that PKs see changes in the relative money prices of commodities taking place independently of changes in the aggregate money price level.

I also use my interpretation of Marx's explanation of the money price of the commodity to critically assess other Marxist interpretations of this explanation. I focus in particular on the interpretations of those Marxists who adopt what I perceive to be a traditional interpretation of Marx's theory of price, referring to them as Traditional Interpretation Marxists (TIMs), and those who adopt what I perceive to be a monetary interpretation of Marx's theory of price, referring to them as Monetary Interpretation Marxists (MIMs). I argue that both approaches have a mistaken interpretation of Marx's explanation of the money price of the commodity stemming from their mistaken interpretation of his conception of the value of the commodity and its link to money. TIMs interpret Marx seeing value having no link to money in the manner of Smith et. al., while MIMs interpret him collapsing value into money in the manner of PKs. This causes both approaches to have correspondingly mistaken interpretations of Marx's conception of money, which in turn causes them to have mistaken interpretations of his conception and explanation of the money price of the commodity. I see the most obvious manifestation of their mistaken interpretation of Marx's conception and explanation of the money price of the commodity is that it requires both TIMs and MIMs to erroneously interpret Marx seeing changes in the relative money prices of commodities taking place independently of changes in the aggregate money price level, at least insofar as they are able to interpret him having an explanation of relative money prices. I noted above that most TIMs accept that Marx has a logically flawed explanation of the relative price of a commodity while most MIMs appear to tacitly argue that Marx cannot be interpreted as having an explanation of trend movements in the relative price of the commodity.

Correction to: Marx's Explanation of Money Price

Correction to:
Chapter 2 in: H. Nicholas, *Explorations in Marx's Theory of Price—Why Marx Is Still Relevant for Understanding the Modern Economy*, https://doi.org/10.1057/978-1-137-56564-8_2

The original version of this chapter was inadvertently published with typographical errors in the first paragraph in page 23. The chapter has been updated with the changes.

The updated original version of this chapter can be found at https://doi.org/10.1057/978-1-137-56564-8_2

H. Nicholas, *Explorations in Marx's Theory of Price—Why Marx Is Still Relevant for Understanding the Modern Economy*, https://doi.org/10.1057/978-1-137-56564-8_10

Author Index

H. Nicholas, *Explorations in Marx's Theory of Price—Why Marx Is Still Relevant for Understanding the Modern Economy*,
https://doi.org/10.1057/978-1-137-56564-8

Subject Index

H. Nicholas, *Explorations in Marx's Theory of Price—Why Marx Is Still Relevant for Understanding the Modern Economy*,
https://doi.org/10.1057/978-1-137-56564-8

www.ingramcontent.com/pod-product-compliance
Lightning Source LLC
LaVergne TN
LVHW010319220926
848484LV00004BB/798

* 9 7 8 1 1 3 7 5 6 5 6 3 1 *